Israel's Silent Defender

ISRAEL'S
S I L E N T
Defender

An Inside Look at Sixty Years of Israeli Intelligence

Edited by
Amos Gilboa
Ephraim Lapid

Associate Editor Yochi Erlich

THE ISRAEL INTELLIGENCE HERITAGE
AND COMMEMORATION CENTER

Cover Design: Leah Ben Avraham / Noonim Graphics
Typesetting: David Yehoshua
Visual Archive of IICC: Jacob Mann
Photo credits: IDF Spokesman's Office, *Bamachane: Israel Defense Forces Weekly*,
Government Press Office, and the Israel Security Agency website www.shabak.gov.il

ISBN: 978-965-229-910-9

1 3 5 7 9 8 6 4 2

Gefen Publishing House Ltd.
6 Hatzvi Street
Jerusalem 94386, Israel
972-2-538-0247
orders@gefenpublishing.com

Gefen Books
11 Edison Place
Springfield, NJ 07081, USA
1-800-477-5257
orders@gefenpublishing.com

IICC
Israel Intelligence Heritage and Commemoration Center
P.O.B. 3555
Ramat Hasharon, Israel 47143
www.intelligence.org.il

www.gefenpublishing.com

Printed in Israel   *Send for our free catalogue*

Library of Congress Cataloging-in-Publication Data

Melekhet mahshevet. English
    Israel's silent defender : an inside look at sixty years of Israeli intelligence / edited
by Amos Gilboa and Ephraim Lapid ; associate editor Yochi Erlich.
        p. cm.
    ISBN 978-965-229-528-6
    1. Intelligence service—Israel—History. 2. Secret service—Israel—History.
    3. Israel. Mosad le-modi'in ve-tafkidim meyuhadim. I. Gilboa, Amos. II. Lapid,
Efrayim. III. Erlich, Yochi. IV. Title.
    UB251.I78M4313 2011
    327.125694—dc23
                                    2011034334

שר הביטחון
MINISTER OF DEFENSE

The Kiriya, 15 Elul 5771
September 15, 2011

Dear Reader,

As a young officer in the IDF, and afterward as commander of an elite unit, I led sensitive, complex and daring operations that were designed to improve Israel's intelligence capability. Intelligence is an extremely vital issue for this tiny country in the Middle East, in its daily struggle for existence, as it is surrounded by terrorist states and organizations that pose a constant threat to the ordinary life of its citizens.

Over the years, and when I served in the most senior positions – as head of IDF intelligence, IDF chief of staff, government minister, and above all during my past role as prime minister and today as minister of defense – I have always valued the contribution of intelligence to building Israel's security.

This book offers its readers a close look at the essence of the Israeli intelligence organization, one of the best and most experienced in the world. It is imperative that professionals throughout the world gain a better understanding of the challenges that Israel faces and the answers that Israel offers the world, in contending with terrorism and threats confronting not only Israel but the entire world today.

In my opinion, this book, written by experienced and professional members of Israel's intelligence organization, is an important gift to Israel's partners in the ongoing struggle against war and terror, and to the advancement of possibilities for peace in the region and throughout the world.

Ehud Barak
Minister of Defense

Meir Amit

1921–2009

This book is dedicated to the memory of Major General Meir Amit, head of military intelligence for the IDF (IDI), director of the Mossad, minister of the Israeli government, and founder, chairman and president of the Israel Intelligence Heritage and Commemoration Center.

Contents

Section Three

EXAMPLES OF INTELLIGENCE OPERATIONS: SUCCESSES AND FAILURES

Section Four

INTELLIGENCE CHALLENGES IN DIFFERENT ARENAS

Section Five

BRANCHES AND COMPONENTS OF ISRAELI INTELLIGENCE

Section Six

THE DYNAMICS OF ISRAELI INTELLIGENCE ACTIVITY

APPENDICES

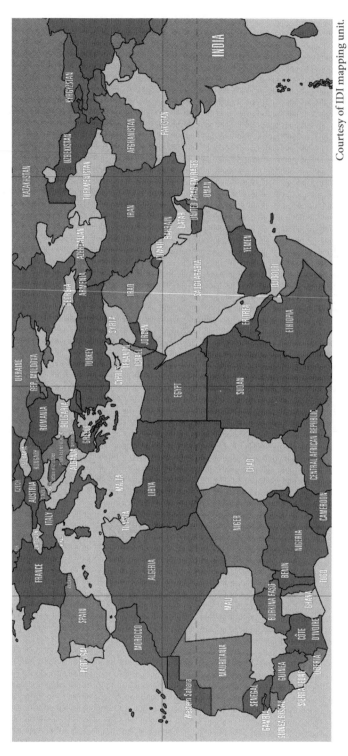

Courtesy of IDI mapping unit.

Editors' Preface

Israel is a country small in area and population, but the challenges before its intelligence community are enormous. Since its founding in May 1948, the Israeli intelligence community has been a central part of Israel's national security and an important factor in its decision-making process. For the past sixty years, it has dealt with all the country's many tactical and strategic challenges. It has also been involved with policy issues vital to the existence of the state: the stability of the regional regimes, radicalization and change, trends toward war and peace in the neighboring countries and the process of working toward political arrangements.

Israeli intelligence makes an important contribution to all the intelligence services around the world, especially that of the United States, in the struggle against the threats from Iran and global terrorism. Everywhere, intelligence officers who are in direct contact with Israeli intelligence esteem its professionalism, the experience it has gained, its daring and its creativity.

With that in mind, the Israel Intelligence Heritage and Commemoration Center decided to provide access to the world of Israeli intelligence for all those interested in it. It was written by the best intelligence officers, almost all of whom served (and some of whom still do, for example Brigadier General Itai Brun and Brigadier General Eli Pollak) in the highest positions of the Israeli intelligence community, each writing about the subject he specialized in for a period of years. For example, former Mossad head Efraim Halevy wrote about the Mossad, and Brigadier General Hanan Geffen, former head of the SIGINT unit, wrote the article about SIGINT.

The history of Israeli intelligence, how it was founded, its achievements and failures, fields of activity, collection agencies, arenas of operations and various other subjects are presented here in articles written by the individuals who dealt directly with them. Only very rarely does Israeli intelligence allow former officers to present an almost official version of their experience to the world at large.

This book provides the most reliable picture of Israeli intelligence that can be made public, given the understandable security limitations. We found it very difficult to decide what to include, especially considering the constraints of space and other factors. We are aware that some of the intelligence community's most outstanding operations cannot yet be revealed. However, we hope that the articles that have been included will make it possible for the reader to partake of the experience of the Israeli intelligence community and learn of the achievements of one of the world's leading intelligence services.

For obvious security reasons, there are very few academic-type footnotes and references. The authors are individually responsible for the contents of their articles.

Various appendices have been included to assist the reader's understanding. There is a timetable of the main intelligence events since the founding of the State of Israel up to the summer of 2010, as well as thumbnail biographies of all the heads of the Israeli intelligence community.

In translating Hebrew terms into English we were careful to use expressions that would be easy for the English-speaking reader to assimilate. The intelligence branch of the IDF's (Israel Defense Force's) general staff – military intelligence, abbreviated in Hebrew as אמ״ן (Aman) – is uniformly referred to as Israel Defense Intelligence, or IDI. The general security service, abbreviated in Hebrew as שב״כ (Shabak), is referred to as the Israel Security Agency, or ISA. The institute for intelligence and special operations is known worldwide by the Hebrew word for "institute," מוסד, and is simply called the Mossad.

In translating terms referring to the bureaucratic structure of the intelligence services and the IDF, we used the following:

- Branch: the uppermost and largest framework.
- Division: the framework directly below the branch.
- Department: the framework directly below the division.

We very much appreciate the contributions of all the authors, who shared their experiences in the hopes of building a better world. Obviously the contents of all the articles are the responsibility of their authors.

The English edition of this book is dedicated to the memory of Meir Amit, who was head of the Mossad and director of IDI, and who passed away in 2009. Its publication was made possible by the generous contributions of the Amit family and of Mozi Wertheim, Israeli businessman and friend of Meir.

Special thanks to Nachik Navoth, a close friend of Meir and formerly deputy head of the Mossad, who used his great talents to recruit the resources to publish an English edition.

Special thanks to Elizabeth Yuval, who translated the Hebrew texts, and to Ita Olesker, who edited the final English manuscript, for their professional contributions.

Thanks to the Israel Intelligence Heritage and Commemoration Center, its chairman, Efraim Halevy, and CEO, Brig. General (Res.) David Tzur, who gave their support to publishing an English edition, and to Ilan Greenfield, Smadar Belilty and Lynn Douek, whose enthusiasm helped market the legacy of Israeli intelligence to the world.

Brigadier General (Res.) Amos Gilboa
Brigadier General (Res.) Ephraim Lapid

Introduction

Efraim Halevy
Former Director of the Mossad

This collection of articles, first published in Hebrew on the occasion of Israel's sixtieth anniversary by the Israel Intelligence Heritage and Commemoration Center, is a first attempt by an Israeli national center to provide the public at large with an insight into the Israeli intelligence community, its structure, operational ethos and achievements during the second half of the twentieth century. Edited and produced by Reserve Generals Amos Gilboa and Ephraim Lapid, and reserve officer Yochi Erlich as assistant editor, all veteran officers of military intelligence, and co-published with Yediot Aharonot, one of the largest publishing houses in Israel, the endeavour was fraught with difficulties and uncertainties.

From the very outset, it was clear to all those involved that regardless of how objective the choice of contributions was, the end result would provoke strong disagreements among both veterans and serving officers regarding commissions and omissions. Indeed, security constraints dictated that the vast majority of the greatest and most successful operations not be revealed at all; thus the contributions of the Mossad, Israel's external intelligence service, and those of the Israel Security Agency would receive less prominence than others. By the time the censors permit wide coverage of the most significant and successful operations of those sixty years, witnesses of and participants in the endeavours will long be dead, and the loss will be irretrievable.

This English edition is dedicated to the memory of the first chairman and a founding figure of the Israel Intelligence Heritage and Commemoration Center, Major General Meir Amit. During his distinguished career, when he served in the positions of both director of military intelligence and head of the Mossad for a total of seven years, British Mandate Palestine–born Amit saw combat in command positions during the War of Independence and played a pioneering role in several areas of defense and civil endeavour. He was one of a number of father figures for the intelligence community. His leadership qualities enabled him to command operations such as the one that brought an Iraqi-piloted Soviet MIG-21 to Israel in the mid-'60s, serving the interests of both Israel and the free world during the long, tense years of the Cold War.

Before delving into the book's diverse contributions, I think it important to draw attention to a few elements of the unique backdrop on which many of the adventures and escapades played. In addition, providing brief descriptions of some of the service chiefs can provide the reader with insight into the nature of our intelligence community, beginning with its founding shortly after our War of Independence. Indeed, I would have preferred to intersperse them with thumbnail sketches of a few of the community's unsung heroes, individuals who snatched glorious victory from the ever-present jaws of defeat, but alas, censorship restrictions will not permit me to do so, even now.

Major General Amit was succeeded as director of Israel Defense Intelligence by Major General Aharon Yariv, born in Latvia, who served as Captain Rabinowitz in the British Army in World War II. Like Amit, he saw action in the War of Independence, rose in the ranks as an infantry brigade commander and for eight years was a legendary chief of the Intelligence Division, including during the Six-Day War. Amongst other contributions, his methodology and razor-sharp mind molded the evaluation branch of the service into its present state. He went on to establish a pioneering think tank in Israel, and when the Yom Kippur

War broke out in 1973 he was hastily redrafted into the army. When the war ended he headed the negotiating team for the terms of the cease-fire with the Egyptian military high command, the first step in the process that culminated five years later with Israel's first peace treaty, with Egypt.

On the other side of the coin, the security service, parallel to MI5, was headed for ten years by Amos Manor, a Holocaust survivor born in Hungary who escaped from one of the last trains taking Jews to Auschwitz. He came to Israel after the war, shortly before the state was born. Within five years his meteoric rise placed him at the helm of a service dedicated to defending the fledgling state against the concerted effort of the Communist bloc's security machine, led by the dreaded, highly successful and motivated KGB, to carry out strategic recruitments in Israel. With no prior experience, Manor quickly devised strategies and a modus operandi enabling his service to unmask agent after agent, and within a few years he was internationally recognized as a unique artist and authority in the field.

German-born Joseph Hermelin headed the security service for eleven years. For the seven years after the Six-Day War he faced a double challenge, the necessity to create a vast, effective security system for collecting intelligence in the densely populated areas of the West Bank and Gaza Strip that had fallen into Israeli hands, and to forge defensive and offensive capabilities to confront nascent but quickly developing Palestinian terrorism. His pioneering successes have become models used worldwide.

The last leader I wish to mention is Isser Harel, who headed the Mossad for eleven years and laid the foundations for both its clandestine foreign intelligence collection and its special external operations. Born in Russia before the Revolution, he came to Palestine as a young pioneer and worked for a short time as a fruit packer. During his long service, he fashioned the Mossad's modus operandi and basic ethos, and the small band of trusted officers he recruited, a few of whom are still alive, acted as a guild sworn to secrecy. His best-known and most publicly acclaimed operation was the search for and apprehension of Adolf Eichmann, the architect of the Final Solution that killed six million Jews, a third of the world's Jewish population. Eichmann was brought to Israel from his hiding place in Argentina in a clandestine airborne operation – the first but by no means last Israeli intelligence community global endeavour.

This very brief and necessarily incomplete introductory sketch provides the reader with a few milestones in the history and achievements of the Israel intelligence community.

I did not randomly select names and subjects, and will readily admit that others might make different choices. But my intent has been to use them to describe the geographic and professional diversity this incomparable intelligence community has had since its inception.

If I were asked to define a major aspect of the "mission" of each service, I would answer that given the unique challenges Israel has faced, and in view of the two thousand years of trials and tribulations that the Jewish people has endured, it has been our sacred mission to play a major role in defending Israel against all threats from all directions.

Forewarned is forearmed: we are duty bound to guarantee that nothing can threaten the existence of the State of Israel, and given our track record, I trust we will stay true to our mission and prevail. I hope the reader will sense that as he or she goes through these pages.

Section One

The Heads of the Intelligence Community Describe Their Visions and Challenges

Introduction

Amos Gilboa and Ephraim Lapid

The Israeli intelligence community is composed of three national services: Israel Defense Intelligence (IDI), the Mossad and the Israel Security Agency (ISA). There is also an intelligence body operating within the Ministry of Foreign Affairs, which is under the authority of the foreign minister.

Israel Defense Intelligence (IDI)

IDI is the largest member of the intelligence community. It is a branch of the IDF's general staff and is responsible for Israel's national intelligence evaluation, as opposed to other countries, where civilian organizations perform the function. The IDI head is the intelligence officer of the Israeli prime minister and government, and helps determine and direct Israel's security and foreign policies. Despite his senior position, the IDI head is subordinate to the chief of staff and through him to the defense minister – unlike the Mossad and the ISA, which are directly under the authority of the prime minister.

IDI is also responsible for the intelligence furnished to the defense minister, the IDF's general staff and the various commands and fighting forces, and for all types of early warning, ongoing security, attack targets and intelligence during wartime.

Various units operate to ensure IDI's ability to carry out its missions. They include a large unit for national intelligence analysis and several units for collection, the most important of which is SIGINT (similar to the American NSA). In addition there are HUMINT, VISINT,

OSINT and mapping units. Manpower, technology, finances and logistics are operated by the chief intelligence officer, who is subordinate to the IDI head.

At the field level of the ground forces and in the air force and navy there are also intelligence units; these receive professional direction from IDI and are integrated into its national security evaluation.

Thousands of enlisted, career and reserve soldiers work for IDI.

The Mossad
The Mossad is responsible for covert activities carried out abroad to preserve the security of the State of Israel and its citizens. It collects intelligence beyond Israel's borders; prevents Israel's enemies from developing and acquiring non-conventional weapons; prevents terrorists from attacking Israeli and Jewish targets abroad; develops clandestine political and other contacts abroad; brings Jews to Israel from locations where Israel's ordinary immigration institutions cannot operate; carries out special operations outside Israel's borders; supports and takes an active part in the operational and intelligence challenges of the IDF and the security establishment; and produces operative and strategic intelligence. The head of the Mossad answers directly to the prime minister.

The Israel Security Agency (ISA, also known as the Shabak)
The ISA is responsible for preventing terrorism and all forms of subversion, whether by hostile enemy forces or by hostile forces within Jewish Israeli society. The ISA is also responsible for all forms of counterespionage, both inside and outside Israel. It is also responsible for the security of national information and for determining the reliability of those who deal with the country's classified information. It protects the country's most important individuals, especially the prime minister. Its role was extended after 1967, when Judea, Samaria and the

Gaza Strip became Israel's responsibility and Arab terrorism increased both in Israel and abroad. The ISA head answers directly to the prime minister.

Coordination

The joint heads of services committee, chaired by the director of the Mossad, coordinates the activities of the intelligence services. It meets at various intervals, and its sessions are attended by the heads of the intelligence services, the head of the national security staff, a representative from the Israel Police Force and the prime minister's military secretary.

Oversight

Parliamentary oversight of the intelligence community is carried out by the Knesset's Foreign Affairs and Defense Committee. The committee also has a secret services subcommittee whose deliberations are confidential. There is no possibility of a hearing, as there is in Congress, and oversight is based on reports from the heads of the intelligence community.

A Final Note: The Israel Intelligence and Commemoration Center

It is the editors' privilege to end this introduction with a note that the Israel Intelligence Heritage and Commemoration Center is responsible for publishing this book. The center is an NGO dedicated to preserving the memory and heritage of the fallen of the intelligence community, those who served in Israel Defense Intelligence, the Mossad and the Israel Security Agency. The center's activities are geared for the general public, particularly for the younger generation. It is also home to the Intelligence and Terrorism Information Center, an NGO that provides the public in Israel and abroad with the most reliable information available about terrorism, particularly Palestinian terrorism.

IDI Faces the Challenges of Tomorrow

Major General Amos Yadlin
Former Head of IDI, 2006–2010

More than sixty years ago, on November 28, 1947, the eve of the UN vote on the Partition Plan, the CIA issued its intelligence evaluation: "The war in Palestine will increase in intensity…. As the Arabs gradually coordinate their war effort, the Jews will be forced to withdraw from isolated positions, and having been drawn into a war of attrition, will gradually be defeated. The Jews will be able to hold out no longer than two years…."

I chose to begin with the CIA evaluation not to indicate another mistake in strategic intelligence assessment (of which we ourselves are not innocent), but to show, on the one hand, how difficult intelligence work is and, on the other, how great an achievement the establishment of the State of Israel was – a historic event in which the Israeli intelligence community played a major role. Now as then, every intelligence worker must be reserved when presenting an evaluation, and focus it on one clear objective: ensuring the security of the country.

Intelligence work is hard and challenging. It is essentially a kind of contest, a battle waged between the ever-changing, growing threats and the developing capabilities of Israeli intelligence to uncover the enemy's capabilities, indicate his intentions, identify his weak spots and enable prevention and victory.

It is therefore no wonder that every head of Israel Defense Intelligence must not only provide early warning for war, national strategic intelligence for decisions and operational intelligence, but must plan for threats before they develop. It is not only a question of considering the enemy's capabilities, but of the broad contexts of the contest. He has to show the decision makers and the IDF what the future possibilities are, the dangers and opportunities, and must also build and oversee the long-term future strength of Israel Defense Intelligence.

The challenges that will confront IDI and the intelligence community in the coming years and the ways of meeting them are the following:

- A nuclear Middle East: Coping with Iran's nuclear aspirations today and in the future requires expertise in a wide range of political, military and technological fields, especially since it is entirely possible that other countries will develop nuclear capabilities.

- The changing military threat: There is still the possibility of a military clash between countries, but one apparently somewhat different from those in the past. There will be less maneuvering and more precise fire; the threat to the home front will be greater, as will the potential for the use of non-conventional weapons. As a result, IDI will have to develop collection, analysis and production capabilities in new areas, while continuing its efforts in classic military research, such as terrain research, modern military doctrines, order of battle, etc.

- Blurred borders between the military and terrorism (asymmetric warfare): The asymmetric efforts of Israel's enemies are not new, but they take new forms. We are currently witnessing the militarization of the terrorist organizations, such as Hezbollah and Hamas, and the use of guerilla warfare by countries such as Syria, which has adopted modes of combat from Hezbollah. Their final objective is to erode Israel's relative aerial and intelligence advantages. As these borders become increasingly blurred, greater cooperation will be required within and between the various intelligence services to meet future challenges: sharing and exchanging knowledge and military and terrorism expertise.

- Crossing borders: Analyzing threats often brings to the surface trends that cross borders. Like the global jihad, which has cells around the world, there are ideas and military developments that do not belong strictly to one country or another. Many examples can be given, such as rockets, from Hamas's Qassams to Iran's Shihabs; the idea of "resistance" (*muqawamah*), which is common to Iran, Hezbollah and Hamas; and the strengthening of the relations between Iran, Syria and Hezbollah, which to a large extent have replaced the former threat of the eastern front.

- Top secrets: The enemy's access to Western technology not only serves him in developing more dangerous military capabilities, but provides him with better protection for his own secrets and enables him to develop intelligence capabilities that can better uncover our secrets. We are constantly required to undertake the Sisyphean task of improving our ability to penetrate the secrets of the enemy, and at the same time must have an active approach to protect our own secrets. I feel it is an Achilles heel for Israel.

- Cyberspace: The threats Israel will face in the coming years will force the intelligence community to remain at the cutting edge of global technology, especially in developing collection capabilities. In addition to extending current capabilities, such as SIGINT, HUMINT and VISINT, Israel Defense Intelligence has already begun collecting intelligence in cyberspace. Moreover, in the long run, cyberspace will have offensive as well as defensive capabilities, and so Israel cannot allow itself to lag behind. That is especially true because the enemy is making efforts to close the cybernetic gap. The increasing use of computers by Israel's enemies all over the globe will increase the volume of information IDI has to cope with, and consequently it has already become necessary to develop information systems more advanced than those we currently have for collection, analysis, storage and circulation.

- Targets: The development of collection and analysis capabilities will not be worth the effort unless it is translated into one of the central goals sought by every intelligence body: relevance. It is my considered opinion that IDI still has a long way to go before it will be able to provide the Israeli defense establishment with solid information for fighting and with exact targets for attack at any given moment. A preprepared stock of exact targets, as well as the ability to create targets in real time, improve field security and upgrade combat intelligence (so that intelligence flows from the general staff to the battalions and vice versa), make for holistic intelligence and will in all probability make it possible for Israel to realize its relative advantages over its enemies. Attaining these goals will be an important step in winning a war quickly and unequivocally.

- Cooperation and foreign relations: More than once, developing threats have made Israel's interests compatible with those of other countries in general, and countries in the Middle East in particular. Lessons learned from dealing with the global jihad have taught that openness between intelligence communities can produce important results. Increased openness with countries in the Middle East and the rest of the world, besides familiar Western allies, can improve our ability to deal with various border-crossing trends and our understanding their societal trends.

- Deterrence and its borders: The strength of Israel's deterrence is elusive and problematic, and it is difficult to predict its future effectiveness. However, in retrospect, it is clear that the enemy has refrained from pulling the trigger or harming the

State of Israel. Basically, Israel's deterrent power rests on how the enemy balances his profits and losses – harming us and the consequences of the challenge he chooses to present. Daily life in Israel is relatively quiet, but that quiet comes with a price tag. The desire to preserve the calm ties our hands vis-à-vis the military buildup our enemies are engaged in. Here a vicious circle is at work, because the enemy gains strength without our interference and consequently feels he has deterrent power, and thus at the end of the day a mutual deterrence has been established.

- Non-military threats: Beyond the military threats, there are new strategic challenges, first among them the efforts to delegitimize the State of Israel and its right to exist. The challenge is presented at various levels, from the most basic, directed at the legitimacy of the state, to the more recent one, which targets Israel's policies and the IDF's ability to act freely to implement them.

- The radicalization of Arab society and the growing challenges to the regimes' stability: While there is no clear and present danger to the stability of regional regimes, one cannot assume the status quo will continue in perpetuity. The dangerous combination of economic distress and an increasingly extremist Arab society is not comforting. It is true that Arab society has in fact been gradually adopting Western technology, more people are wearing jeans and surfing the Internet, and Al-Jazeera TV's discourse is more open than in the past. However, while the trendsetters use cellular phones, their ringtones are Arab, and they disgustedly reject the values of Western democratic society. The concept of Arab nationalism has also lost its luster and is being usurped by Islamism. All of the above pose new challenges for IDI, which beyond classic military and political intelligence must delve more deeply into the changing social trends in the Middle East.

- Guarantees of high-quality intelligence agents: IDI's most important challenge for the future is preserving its relative advantage within the international intelligence community, i.e., the high quality of its recruits, and especially those who remain in the service for long periods of time. The challenge of keeping top quality agents in service will increase, owing to competition from the civilian opportunities presented to those who serve in its ranks (IDI is known as the incubator for Israel's high tech, scientific, academic, legal and medical elites). However, the group as a whole also has to be considered: there has to be transparency, integration and cooperation within IDI and between IDI and the Israeli intelligence community, since it is clear that the intelligence whole is greater than the sum of its parts. This past year we proved how great Israeli intelligence cooperation could be (and I cannot elaborate).

An examination of future threats and the necessary responses shows that the State of Israel will continue to face intelligence challenges. Consequently there can be no replacement for the comprehensive intelligence complex currently being put together by the IDI director, since he is both the national evaluator and military intelligence officer. The more complex the threats become (both outside and inside Israel's borders), the more important will become the special, vital facets of IDI, which provides the decision makers with a full and complete intelligence picture integrating tactical, strategic, military and political understanding.

The IDI director's expertise in actively understanding the discourse between the politicians and the military, the strengths of the IDF and how the defense establishment is constructed will help him contribute to the decision-making process. In the foreseeable future the IDI director will not be able to limit himself to presenting a picture of threats and opportunities; he will have to conduct an instructive dialogue with the decision makers about developing challenges and provide an evaluation of possible options for the actions of our forces and scenarios for the enemy's response to each of them.

Moreover, at a time when threats are international and cross borders, and the distinctions between governments and terrorist organizations are becoming blurred (for example, the Hamas takeover of the Gaza Strip and Hezbollah's involvement in the Lebanese regime), in an early warning of war (IDI's highest mission), beside the enemy's military capabilities, his political, strategic, geopolitical and economic factors must be taken into consideration. Providing the whole intelligence picture and evaluation, therefore, has become a necessity rather than a luxury.

Finally, looking to the future, IDI will have to cope with an increasingly complex and complicated environment. However, I am certain it will be a better, more advanced organization, able to meet every challenge and continue to be the heart of Israel's defensive shield.

The Mossad: Vision and Reality

Major General (Res.) Meir Dagan
Former Director of the Institute for Intelligence and
Special Operations (Mossad), 2002–2011

The Institute for Intelligence and Special Operations – or as it is generally known, the Mossad – is a national organization responsible for clandestine activity abroad whose aim is to ensure the security of the State of Israel and its citizens. The Mossad is responsible for preventing terrorist attacks and threats arising from the use of nonconventional weapons, and it carries out special operations, integrates into and supports the intelligence and operational missions undertaken by the IDF and the security forces, rescues Jews, collects information and produces strategic and operative intelligence.

Since its inception, the Mossad has striven to fulfill its missions. It thwarted the activity of the German scientists in Egypt in the 1960s, fought Palestinian terrorism abroad in the 1970s, foiled Iraq's nuclear program in the late 1970s and early 1980s and brought the Ethiopian Jews to Israel in the 1980s and early 1990s. The Mossad played an important and often exclusive role in these and many other missions – missions it helped make possible through covert operations throughout the world, often joining forces with and profiting from the capabilities of other branches of Israel's defense establishment.

The Mossad's activity relies on secrecy. Secrecy determines its operational restrictions and the considerations influencing its power and capabilities. The Mossad could never have been able, nor be able, to fulfill its mission unless it worked under a cloak of secrecy and compartmentalization. Therefore, obviously, I cannot recount its activities, but I can present some of the premises on which its activities are based.

In recent years various trends have influenced the way the Mossad operates; these trends will continue to influence both the Mossad and the security forces and intelligence community. In general, Israel is at the center of a vast field of complex, multi-dimensional threats. They come from countries as far away as Iran, from various manifestations of the global jihad and from Israel's often precarious position within an environment of threats and opportunities. The international arena is diverse and dynamic, and the balance of power is continually changing. The Middle East has become more complex than ever, and is strongly influenced by religious, political, societal and economic forces, all pulling in different directions.

Israel's strategic environment makes continual evaluation and change imperative. For example, as the threats of the past – such as Jordan before the peace agreement and Iraq before American intervention – fade, new ones emerge, and Israel now has to face the threat of the Tehran-Damascus-Hezbollah axis. However, the axis is not monolithic, but rather composed of many dynamic strata that balance forces, interests and changing trends.

In addition, fundamental concepts undergo constant change, such as the concepts of strategic depth and geographical distance. While we still examine changes in the artillery ranges of enemies on our borders, at the same time enemies further away develop launching capabilities of thousands of kilometers, bringing them closer and posing new threats.

The distinction between "army" and "terrorism" is becoming blurred. Regionally, we are still threatened by large standing armies as well as relatively small terrorist networks. However, both seem to be metamorphosing and merging: the armies conceal themselves and make plans to operate against civilian populations, and the terrorist organizations engage in military buildup, construct hierarchical systems and organize themselves as armies. To respond we have to change our concepts and develop new ways to meet the challenge.

Coping with changing situations and challenges requires a combination of two basic elements. First, a thorough understanding of the new reality. To that end the Mossad invests continuous efforts to increase its collection, analysis and research capabilities, in order to be able to provide a full, authentic, in-depth intelligence picture. Second, in the world of today's threats, an understanding of the situation is not sufficient; we must do our utmost to influence and shape events. To that end we must construct the forces necessary to support our actions and develop responses to challenges and frequent changes, effectively and within the relevant time frame.

We in the security forces will routinely and wholeheartedly examine our organization and preparedness to ensure that our spheres of responsibility and activity, operational methods and distribution of resources provide the correct responses. In the coming years the Mossad will be required to act creatively, with determination and in secret in many areas. That will demand increasing collaboration within organizations, between organizations and even internationally. The Mossad will have to construct new, independent capabilities and at the same time find strategic partners that will allow it to meet future challenges successfully.

The Mossad's main weapon has always been and will always be its personnel, the men and women who know how to operate in a complex world flooded with technology and information. They understand the enormity of the responsibility they bear and are prepared to focus their efforts over a long period of time. They are brave, ideologically motivated, dedicated and loyal individuals.

I look to the future and its challenges, as complex as they may be, with complete faith in the Mossad and its ability to meet them.

The Israel Security Agency:

Challenges and Vision

Yuval Diskin
Former Head of ISA, 2005–2011

The Israel Security Agency[1] has undergone great changes in the past decade. The assassination of Israeli Prime Minister Yitzhak Rabin (1995) and the difficulties encountered in combating the suicide bombing attacks carried out by the Islamist organizations after the Oslo Accords (1993–1994) prompted an in-depth investigation of the ISA's procedures. The ISA was reconstructed and emerged as a leader in activity, capability and management methods. Its guiding principle is *synergetic prevention.*[2] The concept of synergism guides all the ISA's disciplines and makes each unit's relative advantage or capacity subordinate to achieving the common goal. The approach will undoubtedly predominate in the coming decade and undergo constant modifications, continuing as a major factor in the realization of the organization's goals in a changing environment.

Furthermore, this past decade taught the ISA the importance of working in collaboration with other organizations in the defense establishment. It has therefore made efforts with its colleagues in the

---

1.   The Israel Security Agency, or ISA, is commonly known by the acronym of its Hebrew name, *Sherut ha-Bitahon ha-Klali,* or Shabak.

2.   A situation in which the whole is greater than the sum of its parts.

intelligence community to develop a synergistic approach in the war on terrorism and other areas and bring that approach to a universally recognized high level. I am convinced that synergism will make it possible for the Israeli intelligence community to reach its complex goals in the coming decade as well.

The ISA's vision, as recently articulated by its senior leaders, sets the highest standard for its counterterrorism units, whose responsibility is to prevent terrorist attacks, espionage, subversion of the state's democratic regime and the exposure of state secrets.

As impossible a mission as it may seem, the core values contained in ISA's vision are instilled in all ISA personnel. To meet our goals, it is necessary to maintain our technologies at the highest level possible. In essence, the ISA is similar to the other organizations in the intelligence community (the Mossad and IDI), which protect the state's security. However, it differs significantly from them in that it maintains the security of the state and protects its democratic order while working within society itself. We work as a state agency, accountable to the law and with complete allegiance to the values of the rule of law and democracy. The ISA has been granted full authority to achieve its goals, but with that comes the responsibility to employ it with great sensitivity and sensibility, and to adhere strictly to the ISA's ethic of restraint.

The greatest challenge facing the ISA in the coming decade will undoubtedly be recruiting new employees – highly principled, motivated and deeply committed to the State of Israel. That is because we are convinced that the personal qualities of our employees, along with the leadership qualities of our commanders and our core values, are the source of our strength, directly influencing the value of the results we produce.

Section Two

The Roots: How the Intelligence Services Were Founded

The Beginning: From an Information Service to a Military Intelligence Service in the War of Independence (1948–1949)

Yochi Erlich
Former Officer of IDI

The Legacy of the Information Service (Shai)

On the eve of Israel's War of Independence, the leadership in Eretz Israel had no substantial information about the enemy armies, which was a desperate situation. It had not yet constructed a military intelligence apparatus at either the command or field level and therefore relied on what was known as "Shai" (acronym for the Hebrew *sherut yediot*, "information service"). The basic assumption was that the main military activity would be conducted within the Eretz Israel borders against Israeli Arabs, and therefore no preparations were made for collecting information about the Arab armies. Until then Shai's main activity had been providing information about the struggles with the British over immigration (*aliyah*) and settlement, information about local and neighboring Arabs, and about the rogue Jewish organizations, both left and right,[1] which did not accept national authority. When the war

---

1. The Etzel, also known as the Irgun, which followed the Revisionist politics of Ze'ev Jabotinsky; the Lehi, also known as the Stern Gang, whose objective was to force the British out of Eretz Israel; and the Communists.

broke out, the military intelligence corps was established at the general staff level, an accepted practice in every regular army.

Establishing General Command Military Intelligence[2]

During the first half of 1948, Yigael Yadin, the army's first head of operations, began establishing Israel's military intelligence as a department within operations. The key positions were given to members of the Haganah[3] who were familiar with the situation on the ground, including the Arab villages, and not to those experienced in intelligence or who had received professional training. Using the British model, Yadin prepared the foundation for the new apparatus in three stages:

- The first stage was to establish an intelligence department in the general staff within the operations branch (OB/3) and train a corps of intelligence officers at the field unit level (before June 1948). The department collated collected information and circulated it to the field units, and directed and supervised the intelligence action of the field divisions.
- The second was to establish a military intelligence system subordinate to the operations branch for the entire army (July 1948–January 1949).
- The third involved integrating the intelligence system into the general staff with a status equal to the other sections of the operations branch (February–December 1949).

---

2. Based on Zehava Ostfeld, *An Army Is Born* [Hebrew], (Israeli Ministry of Defense Publishing, 1994), pp. 324–81.

3. The pre-state paramilitary organization, which became the Israel Defense Forces after 1948.

The First Stage

During the first six months of 1948 various intelligence units were established and later incorporated into the intelligence service. They dealt with psychological warfare, the military press, censorship, mapping and photograph interpretation. A center was established to monitor and translate Arab broadcasts, which eventually progressed to monitoring enemy signals traffic. There was also a department for collecting and processing material about the armies and economies of the neighboring Arab countries (which later developed into the Arab states military intelligence research unit) and one for collecting and processing information about foreign affairs.

Shai, which operated within OB/3 during the first six months of 1948, was the foundation on which military intelligence was built, but its operational performance was problematic. Only when veterans of the British army took over the command did it become a professional corps.

Intelligence on the Eve of the War of Independence

While Israel did not have all the pertinent information, it was clear that the Arab armies were preparing to invade Eretz Israel and would do so as soon as the British evacuated on the night of May 14 or during May 15. However, only a week before the invasion, the general staff had no organized information about the enemy's strength, weapons and plans, and monitoring the Arab armies was still in its infancy. Intelligence did not improve significantly during the first days of the invasion; the information supplied by Shai was insufficient in many respects and there was no improvement in military intelligence. Reliable information about the invading armies began to arrive only toward the end of May 1948, but by that time the Israeli forces were already fighting fierce battles to halt the enemy's advance. The lack of reliable information at the general staff level meant the various brigades had to deploy for the invasion with almost no intelligence.

There was a desperate need for far-reaching conceptual changes in the structure of the military intelligence corps, its status, composition and methods of operation – changes that had been made essential by the attack of the Arab armies.

The Second Stage

Establishing Military Intelligence:
The Reorganization of the Intelligence Service

The changes in the structure and personnel of the intelligence community were carried out by Ben-Gurion only after the situation on the ground had become extremely difficult and criticism of the field commanders worsened. Most of the changes involved separating political-strategic and internal security intelligence from military and operational security intelligence, and the construction of three distinct branches: political intelligence; internal security, which would report to the Minister of Defense; and a military intelligence service, which would report to the chief of staff.

Accordingly, on June 10, 1948, the deputy chief of staff issued an order to disband Shai and establish a military intelligence service within the operations branch. It would be responsible for combat intelligence, operational security, counterintelligence, censorship and monitoring and translating information. Isser Be'eri – who enjoyed the support of senior members of the leading political party at that time – was put in charge. Chaim Herzog was appointed as his deputy and represented the service in the general staff. A week later Yadin announced that Shai and the operations branch's intelligence service would unite and become "a military intelligence service," divided into departments that included combat intelligence, censorship and operational security. He mentioned only two appointments: Isser Be'eri as its head, and Benjamin Gibli as head of combat intelligence.

Establishing the new service was a watershed:

- There was now military intelligence to support the fighting army.
- The status of military intelligence was elevated; it was no longer a sub-unit of the operations branch, but an independent service within it.
- Once Shai had been disbanded and integrated into the new service, communications took less time and the center of gravity shifted from a civilian information service to an independent military intelligence service with its own sources.

Formulating Methods for Intelligence Work

Once the intelligence service had been established, Herzog began organizing it into an effective professional corps. He was mainly concerned with three issues:

- Constructing a skeleton military intelligence corps as a central, independent body uniting all the existing intelligence units directly answerable to the operations branch, and operating them within one framework according to one program.
- Basing the service on intelligence professionals who during World War II had specialized in fields such as combat intelligence, monitoring and translating information, technical and field intelligence, and research and field security.
- Constructing intelligence sources independent of the civilian intelligence apparatus.

The planned structure of the service included the staff, units for reconnaissance, researching foreign armies, combat intelligence, monitoring and translating intelligence information, field security, counterespionage and a technical unit serving all the army's intelligence bodies.

From that point on intelligence work focused on two main areas. One was strategic intelligence, which studied the strength of the enemy armies, the combat arenas and military potential as the basis for operative planning and determining courses of action in changing situations. The other was operative and tactical intelligence, which gathered information about the enemy and communicated it to the battlefield.

Combat intelligence, headed by Benjamin Gibli, was the most important. It was responsible for field intelligence, and its role was to provide field commanders with reliable, comprehensive information about the enemy. Army veterans who had proven intelligence experience in the British army were assigned to upgrade it. From then on combat intelligence was the main crossroads for the overall intelligence system. It studied and analyzed the enemy's order of battle, aerial photographs, maps, items of intelligence information and reports from the interrogations of prisoners. The various sources were evaluated and the material was processed and distributed to the general staff and field units.

There were additional units that complemented the sources of information. They included electronic intelligence, headed by a former British professional army veteran who reorganized the branch according to methods used by the Allied armies. The field unit dealt with transborder topographical intelligence and identifying strategic targets. The foundations for military mapping were laid at the same time in both the air force and the navy, while aerial photographs became the responsibility of the air force.

The intelligence departments in the artillery and engineering corps were responsible for combat intelligence. The intelligence services of the air force and navy had operative status, but with regard to security, censorship and counterespionage they took their orders from and collaborated closely with the military intelligence service.

Formulating the Intelligence Doctrine and Instituting Uniform Work Methods

The new intelligence doctrine was based on professional material that had been edited and issued in directives and orders; it imposed work procedures and organized methods, and provided intelligence work with a standard, uniform foundation. For example, intelligence collecting objectives were determined, as were priority intelligence requirements (PIR); methods for examining information based on the "four Ws" (what happened, who saw it, when did it happen and where did it happen) were laid out, as well as ways to process and designate information according to needs and levels while preserving compartmentalization and rules for distributing material.

A system for regular reporting to and from the chief of staff and the field units was instituted for all types of intelligence activity. At the general staff level, military intelligence produced and distributed a series of reports, reviews and summaries of comprehensive information about the enemy. Intelligence work evolved and was reshaped. It was carried out in two ways: a doctrine for operating the various intelligence apparatuses was set up, and basic material about the Arab countries and their armies ("Know the enemy") was issued. Thus military intelligence had made a great leap forward from its first days at the end of 1947: from a small nucleus providing random information about Arab gangs and foreigners in Arab villages, it had become a professional corps of intelligence units like those in any regular army.

The Third Stage

The Struggle for Independent Status

Despite the development of the intelligence units, there were still serious differences of opinion regarding their status within the general staff. The minister of defense and the chief of staff were faced with the dilemma of intelligence's being an independent branch within the general staff, or, in accordance with Yigael Yadin's demand, its being answerable to the operations branch. Despite the pressure exerted after the fighting ended in 1949, it remained answerable to the operations branch.

At the end of 1949 David Ben-Gurion, who was both prime minister and minister of defense, reorganized the intelligence services.[4] Military intelligence (now headed by Chaim Herzog) became a department in the operations branch and was turned into a professional military intelligence corps.

A newly established military intelligence based on professionalism and advanced technology supported the IDF during its transition to a peacetime army, when the national objective shifted from a war for the survival of the state to defending its security and borders. Those conditions presented intelligence with two new missions. The first was collecting information about the countries of confrontation in preparation for the possibility of renewed hostilities; the second was routine security intelligence. To that end, toward the final months of 1949 an intelligence corps was established on the existing foundation, but still answerable to the operations branch. Despite the recommendations of those who dealt with the intelligence service's status, Yadin (chief of staff from November 1949 to December 1951) refused to turn it into an independent branch of the general staff in line with the British concept, and only in 1953 were the recommendations of the various committees implemented. The intelligence service achieved, although at a late date, the status and recognition it had aspired to since the end of 1947: it became an independent branch at the general staff level.

Conclusion

In reality the intelligence corps was a new body, even if it did include some of the elements of the underground organizations. Three particularly important figures contributed to its construction and image and left their mark on it. The first was David Ben-Gurion, who was involved in

---

4. See the following two articles about the establishment of the Mossad and the security service.

every stage of its development and intervened at critical junctures. The second was Yigael Yadin, head of the operations directorate, who laid the foundation for the new corps and formulated methods of action at the general staff and field unit levels according to the British model. The third was Chaim Herzog, who was in effect its architect.

The intelligence corps was a new entity and not the product of a continuous process, because there had been no components of professional military intelligence beforehand. After the War of Independence it was generally accepted that intelligence was the front line of the State of Israel's defense, because in the absence of strategic depth, early warning was of prime importance.

Founding the Mossad

Dr. Shimon Avivi

Historian

Overview

Before the establishment of the State of Israel on May 15, 1948, there were various groups in the Yishuv (the Jewish settlement in Eretz Israel before the establishment of the state) that dealt with collecting intelligence abroad. This article will describe the changes that occurred in the Israeli intelligence community before the Mossad was established as an independent operational body bearing the responsibility for overseas intelligence activities.

Disbanding Shai and Founding Other Intelligence Bodies

The groups in the Yishuv that dealt with intelligence were the political department of the Jewish Agency; the Haganah's information service (Shai; see previous article); the Institute for Aliyah Bet (the illegal Jewish immigration during the British Mandate); and the intelligence services and departments of the underground Etzel (Irgun) and Lehi (Stern Gang).

The proliferation of intelligence groups working simultaneously under the British Mandate and the IDF's dissatisfaction with the intelligence it received during the first stages of the War of Independence (1948–1949) prompted David Ben-Gurion – who served as both prime minister and minister of defense – to restructure the intelligence services even as the country was being born.

On May 30, 1948, he informed the general staff that Reuven Shiloah had been appointed by the minister of foreign affairs to head its military and political intelligence departments. During the war he would report to the Ministry of Defense, which would work in close coordination with the intelligence services of the general staff and with those of the other corps. The appointment was strictly personal, because the Ministry of Defense did not yet exist and the Ministry of Foreign Affairs did not have an intelligence department.

The following week, on June 7, Ben-Gurion consulted Reuven Shiloah and Isser Be'eri about the nature of the service. They decided to restructure it completely and base it on three corps. The first would be military intelligence, which would report to the general staff; its directors would be Isser Be'eri and Chaim Herzog. It would be responsible for field security, censorship and counterespionage. The second would be internal intelligence, directed by Isser Harel and Yosef Yizraeli. The third would be external political intelligence, directed by Reuven Shiloah. Until the end of the war it would report to the Ministry of Defense, and after that, perhaps to the Ministry of Foreign Affairs.

Ben-Gurion consulted again with Reuven Shiloah and with Ya'akov Dori, who was chief of staff, and on June 30 instructed Tzvi Ayalon, deputy chief of staff, to disband Shai and establish the new intelligence service under the operations branch at GHQ, which would deal with combat intelligence, operational security, counterespionage, censorship and communications intelligence. The order was carried out the same day, and Be'eri convened the upper echelons of Shai to inform them that the old service would be disbanded and replaced by the new: he himself would head military intelligence, Boris Guriel would direct foreign intelligence and report to Shiloah, and Isser Harel would head internal security and report directly to Ben-Gurion.

The Political Department in the
Ministry of Foreign Affairs

In June 1948 the new political department (sometimes called "the research branch") was established within the Ministry of Foreign Affairs. It was the central body of the intelligence community and would gather political, military and economic intelligence abroad. In addition, it inherited the intelligence functions of the Jewish Agency's political departments in Europe and the United States, of Shai's European branch and the branch in Israel that monitored foreign elements. The department continued the activities of the Jewish Agency department dealing with the Arab countries and Israeli Arabs. It was headed by Boris Guriel and reported to Reuven Shiloah, consultant for special issues in the Ministry of Foreign Affairs and intelligence coordinator for the prime minister and minister of defense, i.e., Ben-Gurion.

The political department was responsible for Arab country policy management and for all Israeli intelligence activities abroad. Most of its overseas branches were integrated into Israel's diplomatic legations and sent their reports to the political department in Tel Aviv.

The Supreme Coordination Committee

The domestic and foreign activities of military intelligence, and the political departments of the Ministry of Foreign Affairs and the Shabak (*sherut bitahon*, Shin Bet, the Israel Security Agency) overlapped in several areas. All of them handled agents and emissaries in Arab and European countries, but without coordinating with one another or dividing tasks. The friction between them meant responsibility and authority had to be defined. Some kind of overall committee had to be appointed, composed of an external authority and the heads of the various services, to direct and coordinate the activities of the intelligence community. In May 1949 the Supreme Coordination Committee was appointed, chaired by Reuven Shiloah. Its members were the heads of military intelligence, the political department, the Shabak and the police force. The committee's authority over the various services of which it was comprised was not clear.

On September 20 Ben-Gurion met with Shiloah, Foreign Minister Moshe Sharett and Shaul Avigur, who had been instrumental in forming Shai and had worked as director of the Institute for Aliyah Bet, to discuss the structure of the intelligence community, how the coordinating committee would operate and what the responsibilities of its chairman would be. However, Shiloah's extended missions abroad made it difficult to establish the committee as the highest authority supervising the community. Sharett agreed that Shiloah would remain in Israel for at least six months to head the committee, but insisted it not be detrimental to the Ministry of Foreign Affairs. Shiloah returned to dealing with the intelligence community but demanded to be allowed to transfer operations from one service to another. Ben-Gurion charged him with examining the existing division of responsibilities and suggesting ways of regulating it.

The Institute for Coordination

On December 13 Ben-Gurion accepted Shiloah's most important suggestions and instructed him to establish an institute (*mossad* in Hebrew) for concentrating and coordinating the activities of the state's intelligence and security services (including the army's intelligence department, the political department of the Ministry of Foreign Affairs, the Shabak, etc.). In addition to his duties as a special operations consultant within the Ministry of Foreign Affairs, he was appointed head of the Institute for Coordination of Intelligence and Security Services. He reported directly to Ben-Gurion, although administratively the institute belonged to the Ministry of Foreign Affairs.

In 1950, after the Institute for Coordination had been established, Shiloah made changes in the intelligence community's structure and the methods it used both in the country and abroad. Its operations inside Israel were transferred from the Ministry of Foreign Affairs' political department to the Shabak; the political department then became responsible for intelligence and operational intelligence abroad. Shiloah was updated about the daily activities of the services but rarely intervened. When it came to routine operations, the services collaborated without the need for the institute's mediation.

A Central Authority for Overseas Intelligence

In 1950, following differences of opinion between Shiloah, Guriel and Arthur Ben-Nathan, who was head of the European operations center, relations within the political department deteriorated. There were disagreements over the delegation of authority, methods of working overseas and the links of the various branches abroad with the department in Israel. In 1951, there was growing criticism of the political department's functioning and of Shiloah's ineffectual control over it and its branches. That led Ben-Gurion to examine personally the demoralization within the political department and the unhealthy relations between it and both the Ministry of Foreign Affairs and military intelligence. He then decided that there would be one intelligence service operating overseas and under one authority.

On February 8, 1951, a fundamental change was made in the structure and functioning of the intelligence community. Ben-Gurion separated the operations department from the political department and the Ministry of Foreign Affairs, and turned it into an independent espionage agency, or, in the words of the Coordination Committee, "a central authority for overseas intelligence." The political department was eliminated, and Chaim Ya'ari (who had worked as head of the special operations department in the military intelligence service) was appointed as head of the new espionage authority. It belonged to the Office of the Prime Minister, had a monopoly over intelligence activity overseas, and one of its duties would be to acquire information requested by the various branches of the intelligence community.

Those events annoyed and upset the overseas branches, creating the situation referred to as "the spies' rebellion." On March 2 they collectively resigned. Among those who quit were Ben-Nathan, employees of the political department and seven branch heads. Shiloah regarded it as particularly serious, not only as an attack on himself but more importantly as an attack on the authority of the State of Israel, and he punished the "rebels." He forbade some of them to work in the Ministry of Foreign Affairs, forbade some from holding any office in the civil service and pardoned some.

On April 11 the Coordination Committee discussed the establishment of a central authority for overseas intelligence, and a week later appointed committees to carry out the transfer of the political department to the new authority headed by Chaim Ya'ari.

Ranking higher than the new authority was the Institution for Coordination and Special Operations, headed by Shiloah and his second-in-command, Isidore Dorot (who had worked for the Shabak), and its name was changed to the Central Espionage Institute. At the end of July the Coordination Committee discussed the institute's political place and decided it would formally belong to the Office of the Prime Minister.

In the summer of 1952 Shiloah left the Central Espionage Institute and was replaced by Isser Harel, who had remained in charge of the Shabak and chaired the committee of the heads of the various services. Chaim Ya'ari resigned as head of the authority and was replaced by Abraham Kidron, who had worked as head of the field security in the military intelligence service.

Conclusion

The Institute for the Coordination of Intelligence and Security Services coordinated between Israel's intelligence and security services. It did not have command authority and did not bear responsibility for collecting intelligence abroad.

The day on which the decision was made to establish an independent operational body that would be responsible for overseas intelligence activities was February 8, 1951, when Ben-Gurion established an independent espionage authority, the Central Authority for Overseas Intelligence. The authority reported to Reuven Shiloah, who at that point was head of the Institute of Coordination. When the institute changed from coordinating to performing missions, its name was changed to the Central Espionage Institute.

Eventually the name was changed again, to the Institute for Intelligence and Special Operations. Coordination was assigned to the Supreme Coordinating Committee, whose name was changed to the Committee of Service Heads.

Founding the Israel Security Agency

Eitan Glaser

Former Head of the History Department of the ISA

Historical Research and Documentation Department

Note: The Israel Security Agency has also been called the Shin Bet (the acronym of *sherut ha-bitahon*, "security service," and the Shabak (the acronym of *sherut ha-bitahon ha-klali*, "general security service"). Its official name is the Israel Security Agency, ISA.

Introduction

The ISA was established on June 30, 1948, with the founding of the Israeli intelligence community after Shai (the Haganah's information service) was disbanded. The community was initially composed of the military intelligence service (Shin Mem); Daat, the political department (which later became part of the Mossad); and Mahatz, the temporary name for the internal security service, which later turned into the ISA. It was originally headed by Isser Harel, known as Little Isser (to distinguish him from Big Isser, head of military intelligence). Before the State of Israel was founded, Harel was in charge of the central and southern districts, including Tel Aviv, for the Haganah's Shai. When that came under IDF authority as a corps within the military, he was given the rank of Lieutenant Colonel.

In his book *Security and Democracy*,[1] Harel wrote that structuring the services and allocating positions were not thoroughly thought out, the people involved did not confer, everything was done in dilettante fashion and almost as a conspiracy with complete disregard for the fundamental principles of a properly functioning democracy. For example, counterespionage was initially the province of the army (Shin Mem 3, field security), the Ministry of Foreign Affairs was in charge of Daat, the political department, and the Shin Bet, as the security service was already being called, was initially responsible only for "dissidents" and communists, to prevent anti-government subversion as the state was being founded.

Two events had enormous influence on the way the Shin Bet initially operated:

- The first was the IDF's sinking of the Etzel arms ship *Altalena* (June 22, 1948).[2] The Shin Bet quickly detained the Etzel leaders involved in bringing it to Israel. In *Security and Democracy* Harel wrote that he knew the Etzel heads were planning future political careers and meant to establish a political party, but some of them were still indecisive and rebelled. Some of the more extreme members even had ideas of carrying out operations on their own, secretly stockpiling weapons and establishing a military headquarters abroad, underground-style. The

---

1.   Issar Harel, *Security and Democracy* (Tel Aviv: Idanim Publishers/Yediot Aharonot, 1989), p. 102.

2.   Menachem Begin, the commander of Etzel, who later (1977) became the Israeli prime minister, was determined to supply his organization with fighters, weapons and ammunitions. The *Altalena* arrived at the Tel Aviv coast about a month after the State of Israel was established. Begin refused to hand the weapons over to the IDF, and Ben-Gurion, fearing that it might lead to rebellion, gave the order to sink the ship.

Shin Bet, he wrote, not wanting to be surprised, monitored their actions.

- The second was the assassination of Count Bernadotte (September 17, 1948), the UN envoy who was sent to reach a stable settlement between Israel and the Arabs. After a short investigation the Shin Bet arrested some of the Lehi[3] members involved, who for cover called their organization the Homeland Front. They were tried, and activating its emergency defense laws, the temporary government declared both Lehi and the Homeland Front terrorist organizations and illegal. Yitzhak Shamir, who was elected Israeli prime minister in 1983, was the Lehi commander at that time.

The rapid and effective undercover actions taken by the security service brought it glory and an aura of omnipotence. From then on, in running the organization Isser Harel had the prime minister's full personal support. The Shin Bet has operated in absolute secrecy from the moment of its founding, with no official public declarations and no documentation. One of the few documents in which it was mentioned was a very short note from Yosef Yizraeli, general director of the Ministry of Defense (July 13, 1948), to the financial and quartermaster branches of the general staff, instructing them to supply Mahatz (as it was then called) with what was needed to conduct its work, without further details. The people who work for it, the places they work and what they do are all secret, and hiding its existence has been a general policy since its inception.

---

3. Lehi is the acronym for *lohamei herut Israel*, "Israel's freedom fighters," an anti-British organization founded and led by Avraham Stern beginning in 1940.

The general public, and especially those who have had dealings with the Shin Bet, know that they are dealing with a body that oversees, monitors, listens, photographs, puts under surveillance, detains (if necessary) and interrogates anyone suspected of activities hostile to the State of Israel. Anyone who asks questions is answered with thundering silence. For almost nine years the Shin Bet's very existence was assiduously denied by the government and its name was never mentioned.

The lack of reference to its existence and the nature of its activity were possible because the Israeli public considers national security of vital importance, and its preservation has always been a number one public priority. Most of Israeli society is "enlisted" and acts in accordance with rules of privileged information and secrecy because of what is perceived as a continual emergency situation. Moreover, Prime Minister and Defense Minister David Ben-Gurion was then at the height of his powers, and after the discovery of the microphone planted by the Shin Bet in the office of Mapam leader Meir Ya'ari in 1953 (because of suspicious connections with the USSR), very few people dared to challenge his categorical statement that there was "no such thing as the Shin Bet." At that time censorship had teeth and concealed – and not necessarily for security reasons – everything the government wanted hidden from the public. Even in the IDF not many people knew of its existence.

The Shin Bet Redefined

When the number of the Shin Bet's tasks increased, and with them its requirements, Isser Harel demanded that the prime minister and the chief of staff coordinate its organization and resources with the demands placed on it, and in effect to upgrade it. First, however, he needed written proof of its existence. He therefore arranged a meeting with the prime minister and the chief of staff on February 8, 1949, to discuss "the intelligence services of the State of Israel," and where it was agreed that a security service would be established. Mahatz would become the Shin Bet, and the following units would be added: Shin Mem

3, which dealt with counterespionage; Military Police Unit 395 (special forces), which at the time specialized in capturing deserters, tracking and undercover arrests, and which eventually became the Operations Unit; and four special military prisons (396, 397, 398 and 399) for mass arrests, should they be necessary. In a letter sent to the chief of staff (February 17, 1949), Harel summarized the meeting and asked that the army be given the appropriate orders. The following day, the first Israeli chief of staff, Lieutenant General Ya'akov Dori, announced the establishment of the Shin Bet, which would be a financially independent unit connected directly to himself, that is, to the chief of staff.

At the beginning of 1949 the Knesset (the Israeli Parliament) enacted the 1949 Security Service Law for IDF recruitment. To distinguish between the law, which pertained only to the army, and the body that carried the same name, it was decided to add the word "general" (*klali* in Hebrew) to the Shin Bet's name, turning its acronym into "Shabak."[4] During the its first two decades it was housed in Jaffa in buildings allocated to it by the Custodian of Abandoned Property, which had jurisdiction over abandoned property.[5] Its headquarters were located not far from the famous Jaffa clock tower and the flea market, in the heart of a noisy neighborhood inhabited for the most part by Arabs. Its subunits were housed in other buildings throughout the city, well assimilated into the civilian environment.

---

4. In 1955 the name was changed in English to Israel Security Agency because the acronym of "General Security Service" would be "GSS," which was reminiscent of "SS."

5. On May 13, 1948, the city of Jaffa was captured by the Haganah and Etzel forces. Most of the Arab residents abandoned the city and left behind empty buildings. The Custodian of Abandoned Property distributed those buildings to many military and government units, which at that time did not have offices and needed a place to get organized.

How do you establish a security service from nothing? What are its tasks? How should it conduct itself? What kind of budget will it have, and what kind of equipment?

A committee of two was appointed to answer those questions: Reuven Shiloah, the first director of the Mossad, and Yosef Yizraeli,[6] and they carefully examined the tasks and the means necessary for carrying them out. They presented their recommendations to the prime minister and the chief of staff (May 9, 1949), including the definition of the Shin Bet's authority, what its work force would be (370 employees, and in certain circumstances, as many as 400), and what its budget should be (15,000 Israeli lira per month).[7]

Operating as an IDF unit, as it did initially, was bound to cause difficulties and fundamental differences of opinion. The army's rigid military framework was not suited to the operations of the Shin Bet, which worked in secret without barracks, uniforms, ranks or roll calls. The army found it hard to accept a unit that in effect was not part of it and whose members were not really soldiers. Moreover, linking the service to the chief of staff, while it was the prime minister and not the chief of staff who had given instructions to the head of the Shin Bet since its inception, caused tension and other problems. The prime minister determined (June 2, 1949) that while it operated from within the army, "from an administrative point of view, it operated as a division of a government ministry in the Ministry of Defense." A joint effort to resolve the issue led to separating it from the IDF on August 1, 1950, and turning it into a civilian organization within the ministry. Its members became civil servants only in 1953.

---

6.   Yosef Yizraeli was born in Russia in 1906 and immigrated to Palestine in 1924. He was active in the Haganah and was put in charge of Taas, the Haganah's military industry, in 1946–1947. A year later he was appointed the first director general of the ministry of defense.

7.   About $27,000 at the rate of exchange at the time.

Most of its various fields of action remained hidden. In addition to its main missions, which were preventing spying and subversion and dealing with the Arab sector, during its first years it dealt not only with purely security tasks, but with many other internal problems that had been defined by the government as national issues with implications for the country's general welfare, such as:

- Aiding in the fight against the black market during the period of austerity (until the early 1950s).
- Preventing goods and money, especially counterfeit currency, from being smuggled from abroad.
- Helping the police prevent new immigrants, living in the transit camps, from rioting in protest of the government's ethnic and economic discrimination. They were easily swayed by the opposition, especially the Communists.
- Helping the police deal with the public disturbances and violence of those who opposed the reparations agreement between Israel and Germany.
- Waging a struggle against the weekly magazine *Ha-Olam ha-Zeh* (This world),[8] which, it was feared, would corrupt its readers, especially the youth. As a counterweight the Shin Bet was behind the publication of the weekly magazine called *Rimon*.
- Locating a boy named Yosseleh Shuchmacher, who had been kidnapped by his ultra-Orthodox grandfather and spirited out of the country. The mission was given to the Shin Bet because it was feared the situation would deteriorate into a civil war between secular and Orthodox Jews.

---

8.   *Ha-Olam Ha-Zeh* was a magazine used to attack the Israeli government by trying to prove corruption and over-bureaucracy. To protect the government, the Shin Bet issued its own magazine to show the bright side of the life in Israel and published mostly positive articles.

During its first stormy years, Israel experienced all the growing pains of a new nation. Lack of experience led the Shin Bet to operate by trial and error. Suspicions still lurked from the time of the pre-state underground organizations, and especially during the period of "*la saison de chasse*," "hunting season," when the Haganah was fighting the Etzel and Lehi,[9] and deep grudges were held by political rivals, considerably influencing political decisions. The Shin Bet's lack of experience also contributed to the strict and at times overzealous search for spies "under every bed" and the increasing surveillance of the entire population, especially foreigners and tourists, and they made people feel that Big Brother was watching them. There were even those who called the Shin Bet the "mechanism of darkness" and the cat's paw of the ruling Mapai party and of its head, David Ben-Gurion.

The Shin Bet Comes Out of the Closet

The turning point in the Shin Bet's functioning and public image came in 1955. The discovery of microphones planted in the offices of a few Communist Knesset members led to the appointment of a ministerial committee to oversee it and ensure that it would serve only national interests and not infringe on civil liberties. At that time the third Shin Bet director, Amos Manor, initiated a thorough house-cleaning and ordered the cessation of all activities not directly relevant to national security.

The general public first became aware of the existence of the Shin Bet and of its power nine years after its founding. The murder of Dr.

---

9. The Etzel and Lehi believed that only military actions would end the British mandate in Palestine. The Haganah, however, believed it was impossible to fight the British Empire and that only diplomacy and compromise would help reach the goal. The differences of opinion led to a cruel, violent struggle between the opposing organizations, and people harbor bitter memories to this day.

Israel Kastner (1957)[10] rocked the country, as did the fact that one of the murderers had been a former Shin Bet source who was fired and later joined a radical group. The Shin Bet then had no choice but to admit its existence and deny the patently false accusation that it was responsible for the assassination. Headlines in *Ha-Olam ha-Zeh* and other papers screamed "Light shed on the mechanism of darkness!" and "Shin Bet!" Isser Harel, who was by then head of the Mossad and in charge of the security and intelligence services, was ordered, for the first time, to appear before government ministers and present them with a comprehensive picture of the Shin Bet's activities.

---

10. Dr. Kastner, a Hungarian Zionist leader during the time of the Nazis, was accused of being a collaborator. He was acquitted by the court but murdered in Tel Aviv in 1957.

Section Three

Examples of Intelligence Operations: Successes and Failures

Operation Suzanna (1954)[1]

Shlomo Nakdimon

Political Commentator and Author of Books on National Security

The Birth of Operation Suzanna

In June 1954, Britain and Egypt were winding up the charged negotiations over the evacuation of the Suez Canal. Seventy years of British control were coming to an end, and much against their will, the British Empire was about to transfer thirty-eight army bases and dozens of military airports, all well maintained according to Western standards, to the Egyptian army.

The Suez Canal had been blocked to Israeli shipping since 1948. Successive Egyptian governments had violated the international commitments, given by the naval powers with the canal's opening in 1888, that ships flying the flags of all nations would be free to pass through it, even during time of war. They also violated the UN's 1951 resolution to end the closure. The original commitment had been included in the agreement with Britain, but Egypt was never required to honor it. The cease-fire agreement signed by Israel and Egypt in 1949 did not end the

---

1. This article is based on personal knowledge, intelligence documents and the books and research work of Hagai Eshed, David Ben-Gurion, Michael Bar-Zohar, Aviezer Golan, Yoav Gelber, Moshe Dayan, Isser Harel, Yehoshephat Harkabi, Avraham Wolfenson, Shabtai Tevet, Haim Israeli, Michael Y. Cohen, Eyal Kafkafi, Meir Amit, Alexander Tzur, Gideon Raphael and Moshe Sharett.

war, which continued in other ways. It became clear that the evacuation of the British forces would make it possible for Egypt to increase its military threat to Israel.

The evacuation of the Suez Canal took place during the Cold War, when the West was preparing for a Soviet-instigated Third World War, and it was seriously feared that the Soviet Union would use a hydrogen bomb. Initially the United States and Britain considered Israel as part of their Middle Eastern defenses, but Israel was later marginalized by the Arab veto. Now, with the British evacuation approaching, the United States formed a regional anti-Soviet alliance with Turkey, Iran, Pakistan and Iraq. Egypt, however, ruled by an officers' group staunchly opposing Britain, not only did not join the new alliance, but also turned toward the USSR and became its main ally in the Middle East.

As of 1954 Israel had a new government, when its founder, Ben-Gurion, retired. The new prime minister was Moshe Sharett, who, despite his rich experience as foreign minister, had to fill the much larger shoes of a man upon whom he had always greatly depended. The new defense minister was Pinhas Lavon, an experienced political leader and brilliant intellectual, but with no experience whatsoever in defense and security. The only two individuals who did have such experience were the chief of staff, Moshe Dayan, and the head of military intelligence, Colonel Benjamin Gibli (and with them the director general of the defense ministry, Shimon Peres). Dayan, despite his activist opinions, was considered a brilliant, sober military commander; Gibli was considered an intelligence star with a promising future. It was now up to the new leadership to deflect or change a regional-international move over which it had no control.

Israel had a very sober view of the fact that when the British forces left the Canal Zone there would be no buffer between it and Egypt. The head of military intelligence accurately described the opinion of Israel's political and military establishments in a memorandum to the defense minister and the chief of staff on June 16, 1954, calling the evacuation of the Suez Canal by the British "the first decisive change in the Middle East since the armistice agreement [1949].... It directly affects [Israel's] security and existence. If practical guarantees for Israel's security and integrity are not included in the agreement, Israel will be forced to reexamine its position and options...." The chances of receiving such guarantees were virtually nonexistent.

Preventing the Evacuation

Israel desired to prevent the evacuation, or at least to delay it. In fact, IDI's production and analysis department submitted its evaluations in two memoranda, on June 7 and 13, 1954, writing that it would be impossible to achieve the objective by conventional diplomatic means. Gibli summarized his recommendations in the documents, which were approved by Dayan, who emphasized that Israel could not accept such a situation. They were in agreement in defining the threats facing Israel, but the question was how to deflect them. The idea to forestall the evacuation had already been discussed within the central defense circles, and its objective was to make the situation untenable for the Egyptians.

One idea was to send an Israeli-flagged ship through the Suez Canal to Israel. If the Egyptians stopped it, they would run the risk of an Israeli military reprisal; if they turned a blind eye, their prestige within the Arab world would be damaged. Israel also hoped for the support of "other forces," such as the opposition within Britain's ruling Conservative Party that had loudly protested the evacuation, called the "Suez Rebels." Their representatives were even in contact with Israel's military attaché in London, Katriel Shalmon, who passed messages back and forth between the Rebels and the army and the Ministry of Defense in Israel.

Sending an Israeli ship through the Suez Canal seemed like a good idea to Lavon. On the other hand, he did not have great hopes for the success of "other forces" beyond the London Rebels, i.e., a media campaign in France and anti-Egyptian psychological warfare.

An IDI evaluation paper predicted the evacuation would begin in three months, that is, time enough to prepare a preemptive campaign. However, the events developed faster. On July 14, 1954, British Prime Minister Winston Churchill told Parliament that the evacuation agreement between Britain and Egypt would be signed on July 23. In Israel, at the Ministry of Defense staff meeting on July 15, it became clear that sending the Israeli ship, named *Bat Galim*, would not be possible before September, but a response to the threat was needed immediately.

Given the situation, those at the policy-making level concluded that the solution was to create a crisis that would show the Great Powers involved that the planned evacuation was unrealistic. According to the information collected, the British government had warned the Egyptian government that the terrorist attacks on British forces in the Canal Zone – which claimed British lives, and in the recent past there had been several of them – might postpone the evacuation. That, perhaps, was behind the idea to carry out terrorist attacks in Egypt that would cause the United States (which supported the British evacuation) and Britain to have second thoughts. A similar idea had been proposed at the beginning of 1954 to sabotage British-Jordanian relations. A suggestion was even made to attack the British consuls in Jordan; the plan was overruled and canceled by Dayan. Inside Israel there was only one force that could carry out such an operation: IDI's Unit 131.

Unit 131 and Preparation for Action

Unit 131 (previously called Department 13) was established during the War of Independence as an operational unit of the Foreign Ministry's political department. Its objectives were diversion and sabotage inside enemy countries during emergencies, and it was to operate under the watchful eye of the Israeli government. At the end of the War of Independence, IDI headquarters demanded that Unit 131 come under its command. In 1950 an agreement was reached, making the unit subject to political (Foreign Ministry) and military (IDI) supervision. Two years later, the members of the supervisory committee were moved to other positions and never replaced, and Department 131 effectively became a military unit within IDI.

Isser Harel, as of 1952 head of the Mossad and receiving a constant flow of information about the unit, knew the supervisory committee was no longer functioning. His attempts to renew the supervision were rejected by the defense minister and chief of staff, each for his own reasons (some of them clearly personal). Instead, they threw him a bone in the form of "authorization from the head of IDI to know what Unit 131 is doing," as he wrote in February 1954 to the acting IDI head, Lieutenant Colonel Yehoshephat Harkabi (Gibli, the head, was studying abroad).

However, when Harkabi asked for Lavon's support to expand the unit and its budget, the chief of staff had reservations. Dayan said that Unit 131 was only supposed to operate in wartime and to be dormant in peace. Dayan, he said, sensed Lavon's eagerness to clip Unit 131's wings, and warned Harkabi against him.

Unit 131 was commanded by Lieutenant Colonel Mordechai Ben-Tzur, whom Gibli had recommended for the position, but who had nothing in his military past to justify his appointment. Avraham Dar, already an intelligence officer, was responsible in Egypt for recruiting young Jewish men to the unit, whom he later sent to Israel for training. He even agreed to take command of the volunteers in Egypt, but after a short time under the command of Ben-Tzur he decided the two of them could not work together, and quit.

Gibli, at Ben-Tzur's recommendation, filled the position left by Dar with Avri Elad, who would command Unit 131 in Egypt. He had belonged to a different unit operating in Egypt and had even become friendly with the interior minister and the head of the secret services. However, he also had a dubious background and had been accused of criminal acts and corruption. He was brought into military intelligence only because of the dearth of suitable candidates.

Ben-Tzur met with Elad in Paris between May 31 and June 3, and put him in command of Unit 131 in Egypt. He explained the mission, "to undermine the faith of the West in the current regime by causing public insecurity and [carrying out] acts which will lead to arrests, demonstrations and retaliation, while totally concealing Israel's involvement." Ben-Tzur hoped that suspicion would fall on the Communists, the Muslim Brotherhood, "malcontents" or local nationalists.

Elad now knew everything about Unit 131. He arrived in Egypt on June 28 and worked diligently on two levels: he met with those under his command, innocent patriots, faithful to the State of Israel and believing utterly in their mission, and was also a double agent working for the Egyptian secret service, a traitor with no compunction about handing the unit over to the enemy.

The young Jewish patriots who were recruited by Dar in Egypt were trained in Israel and returned to Egypt at the end of 1953, eagerly waiting for the signal to act. While they waited they carried out various tasks, all with primitive means. The future operation, as yet amorphous, Israel dubbed "Operation Suzanna," after the wife of one of the unit's members. The commanders who participated in the unit's training were doubtful of its operational capabilities, prophesying that they would be caught and hanged.

Three Actions

The first action under Elad was carried out on July 2, 1954, in a post office in Alexandria, where a small incendiary device was placed, causing a small fire. The second took place on July 14, when members of Unit 131 placed explosives in eyeglasses cases in the reading rooms of the American Libraries in Cairo (next to the embassy) and Alexandria.

On July 11 Dayan left for a five-week trip to the United States and France. The first action was carried out while he was still in Israel, and the second when he was in the United States. While he was abroad, his deputy, Major General Yosef Avidar, ignorant of the operation, assumed his duties. On July 15 Britain announced that the evacuation agreement would be signed on July 23 (the second anniversary of the Young Officers Coup). At the security staff meeting held in Israel on the same day, the question was raised as to Israel's ability to carry out, within a week, an operation that would activate the opponents of the evacuation in Britain, bring about a crisis in London and postpone the signing of the agreement.

On July 17 and 18, according to a signal received from Elad, Ben-Tzur told him to "initiate immediately an action to prevent or postpone the signing of the Anglo-Egyptian agreement. The objectives are cultural, propaganda and economic institutions, official representatives [of foreign countries], their vehicles, British representatives or other British subjects, and anything that can lead to the disruption of diplomatic relations [between Egypt and these countries]. Inform us of the possibility of an operation in the Canal Zone."

However, the missions assigned to Unit 131 were insignificant compared to Ben-Tzur's bombastic plans for July 23. The targets were two movie theaters in Cairo, two in Alexandria, and the left-luggage room at the Cairo train station. During the operation in Alexandria the explosives in the eyeglass case carried by Philip Natanson caught fire and he could not extinguish the flame. The case exploded and Natanson was injured, signaling the beginning of the end. Not only did the unit suffer Elad's treachery, but Natanson's injury as well.

Who Gave the Order?

Technically, the order for all three actions was given to Elad by Ben-Tzur. However, because of the plan's collapse, the public storm in Israel focused on the July 23 action. Only on July 16, Gibli claimed, did Lavon invite him to his private home on Gordon Street in Tel Aviv and, as though the first two actions had nothing to do with them, ordered him to activate the unit in Egypt. On July 17 Gibli summoned Ben-Tzur, probably to his private home in the Tel Aviv suburb of Tzahala, and ordered him to activate the squads in Egypt. On July 18 Ben-Tzur gave Elad the order (quoted above).

Prime Minister Sharett knew nothing of Unit 131's activities in Egypt (according to his diary, he only found out about it by chance, on July 27). Acting chief of staff Avidar also knew nothing, nor did Harel (according to the arrangement and with the knowledge of Lavon and Dayan, Gibli was supposed to keep him informed). Gibli, answerable to Dayan, claimed that he had reported to Dayan (who was then in the United States) close to the time the order was received, that is, on July 19, telling him that the unit had been activated "according to Lavon's order." Dayan claimed to have destroyed the letter and didn't remember whether that particular sentence had been in it, as Gibli claimed. Gibli produced a copy of the letter, but it was a copy that had been retyped to include the "correct" date.

The toll in human life was heavy. Two members of Unit 131 Moshe Marzuk and Shmuel Azzar, were hanged. Four others (Victor Levy, Philip Natanson, Robert Dasa and the young Marcelle Ninio) were sentenced to long prison terms, and Israel's negligible efforts for their release were a disgrace. Intelligence officer Max Bineth, who operated in Egypt independently of Unit 131 and who was not connected to its operation in any way (although Ben-Tzur did try to enlist him) was arrested and committed suicide in prison. An Egyptian Jew, Yosef Carmona, was arrested although he had nothing to do with the network, and either committed suicide or was tortured to death. As the failure became known, Israel was publicly disgraced.

The Eternal Question Mark

Will the mystery surrounding Operation Suzanna be ever solved? To his last day Lavon denied giving the order. Gibli claimed to have answered the question in his autobiography, which, he told me, would be published after his death. Yet he has already died and the book has not been published. In any case, it would make a difference only if Gibli said that the order did not come from Lavon, implying that he [Gibli] had been lying all those years.

For twenty-five years Operation Suzanna, which became known as the Lavon affair, has wrought havoc in Israel's political and security establishments. It caused the schism within Mapai in 1965 and the retirement of its founding father, David Ben-Gurion (who found himself in a quagmire when he reassumed the position of prime minister), as well as the death of the terminally ill Pinhas Lavon in 1976, and it sowed the seeds of the 1977 electoral upheaval in Israel. They were all the results of the order given by "someone" in the summer of 1954.

"The unfortunate affair," as the Egyptians called the catastrophe – what preceded it, the way it was woven together, the way it fell apart – was never investigated by Israel's military intelligence and no lessons were learned. Six official commissions examined its various aspects (the Olshen-Dori Commission, 1955; the Amiad Commission, 1958; the Cohen Commission, 1960; the Ben-Dor Commission, 1960; the Commission of the Seven, 1960; and the Foreign Affairs and Defense Committee of the Knesset, 1960) but none of them found, nor could find, one single official document to clarify the issue or on which to base conclusions. An official state commission of inquiry has never been appointed.

An official investigation would shed light on the warped relationships at the highest political levels of Israel at the time: Prime Minister Moshe Sharett, who was neutralized; Defense Minister Pinhas Lavon, a predatory security shark who bypassed the prime minister; Chief of Staff Moshe Dayan, a generally respected, charismatic commander whose involvement in the affair was never clarified; IDI Benjamin Gibli, whose reputation was already tainted by his having issued an execution order in a field court in 1948. His rocketing career came to a halt after it became known that he was responsible for appointing the inept Ben-Tzur and the criminally implicated Elad as commanders, and that he was suspected of forging a document of critical importance. There was an obvious need to investigate why Dayan and Lavon rejected Harel's impassioned cry to continue the supervision of Unit 131.

Epilogue

In the final analysis, the fear of a Third World War evaporated, as did the regional defense pact. Two years after Operation Suzanna, Israel struck Egypt in collaboration with Britain and France (Operation Kadesh, also known as the Sinai War) and reached the Suez Canal. Eleven years later Israel again reached the Suez Canal (the Six-Day War). Six years after that Egypt, in collaboration with Syria, attacked Israel (the Yom Kippur War) and was initially successful, but in a brilliant move Israel crossed the Suez Canal and took control of both banks. Five years later Israel signed a peace treaty with Egypt that is in force to this day, and Israeli ships sail through the Suez Canal, unlimited and unhindered.

The Israel-Egyptian Rotem Affair (1960)

Colonel (Res.) Dr. Yigal Sheffy

Former Senior Officer of IDI

Between February 17 and 24, 1960, most of the Egyptian field forces rolled into the Sinai Peninsula, with two infantry divisions and an armored division, totaling more than five hundred tanks and tens of thousands troops, and deployed in the eastern Sinai near the Israeli border. The troops had been ordered in by Mushir (Field Marshal) Muhammad Abd al-Hakim Amer, Egypt's minister of war and supreme commander of the armed forces of the UAR (the United Arab Republic, as the union between Egypt and Syria was known from 1958 until Syria seceded in 1961). He ordered the forces to prepare to attack Israel if the IDF attacked Syria. Arab concern about such an attack increased following the deteriorating security situation along the Israel-Syria border (culminating in an Israeli retaliatory raid against a Syrian military post) and false information received by the UAR to the effect that Israel was planning a broader action against the Syrian army.

The Egyptian entrance into Sinai surprised the IDF, which had only a minimal number of troops available in the Negev (Israel's southern region) at the time. Israel Defense Intelligence, which had not expected such a move, was slow to sound the alarm, had not identified the entrance of the Egyptian divisions into Sinai, and even when presented with the information treated it lightly. The result was that the IDF did not deploy in time or with forces sufficient to meet a possible Egyptian attack, doing so only days later when the Egyptians were already in place and prepared, leaving the Negev exposed to attack for several days. Even after the level of readiness had been raised, under the name

Operation Rotem, the force was based primarily on a small IDF stand-ing force, complemented by only a few reservists, with no mobilization of reserve formations.

The Rotem affair stuck in Israel's collective memory as a synonym for IDI's stunning failure to provide early warning of a surprise attack. What is less well known is that the failure could just as well be laid at the doorstep of the decision makers and the operational staff, and that it was in part the result of the fact that, though the decision makers, commanders and intelligence officers were working on clear, accurate information about Egypt's intentions, they were mistaken for too long about its capabilities.

Collection and Basic Assessments

The event took place at a time when the IDF Directorate of Military Intelligence (DMI) relied on a combination of several factors: the assessment that the UAR was not planning a large-scale war in the coming years; past lessons that had taught that during an alert, the Egyptian army customarily reinforced Sinai with small infantry forces for short periods of time, deploying them in the vicinity of the Suez Canal in the rear, not eastward toward Israel; the realization that intelligence collection concerning the Egyptians was scanty, but still believed to be sufficient to give the IDF a week of advance warning; and reliance on human intelligence (HUMINT) for early warning. Signals intelligence (SIGINT), on the other hand, although perceived as a major intelligence collection asset, was not yet relied on to provide concrete early warning.

The gaps in coverage notwithstanding, the DMI believed it could discover the intentions of the UAR decision makers by monitoring the wireless communications between Cairo and Damascus, which had been intercepted and deciphered. The belief was justified when on February 16 a wireless operator of Israeli SIGINT Unit 515 intercepted

Amer's order to the Egyptian army to enter Sinai and be ready to attack Israel within four days if Israel attacked Syria.

Military intelligence was of the opinion that even if it were a question of forces larger than those that had reinforced Sinai in the past, it was doubtful whether the armored formations would leave Cairo at all. In any event, they felt, the Egyptians would first concentrate their forces near the Suez Canal and not move them eastward deep into the peninsula toward the border. Major General Yitzhak Rabin, head of operations; Lieutenant General Haim Laskov, chief of staff; and David Ben-Gurion, defense minister and prime minister, accepted the evaluation as presented by IDI director Colonel Chaim Herzog, especially since they were certain that Egypt's intention was only to respond if Israel attacked first. They also knew that Israel had no such intention.

When foreign intelligence services reported that a strong Egyptian force, including their only tank division, had already crossed the Suez Canal and were advancing into Sinai, the reports were received with skepticism. On the assumption that the Egyptian force would concentrate at the canal, on February 23, two photo reconnaissance planes were sent to the area, although by that time the Egyptians had almost completed their deployment deep within the Sinai Peninsula. It was the first sortie over Sinai or Egypt since the tension began, and it did not reveal military concentrations along the canal. The following day another sortie was sent out, this time over the eastern part of Sinai, and revealed two infantry divisions and 150 tanks, but it did not cover the area around Jebel Libni, where the armored division was deployed, and so the main force was not photographed.

Deployment and Mistaken Assessment

The irrefutable (though, in retrospect, partial) findings finally convinced the general staff to take a series of operational steps. The IDF was put on alert, the air force prepared to halt a possible hostile Egyptian action and all standing formations (basically an infantry, a paratrooper and an armored brigade) were rushed to the Negev.

However, the powers that be felt assured of Egyptian intentions. They also felt that if the Egyptians changed their minds, the Israelis would know about it in advance from monitoring the Egyptian-Syrian communications link. Therefore, they were convinced that the situation was not especially serious. Not knowing exactly where the Egyptian armored division was located also contributed to their sense of confidence (there were still DMI officers who claimed the division had never left Cairo, but even those who were convinced it had and was in Sinai with four hundred tanks, still placed it in the rear). In addition, Ben-Gurion, who was about to go to the United States for his first meeting with American President Dwight Eisenhower, was determined to end the crisis and prevent misunderstandings that might lead to a deterioration of the situation. He therefore did not make impassioned announcements but rather imposed censorship on reports of the situation, and instructed the Egyptians to be informed through diplomatic channels that Israel did not seek war. He also denied the army's request to call up several reservist formations, with the exception of a few reservist units from the infantry and air force that were called up, all based on intelligence he possessed about the other side's intentions. The IDF deployed more slowly than was planned, finishing only on the morning of February 28, with seven infantry battalions and about 150 tanks.

The information that continued to arrive did not clarify the Egyptian deployment, and weather conditions made it necessary to postpone the planned air reconnaissance over Jebel Libni. However, communications intercepts indicated that the Egyptian leadership was of the opinion that the likelihood of an Israeli attack had diminished. Therefore, Laskov and Rabin adopted the operations branch's recommendation to thin out IDF concentration in the south after only three days of alert. So great was their confidence in the information about the Egyptian intentions, they did so even though Israel had received no information about a change for the better regarding Egyptian capability and readiness. By March 3, a significant portion of the forces had left the Negev and only four infantry battalions and seventy tanks remained. Almost all of the eight thousand reservists were demobilized. As far as the IDF was concerned, Operation Rotem was history.

As fate would have it, that same day the reconnaissance flight over the Egyptian forces in Sinai was finally carried out, and for the first time the full picture was revealed: an armored force of more than five hundred tanks was deployed near the Israeli border in an offensive-defensive array. It was a new warning of capabilities, which a surprised Herzog was quick to present, in all its seriousness, to Laskov. However, the chief of staff did not seem particularly impressed, and no immediate counteraction was taken.

Blundering to the End

Within two days the situation had completely changed. On March 5, when in effect the Egyptian state of readiness had been lowered, an IDF reserve armored brigade was hastily mobilized and – along with the standing formations, including the armored brigade – sent to the Negev. This action was the result of a false alarm that combined two pieces of low-level SIGINT, one Syrian and the other Egyptian. They were translated or interpreted to mean that the Syrian army in the Golan Heights and the Egyptian army in Sinai were again on high alert. That, at least, was what DMI head Herzog understood, and he rushed to report to the chief of staff, telephoning him at home. With the balance of forces tipped against the IDF in the south, the report hit Laskov like a ton of bricks. He immediately updated Ben-Gurion and was given authorization to reinforce the Negev by calling up a reserve armored brigade. By the next day the tanks began moving by train from the brigade's base in Haifa, arriving in the south three days later. Even as the Egyptian army reduced the number of its troops in Sinai, the IDF, relying on an early warning of intentions, this time faulty, deployed an even greater armored force than it had originally.

The DMI realized its mistake the following day, but there are different versions as to when the chief of staff was informed. In any case, a few days later, again based on SIGINT and on assessments that dealt with intentions and not capabilities, the forces were sent home for the second time. Ironically, the armored Egyptian division left Sinai only after the Israeli tanks had left the Negev. Operation Rotem officially ended on April 1, 1960.

Conclusion

The Rotem affair made it clear to both IDI and the IDF how vital it was to establish an early-warning system and how important SIGINT was. It was the factor that motivated the establishment of an institutionalized system of collection and analysis to warn of sudden attacks, and contributed greatly to the intelligence achievements of the Six-Day War.

Other lessons, however, were unfortunately marginalized, such as the important role of the decision makers in the early-warning process; the problems involved in relying on a single source, even if considered top-level; and the need to balance warnings of intentions with those of capability. Those were among the pitfalls that the IDF generally and the DMI in particular fell into thirteen years later on the eve of the Yom Kippur War.

Collecting Information in Preparation

for the Six-Day War (1967)

Brigadier General (Res.) Ephraim Lapid

Former Head of the IDI Collection Department and IDF Spokesman

In the 1960s, IDF intelligence was studying and assimilating the intelligence-collecting lessons of Operation Rotem (see previous article). Eli Zeira, the head of IDI's collection department, who had previously held many senior positions and was later to become the IDI director, revolutionized the collection systems by giving priority to SIGINT.

The early 1960s were overshadowed by the Soviet military buildup of Israel's belligerent neighbors, Egypt and Syria. Their advanced weapons systems on land, in the air, in air defense and at sea were for the most part new to IDF intelligence, and intelligence collecting technology had to be used to monitor them. One of the challenges was introducing a new dimension into collection – ELINT (electronic intelligence: monitoring electronic signals containing neither text nor speech).

The United Arab Command and the PLO were established at an Arab summit meeting at the beginning of 1964; therefore, in the mid-1960s most of Israel's intelligence collection effort was invested in tracking inter-Arab deployment. The same meeting also decided to divert the sources of the Jordan River, ushering in an era of incidents in the north that demanded ongoing information collection through SIGINT, HUMINT (human intelligence) and aerial photographs. The Egyptian involvement in the civil war in Yemen gave Israeli intelligence an opportunity to become familiar with Egypt's updated fighting capabilities by means of SIGINT, Mossad agents and connections with regional and global intelligence services.

Intelligence about the order of battle – deployment and activity – was good, and in certain instances very good, especially regarding the Arab air forces and the Egyptian navy. Unlike Operation Rotem, in 1967 the Egyptian army's entrance into Sinai did not surprise Israeli intelligence. However, information about the leaders' intentions was limited, so that during the period preceding the Six-Day War Israel did not know what Nasser was planning.

During the second half of the 1960s every aspect of Israeli intelligence had its virtuosos. There were Lt. Colonel Shaul Shamai, a prodigious decoder of Arabic codes and the only soldier who was decorated by the chief of staff who had not fought on the battlefield; Colonel Zeev Bar-Lavi, of IDI's research and production department, who was an expert on Jordan; Brig. General Yeshayahu Bareket, head of Israel Air Force Intelligence, who focused IAF operations during the Six-Day War; George Hamza, from the OSINT (open source intelligence), known as Unit 550 (Hatzav), expert in Arabic media; Yehiel Leibel, a first-class interpreter of aerial photographs, and many others.

SIGINT (Signals Intelligence)

It was finally recognized that SIGINT data, which had been developing since the 1950s, was an important factor in intelligence collection. Israel therefore greatly increased its coverage of Arab communication systems, including new areas, and created breakthrough collection capabilities.

The Egyptian air force was considered a serious threat to Israel's nuclear reactor in Dimona, and an Israeli response that could be activated in minutes had to be prepared. To that end, it was vital to have new and better capabilities for monitoring the Egyptians. Deployment to face the threat was given the code name Senator, and it presented an opportunity to upgrade the SIGINT unit (then known as Unit 515). Equipment was acquired, the professional staff was expanded, reporting and early-warning procedures were improved, the connection with air force intelligence was tightened, and an improved reporting center was established inside IDI HQs.

New radio-telephone systems were introduced into the Arab countries, and despite these countries' efforts to secure traffic communication, the SIGINT unit successfully intercepted new speech communication channels as well as Morse transmissions. The communications that passed between the Arab countries and their legations abroad were an important source of political information. At the time there were no satellites, trans-oceanic underwater cables or Internet. ELINT went into operation, monitoring both stationary and airborne radar. The directional detection of Arab communications added a new dimension to identifying enemy deployment. During the war, the Israel Air Force contributed to Unit 515's capabilities by destroying the Egyptians' telephone lines, forcing them to use air networks.

An important achievement on the second day of the war was the interception of a conversation between President Gamal Nasser and Jordan's King Hussein. Nasser managed to convince him – against Hussein's better interests – to join the war by telling him, untruthfully, that Israel was succeeding because of American and British help. Nasser said it was important for Jordan to enter the war to split the IDF forces. That posed a dilemma regarding source protection: Aharon Yariv, a forceful IDI head who had served in the position for four years, recommended not publicizing the conversation. Defense Minister Moshe Dayan decided it should be made known. The propaganda and prestige capital attained by Israeli intelligence over the affair was enormous, although it immediately wrought great damage to SIGINT coverage, and many enemy networks ceased operations.

HUMINT (Human Intelligence)

The Human Intelligence Unit (known as 154) was deployed against Egypt, Jordan (which still controlled the West Bank), Syria and Lebanon.

In the absence of aerial photographs, tactical intelligence from agents (including authentic documents and ground photographs) was a good alternative. The unit brought back massive amounts of information about the Egyptian army in the Sinai and the Jordanian army in the West Bank, because in effect the borders were fairly wide open, and also because a new era of fast secret communications had been developed. Lieutenant Colonel Shmuel Goren, who commanded Unit 154 at the time, said he received firm back-up from military intelligence head Yariv, making it possible for him to acquire state-of-the-art equipment and qualified personnel.

The Mossad chalked up two very impressive achievements. One was planting an agent named Eli Cohen into the Syrian upper echelons in the early 1960s; he operated until the Syrians caught and executed him in May 1965. The other was recruiting an Iraqi MIG-21 pilot and convincing him to fly his plane to Israel, which he did in August 1966. The information the Israel Air Force learned from the plane, which until then had been an enigma for Western intelligence services, directly influenced the IAF's performance during the Six-Day War, especially in aerial battles. In addition, giving the Americans and later other intelligence services access to the plane contributed to strengthening inter-intelligence relations.

Even at the beginning of the war, great importance was given to prisoner interrogation, conducted by Unit 560, a special military intelligence unit that had been combined with Unit 154. At the end of the war Israel had more than six thousand Egyptian, Syrian and Jordanian prisoners. Information important for basic and potential intelligence was gotten by enlisting HUMINT sources.

Deception, Psychological Warfare and Electronic Warfare

Emphasis was placed on deception, psychological warfare and electronic warfare. Field security was responsible for deception and operated in conjunction with operational intelligence. Deception was both visual and wireless, and included actively breaking into the enemy's communications networks. Psychological warfare was waged through flysheets and leaflets; the Israel Security Agency and the Mossad participated in some of the activities.

VISINT (Visual Intelligence)

In 1963 a new era in surveillance began with the introduction of 20x120 binoculars. Before the Six-Day War, televised and UAV (unmanned aerial vehicle) surveillance were also developed. Eli Zeira said that he had brought Efraim Arazi from the United States, who had developed new visual systems. Interpretation was the province of the production and analysis department, and they maintained close contacts with the air force intelligence's Aerial Photography Unit. The intelligence officers of the various commands were responsible for the entire system and were answerable to the combat intelligence department.

OSINT (Open Source Intelligence)

Unit 550 monitored the Arab press and radio, which were very valuable sources of information; there was almost no television at the time. Speeches given by Arab leaders, particularly Nasser, were broadcast live and simultaneously translated into Hebrew. The Arab-language specialists in Unit 550, who had been born in the Arab countries, earned a well-deserved reputation for excellence.

Conclusion

On the eve of the Six-Day War, which coincided with the twentieth anniversary of the founding of the state, Israel had a professional, state-of-the-art intelligence corps that directly influenced the war's outcome. The collection and organization activities carried out after Operation Rotem improved Israel's intelligence capabilities in almost every field. The technological breakthrough improved collection capabilities, which made it possible for Israel to achieve its stunning military successes, particularly those of the air force, during the Six-Day War.

A Comparison of the Intelligence between Two Wars: The Six-Day War (1967) and the Yom Kippur War (1973)

Brigadier General (Res.) Amos Gilboa
Former Head of the Production and Analysis Division of IDI

Introduction

This article presents a comparison between Israel's intelligence during the Six-Day War in 1967 and the Yom Kippur War in 1973. It focuses on strategic intelligence and deals with three main challenges: surprise and deterrence, capabilities and intentions, and knowledge of the enemy.

Surprise and Deterrence

It is generally assumed that in 1973, Israel Defense Intelligence was surprised just as it had been in 1967, but that in 1967 there was a period of waiting before the war that enabled the IDF to make preparations. Was that actually the case? I would argue that the surprise of 1967 was completely different from that of 1973. Why?

It is true that in both cases Israeli intelligence assumed that while Egypt wanted a war, it was unprepared to wage one, and that the probability of a war's breaking out in the coming two or three years was low. In 1967 there were two factors that made the assumption convincing: one was that a third of the Egyptian army was fighting in Yemen; the other was Nasser's concept of security, according to which Egypt had passed the stage of taking a firm stance against Israel, was now building its defenses and was not yet ready to attack. In 1973 Israel relied on solid intelligence information (correct to the end of 1972), which indicated that as long as Egypt had not yet acquired the requisite air and missile capabilities from the Soviet Union, it would not initiate a war to conquer most of the Sinai Peninsula.

However, there was a vast difference between the two wars. As far as the Six-Day War was concerned, in 1967 Egypt had not made a decision to go to war. Even when the Egyptian army entered Sinai, there was no information regarding an Egyptian intention or plan to attack Israel, and there is no information that in retrospect indicates that as the army entered Sinai it was planning to go to war. As for the Yom Kippur War, however, in October 1972 Egypt made the decision to attack the following year, in October 1973. Egypt began general preparations for war (and Syria soon followed suit), but Israeli intelligence did not issue a warning, despite the wealth of information it possessed.

Consequently, the surprise of the Yom Kippur War was both strategic and elemental, and it shattered the previous conceptions held by the Israeli population. The initial surprise for Israel in 1967 was the open, unconcealed entrance of the Egyptian army into Sinai, at most a tactical surprise. The intelligence community, as well as the upper echelons of the IDF, were also surprised, but to a lesser degree, because during the first days it was assumed that the Egyptian army was repeating what was known as Operation Rotem, secretly moving a large tank force into Sinai. The rude awakening came with the rapid deterioration of the situation, in both the Egyptian arena (the expulsion of the UN observers from the Gaza Strip and closing the Straits of Tiran on May 23) and in the pan-Arab arena, where Jordan cooperated with Egypt and Syria and joined the Arab forces arrayed against Israel. The closing of the Straits of Tiran was what led Israeli intelligence to conclude that the situation might deteriorate into war.

Capabilities and Intentions in View of
the Seriousness of the Threat

In 1967 and 1973 two different models were used to analyze and evaluate intelligence information. In 1967 the capability model was used, and in 1973, the intention model. The capability model stresses the implications of the changes in the activity and preparations of the enemy on the ground, as well as knowledge of his combat doctrine, training and basic plans. Such analysis provides the IDF with possible courses of enemy action. This model examines what the enemy's capabilities are within a defined geographic area, not what he thinks of doing. For the capability model, knowing the enemy's intention is a bonus.

In May 1967, from the moment the first Egyptian battalion entered Sinai, the previous conception – that Egypt would not go to war for the next two to three years – was discarded, and a process of intelligence evaluation began that emphasized the capabilities of the Egyptian army in Sinai. In the process, Egypt's courses of action changed because of the changes in the order of battle and deployment of the Egyptian forces in Sinai, i.e., defensive until the end of May, offensive from the beginning of June. In effect, the Egyptians chose to employ a possible defensive modus operandi to halt an IDF attack and then to go on the offensive in the Negev. The first day of the war destroyed their plans.

The IDF entered the battle in Sinai with a very good picture of the military-tactical situation, which reflected 80 to 85 percent of the order of battle and deployment of the Egyptian army. Intelligence provided by the air force was the best example of intelligence based on the capability model: targets were determined with the help of photographs and SIGINT (information from intercepted electronic enemy communications), all relying on basic information that had been collected and studied.

In 1973 the situation was completely different. The intelligence picture of the order of battle, deployment and activity of the Egyptian and Syrian armies, as presented to the IDF and the political echelons, was, in fact, as impressive as it had been in 1967. However, the factor of a possible course of action was absent. No attempt was made to analyze a possible Syrian or Egyptian modus operandi from the deployment and strength of their armies. Instead of a basic concept of what they might do, a new concept appeared in Israeli intelligence reports: "The enemy has the technical capability to attack, but the probability that he will attack is very low."

Why was it low? Because the enemy did not intend to attack and start a war. That is the main point: the core of the evaluation was the enemy's intention and not his capability. But if intention is the main point, why pay attention to information about capability? Why analyze possible courses of action?

What caused the difference in thinking between the two wars? Why was capability emphasized in 1967, and six years later, almost the same people emphasized intention and ignored capability? Perhaps in 1967 it was the result of the anxiety of having the enemy twenty kilometers (twelve miles) from Netanya, and it was impossible to rely on intentions, only on what could be seen. Perhaps in 1973 it was the result of pride and conceit, and of the fact that the enemy was far away; and besides, we had nothing but contempt for him, so why bother about his capability?

Knowledge of the Enemy and Its Assimilation

From the early 1960s, one of the main challenges of Israeli intelligence was studying the Soviet doctrine with which the Syrian and Egyptian armies were indoctrinated. The IDF instruction corps brought the subject to all levels of the fighting units, and the Soviet "fortified post" became a key term. Consequently, when the IDF went into the Six-Day War, it had full knowledge of Soviet doctrine and was prepared with the appropriate battle doctrine, completely trained and practiced, and suitably armed.

In 1973, however, the situation was different. While the intelligence community did know about Sagger anti-tank missiles and SA-6 mobile anti-aircraft systems, the IDF had not yet assimilated the knowledge, and the result was that the necessary battle doctrine had not been prepared. Israel went into the war far less prepared than in 1967. Moreover, the warnings of the Soviet invasion of Czechoslovakia were not internalized (using a large military exercise as a cover for attack), which contributed to the strategic surprise.

Conclusion

June 5, the anniversary of the first day of the Six-Day War, was not randomly chosen as the IDF's Intelligence Corps Day. Without a doubt, the intelligence corps basks in the glory of the IDF's successes, but it has its own successes as well. And it was not by chance that the Yom Kippur War became known as "the intelligence failure," bringing in its wake military and political failures as well.

The Intelligence Community during the Yom Kippur War (1973)

Professor Uri Bar-Joseph, Haifa University
Political Science Analyst Specializing in National Security and Intelligence

Overview

The failure of Israel's Military Intelligence Branch – which monopolized national intelligence assessment until 1974 – to provide high-quality warnings prior to the Arab attack on October 6, 1973, is considered both the greatest failure in the history of Israel's intelligence community and one of the greatest intelligence failures in world history. It has been compared to the Soviet strategic surprise when the Germans launched Operation Barbarossa on June 22, 1941, and to the American intelligence fiasco of Pearl Harbor on December 7, 1941.

To put the surprise of Yom Kippur in a larger context, this article first discusses military intelligence's performance in the seven years between 1966 and 1973 and examines whether the experience amassed during that period was properly used by the IDI's production and analysis department before the 1973 war. It will then describe what led to the intelligence failure before the war, and finally it will examine how military intelligence and the Mossad performed during the Yom Kippur War itself.

Prelude to a Debacle: 1967–1973

The seven years before October 1973 continually challenged military intelligence's strategic capabilities. Escalation along the Israeli-Syrian border had been noted since February 1966, when the extremist wing of the Baath Party took over the Syrian government, and Israel was considering the possibility of exerting military pressure to topple the regime. The key question was how Egypt would respond. Since 1962 the IDI production and analysis department felt that Nasser would not use force as long as a third of his army was involved in the civil war in Yemen.

On the basis of that assumption, the IDF increased its pressure on Syria – pressure that reached its height in April 1967, when six Syrian MIG-21s were shot down, three of them over Damascus. In those new circumstances Nasser had to take military action despite the fact that his army was still in Yemen, to assist Syria and save his image as the leader and the protector of the Arab world. The assumption that Nasser would not respond ceased to be valid, and the crisis initiated by Nasser in mid-May 1967 came as a surprise to Israel. His public announcement of the closure of the Straits of Tiran, Israel's southern access to the Red Sea through the Gulf of Eilat and a well-known Israeli casus belli, came only a few hours after the production and analysis department announced that in its assessment, Egypt would avoid such a move.

Israel's stunning victory in the Six-Day War buried the intelligence failure that preceded it. The war also completely changed Israel's strategic environment, creating new threats and new opportunities. The first of these was the possible renewal of a shooting war. While immediately after the Six-Day War military intelligence was essentially mistaken in its evaluation that defeat would deter the Arabs from taking up arms again, it later corrected the mistake. Its greatest achievement was the early warning in the fall of 1968 that in spring of 1969 Egypt would "renew fire." In intelligence terminology that meant both a possible static war along the cease-fire line or an Egyptian attempt to cross the Suez Canal. Based on the warning, the IDF planned for a new Egyptian military initiative, and the target date for completing preparations was March 1, 1969. One week after the expected day Egypt launched the War of Attrition, which lasted until August 1970.

On the other hand, IDI incorrectly evaluated the Egyptian position regarding a political settlement of the conflict as more belligerent than in fact it was. The result was that until the Yom Kippur war (and actually, until Anwar Sadat's 1977 peace initiative), it assumed that every indication of Egyptian readiness to settle the conflict by peaceful means was merely a tactical move. Another failure concerned the lack of warning prior to the Soviet intervention in the War of Attrition in early 1970, a subject discussed by Dr. Dmitry Adamsky's article later in this volume.[1]

The intelligence failures before the fall of 1973 are highly relevant for an understanding of the fiasco of the Yom Kippur War. That is because military intelligence's failures – such as its underestimation of the possibility that Nasser would make aggressive moves in 1967 or that the Soviets might intervene militarily in the War of Attrition in 1970 – were rooted in the military tendency to view the opponent's behavior solely through the prism of a balance of military forces, without taking the political dimensions of the problem into consideration. Thus, for example, lack of understanding of Nasser's political inability to accept the IDF's growing pressure on Syria prior to the 1967 crisis prevented military intelligence analysts from seriously considering the possibility that he might initiate a crisis even though a third of his army was still in Yemen. The same is true with regard to the assessment of the military risks that the Kremlin was willing to take in late 1969 to prevent the political repercussions of the collapse of its main client in the Middle East. Since military intelligence did not properly study the period prior to the war of 1973, it did not learn from its failures.

---

1.   See page 178.

The Intelligence Community and the Yom Kippur War

When the War of Attrition ended in August 1970, the possibility of an Egyptian renewal of hostilities with Syrian participation ranked high on IDI priorities. Providing a high-quality warning of such a threat was the first concern of both IDI and the Mossad. The Mossad was highly efficient. One of its main sources was Ashraf Marwan, Nasser's son-in-law and a close personal aide of President Anwar Sadat, who offered his services to Israel in 1969. Marwan (code-named The Angel) was an unstoppable source of highly secret information, including the war plans of the Egyptian army and its order of battle, the minutes of the meetings of the Egyptian cabinet and high command and the protocols of the talks between the Egyptian and the Soviet leadership, which focused primarily on Sadat's demands for the more advanced weapons systems in the Soviet arsenal. The documents, as well as Marwan's verbal communications, clearly indicated Sadat's strategic dilemma: on the one hand, he could not accept the status quo of neither war nor peace; on the other, he knew that Israel's superiority in the air doomed to failure any Egyptian attempt to cross the Suez Canal. Information from other Mossad and IDI sources confirmed the dilemma.

In late October 1972 Sadat decided to deal with the problem by waging a limited war. Its territorial objectives would ensure that the Egyptian army did not advance beyond the air-defense umbrella provided by its anti-aircraft deployment along the western bank of the Suez Canal. Despite the fact that on a number of occasions Mossad sources in Egypt, including Marwan, reported a change in the Egyptian concept regarding a war, military intelligence's top analysts refused to give up their assessment (known as "the concept") that Egypt would not go to war before acquiring long-range attack plans and Scud surface-to-surface missiles that would deter Israel from attacking targets deep inside Egypt.

In April 1973 a number of Mossad sources, as well as Jordan's King Hussein (who routinely met with senior members of the Israeli leadership) reported that Egypt intended to initiate a war in mid-May. Despite IDI evaluation that Egypt would not go to war because it still lacked attack aircraft and Scud missiles, the chief of staff, Lieutenant General David Elazar, and the defense minister, Moshe Dayan, decided on a state of high alert, to mobilize two reserve tank brigades and to accelerate preparations for a war – an operation known as the Blue-White Alert. When war did not break out in the spring, it increased the self-confidence of the analysts who predicted Egypt would not go to war because it lacked the essential weapon systems. Dayan and Elazar, who had assessed the situation differently, had to accept that they had erred and that IDI director, Major General Eli Zeira, had been correct. In retrospect, the April warnings apparently reflected Egypt's true intentions, but the war was postponed until the end of the summer because the Syrians had not yet completed military preparations.

During the second half of the summer of 1973 there were increasing indications that the Syrians were engaged in unusual activities. For years they had thinned out their forces along the border before winter, but that summer they reinforced them. Some of the moves were undertaken without prior warning. In view of the proximity of civilian settlements to the border, the IDF increased its alert along the northern front. Israel's main concern was not a general war but a limited Syrian initiative, aimed at the occupation of a stronghold or two, or destroying a civilian settlement. A Syrian war initiative was ruled out because it would necessitate an Egyptian decision to go to war, and war, in IDI assessment, was not on the Egyptian agenda. Nevertheless, after being warned by King Hussein that the Syrian army was fully deployed, on September 26 the IDF began reinforcing the Golan front. By Yom Kippur, the 7th Armored Brigade and other forces were fully deployed. However, the order of battle was far less than the one planned for a full-scale war.

Toward the end of September, while Israel was occupied with the Golan Heights, the Suez front was considered completely quiet. The

Egyptian army had already started deploying for war but did so under the cover of preparations for a routine exercise, *Tahrir* 41 ("Freedom 41"). A day before the exercise started, a Mossad source in Egypt reported that Tahrir 41 was merely a cover for war. Reports from posts along the Suez Canal as well as from SIGINT sources showed not only the exceptional magnitude of the military activity but the fact that it was very different from the familiar pattern of similar exercises in the past. It included the transfer of large quantities of live ammunition to the front, the clearing of mine fields near the canal, the preparation for taking to the water and the accumulation of crossing equipment along the waterline, all of which implied offensive intentions. Nevertheless, military intelligence's assessment remained the same: Egypt did not view itself as capable of going to war.

Consequently, from the perspective of the chief of staff, who was entirely dependent on intelligence reports and evaluations, the situation on the Egyptian front was entirely normal until two days before war broke out. Two events changed his evaluation. One was an Israeli reconnaissance flight along the canal, which showed that the Egyptian army was fully deployed; the other was the sudden evacuation of Soviet families from Egypt and Syria, which began on the evening of October 4.

Based on the new information, the chief of staff put the IDF on red alert on the morning of Friday, October 5. In discussions held throughout that day (the eve of Yom Kippur), he said that although the situation was tense, war would not break out before additional intelligence arrived. For that reason he did not demand the mobilization of the reserve army. What Elazar and Dayan did not know was that certain "special means of collection," which they understood from the director of military intelligence to be operational, had not been activated. Since they believed that war would not break out without a warning from those "special means," they underestimated its likelihood. Zeira, convinced that war was unlikely, prevented the dissemination of the clear warning that had become available twenty-one hours before the war started.

The warning that completely changed the situation came about ten hours before war broke out. It was an unambiguous warning from the chief of the Mossad, Zvi Zamir, who some two hours earlier had met in London with his best Egyptian source, Ashraf Marwan. Marwan informed him that a war would begin on sunset that same day. The chief of staff consequently demanded authorization for the Israel air force to carry out a preemptive strike against the Syrian air force and for a call-up of all the reserve forces. After a delay of a few hours Prime Minister Golda Meir authorized a large-scale mobilization of the reserve army but did not authorize the strike.

When war broke out at 2:00 p.m., the IDF in the Golan Heights had not yet fully deployed. A different deployment might have prevented the collapse of the line in the front's southern sector fourteen hours later. The canal front was completely unprepared, and only a few tanks were in position when the war began. The rest of the three hundred tanks of the regular division in Sinai, Division 252, were on move toward the canal. The Bar-Lev line was manned by a relatively weak force of reserve soldiers instead of the regular service paratroopers who were supposed to meet the crossing forces. The lack of preparedness led to the encirclement of the Bar-Lev line only a few hours after the fighting began. In an effort to support the strongholds, Division 252 lost two hundred tanks within sixteen hours.

In the early morning hours of October 7 Israel was left with hardly any forces to defend the southern sector of the Golan front. The Syrian army could cross the Jordan River into Israel along its pre-1967 border, encircle the Israeli forces in the northern sector and thus occupy the entire Golan Heights. At the same time the IDF was left with hardly any forces capable of defending the Sinai, and the Egyptian army could launch a strike deep into the heart of Israeli-held territory. Only the rapid arrival of reserve forces prevented those threats from being realized.

The Intelligence Community during the War

The intelligence fiasco that preceded the war had a major impact on intelligence community performance during the war. Branch 5 (Syria) of the IDI's production and analysis department, which before the war had argued that the Syrian deployment in the Golan Heights was most likely a preparation for war, functioned well once hostilities commenced. On the other hand, Branch 6 (Egypt), whose head had failed entirely to read Egypt's intentions, functioned ineffectively after the war started as well. Following the failure of the IDF counterattack on the canal front on October 8, the chief of staff ordered the branch head to be replaced, which improved its performance throughout the remainder of the war.

The war revealed various shortcomings in Israel's intelligence community. One of them was the ineffective flow of intelligence information to the ground fighting units and the Israeli air force. As a result, the ground forces in the Golan were surprised by the arrival of Iraqi expeditionary forces on the battlefield, although sufficient information about them was available in Tel Aviv and had been transferred to the northern command. Similarly, since the available information about the Egyptian concentration of forces near the bridgeheads along the canal was not transferred to the Israeli air force, it did not exploit its ability to destroy them.

The impact of intelligence on the way the war was conducted was manifested by two critical events, one negative, the other positive. The first was the mistaken assessment of the Egyptian war plan at the beginning of the war. That significantly hampered the IDF's effectiveness on the southern front during the first three days of the war. The second was the warning the Mossad received on October 12 about the Egyptian intention to carry out an offensive into the Sinai two days later. That warning prevented the Israeli leadership from making strategic mistakes and enabled the IDF to defeat the Egyptian offensive and then take the initiative by crossing the canal.

The Egyptian War Plan

In light of its air inferiority, Egypt constructed a war plan to prevent the IAF from attacking its ground forces. The plan was based on limited territorial objectives, i.e., the occupation of Israeli-held territory east of the Suez Canal to a depth of ten kilometers (6.2 miles). The Egyptian ground forces in the strip along the canal were still protected by the anti-aircraft layout on the canal's western side. Any advance eastward would allow the IAF to freely attack the ground forces. The Egyptians did not reveal their limited war objective to their Syrian allies lest they refuse to join a war in which the Egyptian army's advance would halt after a few hours and the main bulk of the war effort would fall on Syrian shoulders. Therefore, the Egyptian plan presented to the Syrians before the war consisted of two stages: the first stage a crossing of the Suez Canal, and the second a breakthrough of the 4th and 21st Armored Divisions to the Gidy and Mitla passes and an incursion deep into Sinai. IDI had been familiar with the plan at least since the summer of 1972.

Shortly before the war broke out, Ashraf Marwan gave Israel the Egyptian plan that had been kept secret from the Syrians. Meeting with the chief of the Mossad on the night of October 5, when he warned that war would start the following day, he again provided its details. On October 6 at 1:45 p.m., fifteen minutes before the war started, the IDI's production and analysis department issued a short notice to the effect that the Egyptian war objective was "to take over the eastern bank of the [Suez] canal and occupy the territory along it, ten kilometers to the east. The results [of the assault] will determine further developments. In any case, at this stage they do not intend to reach the passes."

Unfortunately, as soon as the war began and intelligence on the southern front became chaotic, that piece of critical information was lost. Instead, military intelligence continued to evaluate the situation on the basis of the Egyptian plan that had been presented to the Syrians, calling for an armored attack immediately after the crossing, and the agency's senior officers briefed Elazar accordingly. A few hours after five Egyptian infantry divisions crossed the canal, the IDI director and his aides reported that the 4th and 21st Armored Divisions had also begun crossing. Their reports contributed to the grave concern, on the morning of October 7, that the main Egyptian armored force was about to cross or had already begun crossing the canal and would launch an attack within hours. Given the circumstances at the time, it was clear that the slim forces of the 252nd Division could not stop such an offensive. Therefore Dayan, who had gone to the southern command's war room, suggested a deep retreat eastward into Sinai. Fortunately, his suggestion was rejected. Later that day, in the chief of staff's assessment the reserve forces that had been streaming into the Sinai since noon were sufficient to repel any Egyptian attack and no further retreat took place.

Military intelligence's mistaken evaluation of Egypt's war plan continued to influence the conduct of the war afterward as well. The chief of staff did not know that the Egyptian army had limited territorial objectives and therefore accelerated the counterattack on the canal front, concerned that once Egypt's armored forces crossed the canal, the IDF would face a far more difficult challenge in reoccupying the territory it had already lost. Consequently he decided that the counteroffensive would take place on the morning of October 8. It is entirely possible that had he known at that stage that the Egyptians were not planning to move their armored divisions eastward, he would have waited until the reserve forces were better organized, and the counterattack could have been launched on October 9. However, that was not the case, and the IDF's October 8 offense was a complete failure. Following the fiasco, the former chief of staff, Lieutenant General (Res.) Haim Bar-Lev was sent to take over the southern front. Before he left for his command he met with the Mossad chief, who had just returned from London. Zamir gave Bar-Lev a copy of the real Egyptian war plan, the one military intelligence had had in its possession for weeks. Bar-Lev studied it on his helicopter flight from Tel Aviv to Sinai. He subsequently operated according to it, and the results were manifested on the ground immediately.

The Warning of the October 14 Attack

On October 12 Israel's top leaders met to discuss the situation on the southern front. They had three options: first, to accept a cease-fire and admit that Israel had lost the war; second, to wage a costly and probably unsuccessful counterattack on the Egyptian force, which so far had suffered few losses and was at the height of its power; and third, to wait for the next phase of the Egyptian attack, the second offensive, according to the plan delivered by Marwan, defeat it and then counterattack the weakened Egyptian forces. While the consensus was that the third option was the best, the question was whether or not the Egyptian army would resort to another offensive. Under those circumstances the general tendency was to accept a cease-fire and admit defeat.

During the deliberations, the chief of the Mossad, who was present at the time, was informed that one of his sources in Egypt had just delivered a warning that the Egyptian army was making preparations to carry out the second offensive. Zamir immediately reported the information, which was critical and completely changed the course of the deliberations. It was now decided to end the meeting and wait for Egypt's next move.

When the Egyptians attacked on October 14 they found the IDF ready and waiting, and the attack was repelled. The Egyptians lost 250 tanks as well as hundreds of armored personal carriers and other military equipment, while the IDF suffered relatively few losses. The outcome made it possible for the IDF to take the initiative, and a day later Israel began crossing the Suez Canal to the west, an operation that entirely changed the situation on the southern front.

Intelligence for Operation Yonatan (Entebbe) (1976)

Brigadier General (Ret.) Gadi Zohar
Former Head of the Terror and Palestinians Department
in the IDI Production and Analysis Department

Background

"Where the hell is Entebbe?" That was my first reaction at four o'clock on Monday morning, June 28, 1976. We were sitting in the war room of Terror and Palestinians Branch of IDI's research and production department. Air France flight 139 had been hijacked on its way to Paris from Tel Aviv after having taken off from a stopover in Athens, and I had been following the developments day and night.

A few hours before, it had landed in the unknown Entebbe. It had taken off from Benghazi, Libya, after Qaddafi had allowed it to re-fuel but refused to let it remain on Libyan soil. In Benghazi an Israeli woman with British citizenship was removed from the plane after she convinced the hijackers that she did not feel well, becoming the first intelligence source for what had happened inside the plane. Intelligence was very important, but in this case we had to rely on extremely uncon-ventional sources.

Air France 139 was not the first plane hijacked by Palestinian ter-rorists. The first was in 1968, when an El Al flight was hijacked en route from Rome to Tel Aviv and forced to land in Algeria. However, at the end of 1975 the PLO and other Palestinian organizations halted their terrorist activities abroad, having come to the conclusion that it did the

Palestinian cause more harm than good, and yet here was another example of a hijacked plane with Israelis aboard.

In February 1976, before the hijacking, an attempt to fire a shoulder-launched missile at an El Al plane in Nairobi was foiled. In retrospect it turned out that the prevention of the attack and the arrest of the terrorists were what prompted Wadia Hadad's group to hijack the Air France plane.

Essential Intelligence Information during the Hijacking

As soon as the hijacking became known, from the takeoff in Athens to the landing in Entebbe, we concentrated on the essentials:

- What was the hijackers' objective? Were they planning to land the plane in Israel?
- Who were the hijackers? What was their organization? What weapons did they have?
- Were the hijackers in contact with their headquarters? Where was the attack's control center?

With the above in mind, the relevant agencies immediately began preparations for a landing in Israel or an attempt to crash the plane, and obviously every item of advance information was critical. The picture was bleak. The best updated information came from debriefing the woman who had extricated herself from the situation in Benghazi. She provided both the media and British intelligence with the first description of the hijackers, how many there were, what their nationalities were, what weapons they were carrying, what the atmosphere inside the plane was like and what the hijackers had said.

From the small amount of information the Mossad had, and especially from an intelligence evaluation based on prior knowledge of the terrorist organizations' modus operandi, we concluded that we were dealing with the organization of Wadia Hadad. Hadad had formerly been an operations officer in George Habash's Popular Front for the

Liberation of Palestine, but left it because it had decided on a moratorium of terrorist attacks abroad. It was he who had orchestrated the plot to shoot down the El Al plane in Nairobi in February 1976.

After a few uncertain hours, open sources reported that the plane had landed in Entebbe, Uganda. There were 247 passengers on board, both Israelis and other nationalities, a French crew and four hijackers – two Germans, male and female, and two Palestinians, armed with pistols and hand grenades. Other terrorists joined them once the plane was on the ground.

Essential Elements of Intelligence Information after the Landing

When the plane landed in Entebbe that morning we knew very little about the terrorists' intentions or about the place itself. When we started collating the existing information, I sent an officer to a bookstore to buy an old tourist map of Uganda. We found Entebbe as a tiny dot; it was the airport of Kampala, the capital city, but not much more than that. Researchers from Israel Air Force Intelligence found it listed in the *Jeppesen Flight Guide*, a basic international reference work for navigation and landing information about every airport around the globe.

On that day, June 28, we still weren't talking about a rescue operation. The IAF was calculating routes and the possibility of flying to Entebbe, but no instructions had been given for an operation. Intelligence, research and collection only monitored the event and decisions were far in the future.

Uganda, despite Idi Amin's particular and colorful personality and the terminating of Israeli-Ugandan diplomatic relations in 1972, was not perceived as actively sponsoring terrorism and was not an intelligence objective for the Israeli intelligence community. Therefore, the basic information we had at the beginning of the event was particularly thin.

At that stage we dealt primarily with the following intelligence gaps:

- Was Entebbe the hijackers' final destination?
- The terrorists: how many, what weapons, were they in contact with their headquarters and what was their plan of action?
- The Ugandan army: what were its involvement, deployment, weapons and capabilities?
- Where exactly in the terminal were the hostages being held?
- Was the terminal booby-trapped, and if so, where were the explosives placed?
- What intelligence was necessary for an IAF flight's landing on the Entebbe airport runway?

The terrorists stated their demands: they wanted the release of the terrorist operatives who had been arrested in Nairobi at the beginning of the year, verifying our assessment that Wadia Hadad's organization was behind the hijacking. Their ultimatum was that the release of the terrorists had to be effected by 1400 hours on July 1, otherwise the hostages would be killed. That is, we had a little more than forty-eight hours and no intelligence for an operation to rescue the hostages.

Starting to Think about an Operation

In the early morning hours of June 29, when all the relevant research and collection personnel had gathered in the office of the deputy head of operational research, Colonel Ehud Barak, we had more questions than answers. This was the first time, however, we considered a rescue operation. We had to verify what intelligence we had, what we lacked and what the chances were that we could complete our preparations before the ultimatum ran out.

At that stage, Tuesday, June 29, the main sources of information were IDF and IAF soldiers and officers who had been in Uganda in the past. They arrived, on their own initiative one after another, during the night and until the operation itself, and without their contribution the rescue operation never would have taken place. Although they had been hurriedly evacuated in 1972, they had a great deal of information and many photographs, maps and movies, all of which were extremely valuable. In addition, Idi Amin's pomposity and frequent media appearances were important to intelligence collecting, and the telephone conversations he held with "Bourka" – Baruch Bar-Lev, Israel's last military attaché and a personal friend – were an excellent source of intelligence.

The foreign hostages, who had been separated from the Jews and Israelis, were released on Wednesday, June 30, and flown to Paris on July 1. Clearly they were an important intelligence source. With the aid of the Mossad, which provided the logistics and contacts with French intelligence, a team was dispatched from Israel to debrief them, having been instructed by the production and analysis department and the officers of the operational units that had been alerted.

Intelligence Deployment for the Operation

A great deal of information was collected from the hostages, but since they were not regular sources and had been traumatized by their ordeal and then pressured by the debriefing, they sometimes contradicted one another, and the results were inconsistent. Nevertheless, as we already had the basic information about the site, a picture of the situation inside the terminal was beginning to take shape.

On Wednesday the 30th, and from then until the operation, missions were assigned to the intelligence community, and by the end of the day we had a good idea of the event and our destination (the airport and terminal), although still not at the operational intelligence level.

The work was divided as follows:

- The production and analysis department provided the integral picture: the terrorists, the Ugandans, the hostages, the terminal, and the Arab and international arenas.
- Air force intelligence department: flight routes, runways, refueling, etc.

- Naval intelligence department: Lake Victoria (examined as an operational option).
- Intelligence specific to the operation was provided by the infantry and paratroopers' chief intelligence officer and the intelligence officers of the operational units who were assigned to the mission.
- With regard to collection, there was no reliable source covering the event, so most of the material came from chance and open sources: the media, officers and soldiers who had served in Uganda, Israeli civilians who had been there in the past and the hostages who had been released.

The Mossad provided good, updated coverage at the last minute: organizing quickly, it brought an agent to Nairobi, a pilot who rented a light plane and took off for Entebbe pretending to be a civilian flight. He circled above the airport taking pictures, and then returned to Nairobi. The photographs were immediately sent to Israel and shown to the government on the morning of the operation, reinforcing the decision to authorize it as the planes took off and made a stopover in Sharm el-Sheikh. For the first time there was independent visual corroboration of the intelligence picture we had presented based on other sources.

The aerial photos were given to the operation's intelligence officer on the last plane to take off for Sharm el-Sheikh, but there was no way of circulating them among the commanders of the forces, so their contribution as intelligence for the operation was partial, but it was essential for the decision makers.

The Operation Gets Underway

On July 1 the ultimatum expired and the government of Israel had to decide how to respond. Despite the efforts of the French government to negotiate an end to the affair, separating the Israelis and Jews from the other passengers only increased the threat that the terrorists would kill the hostages. The government had no other assessment or intelligence, and in the end decided to agree to the ultimatum and negotiate with the terrorists under French aegis, even sending Major General Rehavam Ze'evi (nicknamed "Gandhi"), the prime minister's advisor for terrorist affairs, to Paris.

Satisfied by the Israeli readiness to negotiate, the terrorists agreed to postpone the ultimatum to 1300 hours, Sunday, July 4. The additional days were vital for making final preparations for the operation and high-level political and military decisions. On the afternoon of Thursday, July 1, authorization was given in principle, and preparations continued until Friday, July 2. On the night of July 2 we issued the summary of intelligence for the operation to all parties involved, including the government, updated to July 1. When the planes took off for Sharm el-Sheikh on Saturday afternoon the final government authorization for the operation had not yet been given.

The Main Gaps in Intelligence for the Operation

The planes took off for Entebbe on July 3 with intelligence updated to July 1, with the exception of the Mossad photographs, which, as noted, had been presented at the government meeting but not circulated to the operation's commanders. The main gaps in intelligence were closed by the assessment of our analysts, and to our good fortune proved correct:

- Which room in the terminal were the Jewish and Israeli hostages being held? Before the foreign nationals had been released, the Jews and Israelis were held in the small room. It was assumed that they had been moved to the large room, where it was easier for the terrorists to assume control.
- Was the terminal booby-trapped? The terrorists claimed to both Idi Amin and the hostages that the terminal was booby-trapped, and even positioned boxes from which electric

wires protruded. From the debriefings of the hostages, it was concluded that they were fakes.

- Were the runways interconnected? The terminal in which the hostages were being held was located on the runway of the old airport, and we knew the airport had been expanded and that another runway and new terminal had been built. The operational plan was to land on the new runway, and even though according to our maps the runways were not connected, we assumed they were, and the Mossad's last-minute photographs indicated that that was, in fact, the case.

Conclusion

The operation in Entebbe was unique with regard to operational planning, intelligence and the way decisions were made. The massive Israeli presence in Uganda before 1972 and the release of the non-Jewish, non-Israeli passengers were what made it possible to construct a reliable intelligence picture about what was happening at the target destination. Daring operational planning and the ability to make political decisions based on partial intelligence were responsible for the success of this unique operation.

Strategic Intelligence for the Attack on the Iraqi Nuclear Reactor (1981)

Major General (Ret.) Aviezer Yaari
Former Head of the Production and Analysis Division of IDI

Background

In 1974 Saddam Hussein signed a deal with Jacques Chirac's France for the construction of two nuclear reactors. They were to be built in Iraq by the French, who also took it upon themselves to oversee their operation. The reactors, which were called "research reactors," were built near Baghdad. One was suitable for producing no more than ten megawatts, and the other, up to seventy megawatts. Construction was scheduled to be finished by the end of 1980, but was rescheduled to 1981. In June 1981, the Israeli air force attacked the larger nuclear reactor and destroyed it.

Israel's immediate concern was the reactor's potential for manufacturing fissionable material suitable for military purposes, and it was shortly proved that that was indeed the Iraqis' intention. They built laboratories and other installations nearby, one of which was a hot cell laboratory capable of extracting plutonium from radiated rods. In addition, the French supplied them with highly enriched (93 percent) fuel, increasing Israel's concerns. Israel was familiar with Saddam Hussein and his ambitions for power and control of the Persian Gulf. In addition, he was motivated by Iran's efforts to build nuclear reactors at Bushar, which had begun during the reign of the Shah. Those efforts, which stopped with Khomeini's Islamic Revolution, were renewed later and are today a clear and present threat.

Israel's scientific and intelligence relations with France during the 1950s and '60s helped complete the picture. An understanding was gained of the plans, structure and magnitude of Iraq's nuclear project, and the stages were monitored as work progressed.

Once the deal with France had been completed, the Rabin government took steps to try to change the French position on the contract or to cancel it. The efforts were unsuccessful, and in 1977 the matter was handed over to the Begin government. Rabin gave Begin detailed information about what had been done up to that point, and Begin started pressing for action at every level. He was deeply convinced that an enemy of the State of Israel had to be prevented from building a nuclear reactor that could be used not only to threaten the existence of the state but to threaten the Jewish people with a second Holocaust.

Strategic Intelligence Issues

Israeli intelligence was faced with three major tasks.

The first was to monitor the project's progress. To that end it used HUMINT and other sources; contacts with scientific communities, especially in countries that had supplied Iraq with equipment; connections with intelligence colleagues abroad; political activity conducted with certain European and other countries; visual operations; surveillance; and ground and aerial photographs.

Israel tracked purchases made throughout Europe for the various components needed to construct the nuclear reactor and the attached laboratories, and also monitored the infiltration of Iraqi students into Western institutions for advanced scientific study and of Iraqi workers into nuclear facilities; both groups were being trained as a generation of specialists and operators. Notice was taken of the routes used to convey equipment to Iraq, and the possibility of disrupting them was examined.

Finally, Israel had to follow the flow of funds from Iraq used to grease the wheels and bribe vendors abroad.

The second task was to examine the feasibility of either preventing the reactor from working or obstructing its operation.

The third task was to process the information for a possible military operation and to form a general assessment. Processing and evaluating the information was carried out by various small teams that were party to the secret within military intelligence, the Mossad, the scientific community and a committee of advisors appointed by Begin. In addition, an inter-agency think tank, of which I was a member, was established, headed by deputy Mossad chief Nahum Admoni, to examine and evaluate information from all the sources and make it available to the relevant agencies. The group also monitored operations undertaken to disrupt the reactor's construction, and during the final months of the summer of 1980 it concluded that the efforts had been only partially successful. At that point, and before a report was made to the government, the lion's share of the work was transferred to the research departments of IDI and the Mossad.

Intelligence and the Politicians: To Attack or Not?

The government deliberated responses to the nuclear threat and decided on an aerial attack. However, at that time, early in 1980, other options were also discussed. Begin appointed a committee headed by Aharon Yariv (former IDI chief) to examine the alternatives. The committee finally recommended not to attack, and some members of the intelligence community also had reservations about attacking. Opinions in IDI and the Mossad were divided, especially when the time came to decide. The IDI production and analysis department was in favor of the attack while the IDI chief opposed it, and the situation in the Mossad was similar. On October 28, 1980, I was summoned to give the government an intelligence evaluation before the final decision was made. I explained the production and analysis department's opinion in favor of an attack, and Nahum Admoni from the Mossad said the same. The IDI and Mossad heads had expressed their opposing opinions at a previous meeting.

Arguments against an Attack

- Bombing the reactor would make world public opinion hostile to Israel, especially if the reactor were already active at the time of the attack. Israel would be accused of violating the international consensus against attacking nuclear reactors.
- Israel would be accused of disrupting the peace process that had been begun with Egypt two years previously.
- Bombing the reactor was liable to unite the Arab world into waging a new war against Israel.
- The international community, including the United States, was liable to impose sanctions on Israel, to limit relations with it and foster relations with the Arab world.
- Finally, from the practical scientific standpoint, destroying the reactor might not prevent and might even accelerate Iraq's efforts if it were really intent on acquiring a nuclear weapon.

Arguments in Favor of an Attack

- At the time (October 1980) all the structures had been built and the installation of the facilities was almost complete. Since the reactor was not yet operative, it alone would be destroyed and there would be no collateral environmental damage.
- A month previously, the Iraq-Iran war had broken out and the foreign experts had left Iraq (harming the French experts was one of the arguments against an attack).
- The reactor's aerial defense system had not yet been completed and the Iraq-Iran war was delaying it further.
- Twice during the previous month Iranian Phantom jets had attacked the reactor without success. The attacks made it possible for our planes, which were also American (F-16s), to be

confused with the Iranian jets and so delay and moderate immediate world criticism.

- At that point the IDI production and analysis department did not envision the Arab world uniting against Israel over the destruction of an Iraqi nuclear reactor.
- The world, and particularly the United States, would have a severe political response, but not to the point of genuine sanctions against Israel.
- Those in favor considered an attack on the reactor as potentially causing a long delay in Iraq's acquisition of nuclear capabilities, or potentially even stopping it (in effect, the assessment was for at least five years). That would enable Israel and the rest of the world to work to abort the project.

In Retrospect

Twenty-nine years later, an evaluation of the intelligence operation and its collection and analysis contribution, as well as the contribution of the committee of experts, make it possible to conclude that Israeli intelligence, even though its capabilities were unlike those of today, was sufficiently professional and collected the relevant information. The analysis, evaluation and presentation of information helped in the decision-making process.

In retrospect, those who opposed the attack were correct in their assumption that Iraq would continue its nuclear efforts. However, the nuclear projects it did complete were destroyed eleven years later in the First Gulf War, 1991.

On the other hand, those who supported the attack were correct in their assessment that it would cause a delay in Iraq's nuclear capability, which, if properly exploited, would be long enough to make it possible to prevent Iraq from acquiring nuclear arms. As noted above, that was what happened. They were also correct in their assessment that the Arab world would not respond seriously to the attack, and that the international community would loudly condemn Israel, but no more than that.

Only a few years after the attack, an increasing number of world leaders justified and eventually praised Israel's action, and there were those who used it to develop a theory of preemption. To this day Iraq does not have nuclear capabilities.

Aerial Intelligence for the Attack on Iraq's Nuclear Reactor (1981)

Lieutenant Colonel (Res.) Shamai Golan
Air Intelligence Officer of the Attack Operation

Overview

Plans for the aerial attack began in 1979. All we had at the time was general information that the reactor was located south of Baghdad, and an American map with a scale of 1:250,000. Intelligence was required in three fields:

- The reactor itself as a target: the materials used to construct it, its depth underground, its most vulnerable spot, the most suitable weaponry and fuses, i.e., everything that would ensure its destruction.
- Its aerial defenses and the areas around it, knowledge that was necessary to coordinate an attack profile: surface-to-air missiles, anti-aircraft guns, radar, defenses and camouflage.
- Data about the flyover zones between Israel and Baghdad: straight across Jordan, from the north over Turkey or through the south over Saudi Arabia?

The Reactor

As an intelligence objective, the reactor itself was relatively easy prey. The precise information needed and how to procure it were obtained quickly, and the Office of Scientific Relations provided exact sketches of the reactor's structure and components. The sketches made it possible to choose the kind of ordnance required and to calculate the number of explosive devices necessary to ensure the reactor's complete destruction. The information was graphically reworked to make it suitable for the pilots' visual angle from the air.

Aerial Defenses

Knowledge of the target's aerial defenses was essential for coordinating the attack profile, and was an intelligence challenge of the first order. The Israeli intelligence community was not required to provide information about the entire battery of surface-to-air missiles nor where each and every anti-aircraft gun protecting Baghdad and its environs was positioned. We made do with an inventory of the missile batteries and anti-aircraft units in the region.

In trading information and seeking cooperation from other intelligence branches, we did not go into the kind of detail necessary for an attack. It was also clear that by asking for very detailed information we might reveal our intentions. In any event it was not certain that the information would be provided, and in this case time was on our side. A few meetings with the intelligence agencies of friendly countries enabled us to paint an exact picture: the reactor was girded by a ring of eleven batteries of SA-2/3 surface-to-air missiles. As far as anti-aircraft guns were concerned, general knowledge about the types of guns was sufficient, and we assumed they were deployed throughout Baghdad as well as around the reactor and its environs. At the time the Iran-Iraq war was being waged, and a few days before the operation we found out that the SA-6 surface-to-air missile unit had been moved from the Iranian front to the defense of the reactor.

Choosing an Air Route

From the intelligence point of view, choosing an air route was perhaps the most complex issue. The most important factor was preventing the planes from being detected, and if they were detected, concealing their destination. Flying time from Israel to the target was about an hour and a half, and early detection would alert the Iraqi aerial defense system and create a very serious situation.

After lengthy deliberations it was decided that the planes would fly over northern Saudi Arabia. That gave rise to certain problems. Obviously, a location had to be found where the border could be crossed at a low altitude without exposure to military forces that would report to a Saudi control post, which in turn might warn Iranian and Iraqi neighbors. Examination showed that no location existed that was not exposed to observation at least once. We would have to lull the suspicions of the observers and military posts, which we did: for months the Israeli air force flew occasional sorties that scraped along the Jordanian and Saudi borders, accustoming their military forces to our aerial presence. In the final analysis, however, it was obvious that a border crossing would be detected wherever it occurred.

The next critical stage was crossing the Saudi Arabian–Iraqi border. We had to map the Saudi and Iraqi forces stationed along the border and the oil pipeline, because the detection of our planes as they crossed the border was liable to alert the system and it was still a long flight from there to Baghdad. A few reconnaissance flights were flown to determine where their radar stations and military posts were situated, even the location of the civilian camp where the oil crew lived, any information that could be gleaned. Here as well, lest our intention be discovered or a complication arise that might lead to a dogfight in Saudi air space, at a certain point the flights were discontinued, and a crossing point was chosen at a spot where intelligence of the area was known, even if there were radar and observation posts in the area.

As noted, flying time to the reactor was about an hour and a half, and the planes had to fly at the lowest possible altitude to prevent them from being tracked and avoid detection before they were over the target. Accordingly, high tension wires had to be located and mapped, requiring intensive intelligence collection and interpretation.

The operation was scheduled for the late afternoon, allowing the planes to attack as daylight faded. That guaranteed that the target could be identified and that the planes would return to Israel in the dark, minimizing the danger from Iraqi planes stationed at airfields along the Jordanian-Iraqi border. There were limited amounts of information that could be acquired about the enemy planes and radar stations, and about tactical intelligence in real time, and collection sources had to be deployed, especially airborne sources.

Field Security

Until the last minute, it was a strictly "need to know" operation, and even so the full picture was never revealed. For example, the intelligence officers in the control booth knew about the operation only when the planes took off, and as for the final target, only during the flight. From an operational point of view, there was no need for them to know beforehand. The collection units took the necessary steps close to the time of the operation, advising of a general activity without mentioning the target itself.

The Operation

The operation was carried out as planned:

- The Israeli air force planes were detected as they crossed the border south of Aqaba by none other than King Hussein of Jordan. At the time he was sailing in the bay and he reported eight Skyhawks flying eastward. The report was received at the Jordanian control post in Amman, and there was a genuine fear that it would be passed along to Baghdad, because the Iraqis had an air force liaison officer in Jordan.
- Intelligence mapping of the routine air activity and aerial defense deployment of Jordan, Saudi Arabia and Iraq in the H-2/3 airport sector was carried out. Ongoing monitoring over the previous year and a half had made it possible to create

an aerial intelligence picture. When the planes had flown for half an hour and crossed the Saudi-Iraqi border and no change was reported even though the planes had been sighted, the intelligence evaluation was that an alert had not been sounded and the operation continued as planned.

- The planes reached their destination without being detected. The few anti-aircraft guns and surface-to-air missile batteries in position could not provide a response and all eight planes attacked and returned to Israel safely. On the way back a MIG-21 was seen taking off from the Rashid airfield near the Iraqi-Jordanian border, but it returned to base as soon as Israeli warplanes flew toward it.

Conclusion

Intelligence played an important role in the destruction of the Iraqi nuclear reactor, from determining the type of ordnance necessary, to deciding which route to take to Iraq, to the profile of the attack flight. The preparations for the operation were kept at the utmost secrecy. Therefore a very small number of people (who were in on the secret) were involved in the collection activities. So it may be that some information was missed. Nonetheless, we believe that in this case, secrecy outweighed any possible additional information.

Operators in the SIGINT unit, October 1948

IDI headquarters in "the Green House," Jaffa – the beginning, 1948

Israeli intelligence began in this building

An interception station of the Haganah in Jerusalem

A monitoring device in a bunker near Tel Aviv, 1948

A monitoring mobile squad on the southern front – the beginning, 1948

Israeli reconnaissance soldiers during the War of Independence, 1948

*Israeli and Jordanian officers in armistice negotiations
at the end of the War of Independence, 1949*

Reuven Shiloah, the founder of the Mossad

Preparing a military map in the IDI's mapping unit

First Israeli prime minister and defense minister David Ben-Gurion and his wife Pola, meeting intelligence officers at their home in Kibbutz Sde Boker in the Negev

Undercover ISA operations agent at work

A mobile observation of ISA's operation unit, 1950s

US assistant secretary of state Henry Byroade is briefed by an Israeli intelligence officer at the Syrian border, 1952

Collecting visual intelligence along the border of the Gaza Strip, 1953

The northern command intelligence department exploring targets, 1955

Senior collection officer with Bedouin sheikhs near the Egyptian border, 1960s

An Israeli secret agent in an Arab country

Prime Minister David Ben-Gurion and the team of Mossad and ISA who captured Adolf Eichmann in Argentina in 1960 and brought him to trial in Israel

The American Jewish comedian Danny Kaye visiting
Aharon Yariv (sitting on the table), who later became head of the IDI, 1964

A MIG-21 fighter, landed in Israel by an Iraqi pilot
in a secret operation of the Mossad, 1966

*Mossad combatant Eli Cohen on the balcony of his house in Damascus
shortly before being captured by the Syrians and executed, 1964*

Senior intelligence officers in the northern command overlooking Syria, 1967

Kurdish revolt leader Mustafa Barzani visiting Israel, with Defense Minister Moshe Dayan and Mossad director Meir Amit (second from right), 1967

*Israeli president Zalman Shazar and Mossad director Meir Amit (first on left)
at a reception in honor of Wolfgang Lutz, Mossad agent, after his release
from Egyptian prison, 1968*

*Israeli president Zalman Shazar hosting Marcel Ninio (center), Victor Levy and
Robert Dasa (left) after their release from Egyptian prison, 1968
(Operation Suzanna, 1954)*

Major General Eli Zeira (center) replaces Major General Aharon Yariv (right) as head of the IDI, as the chief of staff, Lieutenant General David Elazar (Dado) looks on, 1972

A Soviet SIGINT ship off Israeli shores during the War of Attrition, 1970

Prime Minister Golda Meir, chief of staff Lieutenant General Haim Barlev (left) and head of the IDI Major General Aharon Yariv (center), 1972

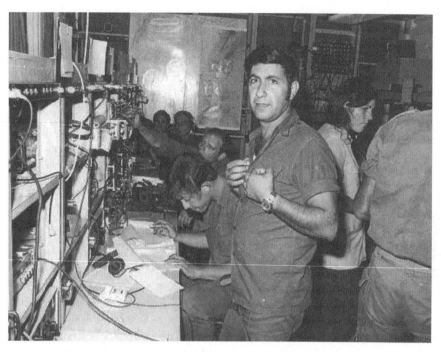

The Yom Kippur War – an intelligence monitoring station, 1973

SIGINT base in Sinai during the Yom Kippur War, 1973

*A war room of a combat intelligence unit in the field
during the Yom Kippur War, 1973*

Aerial SIGINT

The Agranat Commission – a state commission appointed to examine the failures of the Yom Kippur War, 1974. Right to left: Lieutenant General Haim Laskov, former chief of staff; Isaac Neventzal, former state comptroller; Shimon Agranat, president of the Supreme Court; Moshe Landau, Supreme Court justice; and Lieutenant General Yigal Yadin, former chief of staff.

Israeli-Egyptian peace talks, 1978. Right to left: head of the IDI Major General Shlomo Gazit, Egyptian chief of staff Field Marshal Abd al-Ghani Gamasi, and Minister of Defense Ezer Weizman.

Major General Shlomo Gazit, head of IDI, greeting released hostages of the Entebbe hijacked airplane, 1976

Rescuing Ethiopian Jews, the Sudanese coast. Courtesy of David Ben-Uziel.

Mossad operation "Brothers" – Ethiopian Jews on their way to Jerusalem

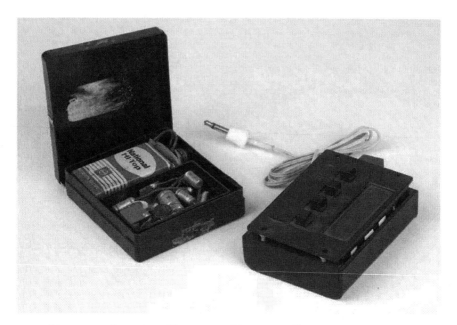

Monitoring devices used by agents of foreign intelligence services, 1980s

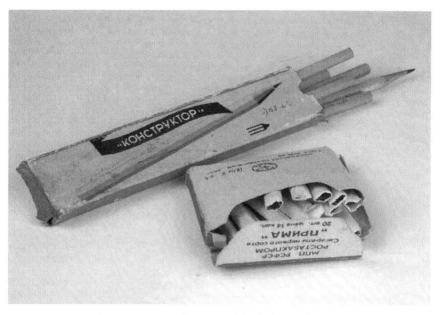

Soviet caches in innocent objects used for hiding information, 1980s

The first drones in the service of IDI and the air force, 1980s

Israeli intelligence – a pioneer in the space program

IDI in the military operation Cast Lead (December 2008–January 2009) in the Gaza Strip

Modern-day Israeli soldiers in advanced observation posts near the Gaza Strip

The ship Karin-A *smuggling military equipment from Iran to Gaza,
captured after an Israeli intelligence operation, 2002*

Major General Amos Yadlin, former head of IDI, with a new intelligence officer

Intelligence staff at work

Intelligence staff at work

Briefing of intelligence soldiers in a combat unit

A combat surveillance unit

A combat observation unit on the front

Section Four

Intelligence Challenges in Different Arenas

Intelligence and the Lebanese Arena

Brigadier General (Res.) Amos Gilboa
Former Head of the Production and Analysis Division of IDI

Overview: What Makes Lebanon Special?

Israel and its defense establishment have been more deeply involved in Lebanon than in any other Arab country, and it is the area that the Israeli public argues over the most. Israel has had three wars with Lebanon, there have been hundreds of large and small military operations, the IDF spent its longest period of time and suffered the greatest number of non-war related casualties there, and Lebanon motivated two investigation committees. It was the first arena that turned the Israel home front into the front line, and the one that Palestinian terrorism uses as a model and where suicide bombing was employed for the first time. Lebanon was also the second Arab country that signed a peace agreement (since cancelled) with Israel.

Israel's involvement with Lebanon, by its very nature, posed many strategic, operational and tactical challenges for the intelligence community (IDI as the leading body, the Mossad and the ISA). However, four other factors have made Lebanon's challenges special.

Society and Regime

Lebanese society is the most factionalized and varied in the Middle East, especially with regard to religion. That has also made the central government the weakest in the region; it does not have the tools for effective control, the most important of which is a strong army. In Lebanon, military strength is in the hands of the various militias of religious factions and other political organizations. Until 1982 that strength was concentrated in the hands of the Palestinians, but in the 1990s Hezbollah became the strongest organization. Hezbollah is a multidimensional political and military organization, as will be seen below. Unlike the Palestinian organizations, it managed to penetrate the vulnerable socioeconomic space left unguarded by the central government's weakness.

Ideology

Lebanon lacks a central ideology. It hosts religious and secular radicalism, Nasserism, Baathism and liberalism, as well as a pragmatic, opportunistic "ideology" followed by criminal and clan gangs.

External Influences

Lebanon, more than any other Arab country, is influenced and interfered with by external factors. There are regional forces, such as Syria, Egypt and Saudi Arabia, and international forces as well, which use Lebanon as a proxy. Israel was directly and indirectly involved in Lebanon between 1976 and 2000, and its influence is felt to this day. Finally, Iran has become extremely influential in Lebanon in recent years as the patron of Hezbollah.

Disorder and Confusion

The three elements noted above have caused disorder and confusion. There have been two civil wars (one in 1958, the other from 1975 to 1989), and local clashes and frequent political crises in the interims. Violence has become an integral part of the political culture, focusing on the assassination of rivals. Frequent new political alliances shuffle the deck, there are changes in orientation (for example, the Maronite Christians sometimes align themselves with Syria, sometimes with Israel, and sometimes some of them even enter into an alliance with Hezbollah), and there are gang wars in which politics and crime are interrelated.

This article will present the main stages of sixty years of Israeli intelligence in the Lebanese arena, with an emphasis on the special challenges it has had to face, and explain the main implications Lebanon has for Israeli intelligence.

Stages and Main Challenges

During the State of Israel's first twenty years, 1948–1967, Lebanon did not particularly interest Israeli intelligence and was generally ignored. It only came into focus toward the beginning of the 1970s, when its internal situation became turbulent. It was gradually given a high place in the priority information requirements (PIR) of the Israeli intelligence community, and consequently intelligence activities inside Lebanon became a growing priority.

1967 to 1982: The Period Preceding the First Lebanon War – A Mosaic of Challenges and Watershed Responses

The Palestinian Challenge and Its Terrorist Core

In 1969 the PLO moved most of its activity to Lebanon. Following the Black September of 1970[1] in Jordan, it moved the rest of its activity there, and Lebanon became the home base for anti-Israel Palestinian terrorism. Israeli intelligence focused on the following issues:

- Early warning of terrorist attacks became the PIR's top priority and began a new era in collecting and analysis, at both the northern command and IDI levels. There were successes but also failures (for example, the terrorist attack in the northern

---

1. September 1970 is referred to by the Palestinians as Black September. King Hussein moved to stamp out the military Palestinian organizations and restore his monarchy rule over the country. Armed conflict lasted until July 1971, when the PLO and thousands of Palestinian terrorists were moved to Lebanon.

development town Maalot in 1974, and the attack from the sea on the coastal road from Haifa to Tel Aviv in 1978).

- A list of military, political, infrastructure and other targets was prepared (for air, land and sea attacks). It was a time of hundreds of attacks and raids against hostile terrorist targets (one of the most famous was Operation Springtime of Youth in Beirut in 1973, an attack from the sea carried out by the General Staff Commando, which killed three senior terrorists involved in the 1972 Munich massacre). It also was the time of the first rocket war between the IDF and the PLO, and for several days the PLO attacked Israel's entire northern region, particularly Kiryat Shmona.

- The Palestinian military infrastructure and the territory of south Lebanon were studied and the lessons internalized. Before the First Lebanon War, there were more than 10,000 Palestinian terrorists organized like an army, with thousands of rockets and mortar shells and hundreds of artillery, some of them in fortified positions. A large proportion of the terrorists were based in south Lebanon. During that period, south Lebanon was high on the IDF northern command's list of intelligence priorities, especially providing the troops on the ground with all the required intelligence about the enemy and the terrain.

The Syrian Military-Political Challenge

In June 1976, the Syrian army invaded Lebanon, beginning a new era that ended only twenty-nine years later when the Syrian military force pulled out. Israeli intelligence now had a new arena for conventional warfare (in addition to the "old" one of the Golan Heights) with everything that entailed, including the study and monitoring of the Syrian army's capabilities there. Moreover, it opened a new early warning front. There were two strategic intelligence questions: Was the division of the Syrian army into two fronts (Lebanon and the Golan Heights) "good" for the IDF, or did it increase the Syrian threat? And what brought Hafez Assad to Lebanon in the first place? Security considerations? Aspirations for a "greater Syria"?

The Internal Lebanese Challenge

In April 1975 the Lebanese civil war broke out, continuing until 1989. Throughout the war there were attempts to reach a cease-fire and find some kind of compromise. The Lebanese government collapsed, the army fell apart and various societal and political events rocked the country, for example the decline of the importance of the Christians (and later, after 1982, the rise of the Shi'ites). All these factors forced Israeli intelligence, at both the collection and analysis levels, to deal with issues previously unknown – to develop an understanding of the social, economic, cultural and political processes taking place in Lebanon – issues far different from classic political-strategic intelligence matters such as foreign policy and defense capabilities. Moreover, a new military challenge presented itself: how to evaluate the balance of power between the various rival groups, an evaluation which was liable to be chaotic.

The Mossad

The Mossad had contacts with central Lebanese public figures during the 1950s and '60s, but from 1976 until 1982 those relations became a vast military and political system. That meant indirect Israeli involvement in the Lebanese civil war, which later became direct involvement. From 1976 until after the First Lebanon War, the Mossad was the main Israeli factor in the Lebanese arena: it was responsible for all the connections with the Christians (who pushed for greater direct Israeli involvement as a way of getting the Syrians out of the country) and other religious groups. It was also responsible for arming and training them (through the IDF), and for intelligence evaluation concerning Lebanon (with IDI).

The Collection of Information

The intelligence challenges naturally encouraged new collecting procedures. Most conspicuous was the increase in the importance of VISINT (visual intelligence), especially the use of unmanned aerial vehicles (UAVs, also known as drones). The Lebanese arena gave birth to the drones; it was their testing field and a few years before the war in Lebanon, their first operative sphere. Moreover, to a great extent Lebanon heightened the importance of VISINT as an intelligence apparatus in the war on terrorism and illustrated the problems of intelligence collaboration with the Christians, who provided disinformation.

1982 to 1985: From the First Lebanon War until the Withdrawal to the Security Zone

The years 1982 to 1985 were overshadowed by the war: the intelligence preparations before it, tactical-operative-strategic intelligence during it, and coping with Lebanon's internal complexities.

- Intelligence preparations were carried out for a land war with the Palestinians and the Syrians. The preparations were drawn out, and the forces were provided with updated intelligence, which included a clear picture of enemy deployment.
- The main tactical-operative intelligence problem was how to transmit updated intelligence rapidly to the fighting forces in real time in the dynamic situations created on the ground.
- At the strategic level there were two opposing intelligence evaluations. One, represented by military intelligence, was that the Christians could not be trusted and that a pro-Israeli Christian Lebanese regime could not be relied on. The other, represented mainly by the Mossad, was that the Christians could in fact be trusted, and therefore the quest for such a regime was desirable.

- Within the chaotic internal Lebanese situation, most intelligence dealt with the bloody conflicts between the Druze and the Christians, and the Christians and the Syrians.
- At that time a new dimension was introduced into the internal Lebanese fray: the political rise of the large, oppressed Shi'ite community, which had not participated in the Lebanese civil war. Military intelligence was aware of the process. As a result, it began studying and researching the Shi'ite issue and developing links with the heads of the Amal movement (the main Shi'ite political stream at the time, before the ascendance of Hezbollah). During the war and toward its end, another factor entered the picture: the ISA, which took intelligence responsibility for south Lebanon. Therefore there were three Israeli groups dealing with the Lebanese arena: military intelligence, the Mossad and the ISA, and there was no small amount of friction between them.

1985 to May 2000: From the Withdrawal to the Security Zone until the Withdrawal from Lebanon – the Appearance of Hezbollah

Three main factors influenced intelligence challenges from 1985 to May 2000. The first was that in 1989 the Lebanese civil war ended, the Taif agreement was signed (which officially terminated the civil war and introduced changes in the political framework of the regime to the detriment of the Christians) and Lebanon became a Syrian protégé. The second was that Hezbollah, after a series of battles with Amal at the end of the 1980s and after the Taif agreement, remained the only armed organization in Lebanon (except for the army) and the dominant Shi'ite factor, ruling south Lebanon and other areas of the country. The third was that Israel's interest in general, and Israeli intelligence's interest in particular, in the chaotic internal Lebanese situation cooled off dramatically, while Syrian and Iranian influence increased.

Hezbollah, the security zone and its proximity to Israel became the focus of intelligence activity, while fewer resources were invested in the Syrian army. Throughout the 1990s, military engagement was with Hezbollah, and the large Israeli military operations, Operation Accountability in 1993 and Operation Grapes of Wrath in 1996, were carried out by standoff fire power. The challenges of dealing with Hezbollah were like those of previously dealing with the Palestinians in Lebanon: early warning concerning possible acts of terrorism and activities against the IDF, locating and identifying targets (strategic and tactical) and studying and assessing Hezbollah's military capabilities, in which the northern command and combat intelligence played an important role.

However, unlike the Palestinians, the intelligence challenge posed by Hezbollah was not only local but included Iran, making it much larger and more complex. Hezbollah is an organization motivated by Iranian ideology, by deep religious fervor; it is obedient, departmentalized, closed and keeps a low profile. It has advanced technological capabilities and a great deal of fire power. It is a multifaceted, guerilla-terrorist organization, semi-military and at the same time political, and its military power derives from Syria and Iran.

The IDF withdrawal from south Lebanon in May 2000 posed a challenge for intelligence forecasting: What would happen along the northern border after the withdrawal? Would Hezbollah continue its jihadist policies and carry out terrorist attacks (directly, or indirectly through the Palestinians)? Would it continue its military buildup, or turn its attention to insinuating itself into Lebanese political life? What would happen in south Lebanon and along the international border? Who would rule south Lebanon, Hezbollah or the Lebanese army?

Events showed that the intelligence forecasts were too gloomy, but were correct in their assessment that Hezbollah would not relinquish its jihadist aspect, with everything it implied (military buildup, tightening the ties with Iran, turning south Lebanon into a giant underground bunker, etc.).

May 2000 to July 2006: From Withdrawal
to War with Hezbollah

During the six years of 2000-2006 the State of Israel, the IDF and the intelligence community shifted the focus of their interest to the Palestinian arena when the intifada (or terrorist campaign) broke out. It received top priority and was where intelligence invested most of its efforts and resources.

Lebanon presented the following challenges:

- Hezbollah's military buildup, targeting its military capabilities, understanding its defensive strategy and becoming familiar with its deployment.
- Hezbollah's policy of opening fire and attacking Israel and the potential for a deterioration of the situation.
- Early warning of various attacks, most importantly the abduction of IDF soldiers.
- The relations between Hezbollah, Iran and Syria.
- Internal developments in Lebanon after UN Security Council Resolution 1559, passed in September 2004, one of whose provisions was the disarming of Hezbollah and the withdrawal of Syrian forces from Lebanon.
- The administrative challenge: how to create the proper balance in allocating resources (collection and manpower) between the complex Lebanese arena, with its potential for imminent conflict, and the Palestinian arena, whose potential for conflict was realized shortly after the IDF withdrew from Lebanon and Hezbollah began pouring in support.

As to how those challenges were met, the Winograd Commission[2] said that in general, during the years before the war, IDI supplied a genuine

---

2. Eliyahu Winograd, a former Israeli Supreme Court judge, was appointed by the government to head a commission to investigate the Second Lebanon War.

picture of Hezbollah for military and political needs, but was lacking in field intelligence.

Summer 2006: The Second Lebanese War

The nature of the Second Lebanon War posed a series of new challenges for Israeli intelligence. Instead of a conventional war, it was asymmetric, fought against an organization and not a country, and against guerilla forces with the fire power of a large country. The main strategic-operative challenges were:

- To acquire intelligence about an enemy that had assimilated into the villages and "disappeared," lived in underground tunnels and fought from within the civilian population, and operated as a network without a hierarchical structure.
- To locate, identify and report in real time about thousands of short- and long-range rocket and missile launchers, most of them situated in urban areas.
- To provide a strategic-operative evaluation of Hezbollah's concept of waging war and of its determination and perseverance.
- To assess Syria's intentions, especially whether its army would intervene in the war to support Hezbollah.

For the intelligence lessons learned in the war, and the successes and failures, see below the article by Brigadier General Daniel Asher, "From Lebanon to the Gaza Strip." To sum up the Winograd Commission's findings concerning strategy in as few words as possible, it can be said that the intelligence community presented a good military and political picture (including its considered estimation that Syria would neither initiate nor be drawn into the war), but at the tactical level, combat intelligence was faulty.

There are two strategic-operative points to be made, one a great success and the other a resounding failure:

- The success occurred on the first night of the war, July 11, 2006, when the Israeli air force destroyed about half of Hezbollah's long-range rockets (Iranian Fajr rockets) positioned in south Lebanon, hidden and protected in civilian residences. It was the result of years of determined, individual, gray, exhausting intelligence work, and one of Israel's greatest successes in target intelligence.
- The failure occurred on the night of July 14, 2006, when Hezbollah launched two C-802 shore-to-ship missiles from the Beirut beach at Israeli missile boats patrolling in Lebanese waters. One ship was hit and badly damaged, but miraculously did not sink. Four crew members were killed. The missile launch came as a complete surprise, but a greater surprise was the fact that Hezbollah possessed them.

A few words about C-802 missiles: They were originally manufactured by China and developed by Iran, apparently reaching Hezbollah in 2003. Israeli navy intelligence did not have hard evidence about them. Based on snippets of information, naval intelligence conducted an examination and concluded (falsely, in retrospect) that Hezbollah did not possess them. As a result the Israeli navy was not deployed to deal with C-802s, and was painfully surprised when the ships were attacked. The interesting question is why naval intelligence was so wrong, but the answer is not within the scope of this article.

Major Implications

In conclusion, I would like to examine three central consequences for intelligence – alongside many others – resulting from the special nature of the Lebanese arena. The first is the enormous and sometimes too great burden placed on military intelligence as the "national estimator." An examination of its roles shows it has to deal with almost more than it can handle, making it difficult for it to function as the strategic national estimator. IDI was responsible for providing tactical intelligence and targets for aerial and other attacks as well as for military assessment and political evaluations. At the same time it took part in the peace negotiations with the Lebanese, participated in various contacts with them and others, and naturally was involved in all operational planning and activities – in a nutshell, an overwhelming burden.

The second consequence is the problems of relations with the decision makers. There are many such problems, but in the case of Lebanon, which is particularly complex and complicated (and apparently in other cases as well), there was the problem of getting the decision makers to assimilate the intelligence picture and its implications. That happened in the Lebanese civil war, where it was hard for them to grasp the frequent changing alliances of the Lebanese factions and to understand Lebanon's intricate political scene. It happened again before the Second Lebanon War broke out, especially when they did not grasp the strategic significance of Hezbollah's firepower. Judging from my experience, one of the major factors behind the problem may be the frequent changes in decision-making personnel.

The third consequence is the difficulty in collecting and analyzing intelligence. The classic division of collecting and analyzing for a regular country (in the military, political and economic spheres, and focusing on the center where decisions are made) does not work for Lebanon, because its various, complex systems are multidimensional. Therefore, military analysis of the Lebanese army is not enough; the Syrian army has to be taken into account as well and various semi-military bodies have to be researched and intelligence about them has to be collected. Studying Hezbollah means dealing with terrorism, regular military affairs, religious-social issues and politics. Moreover, both collecting and analyzing intelligence necessitate understanding and knowledge of external influences on Hezbollah, the interaction between these influences themselves, and their interaction with the other Lebanese forces.

The implications are relevant for both the present and the foresee-able future, since both the State of Israel and its intelligence community will have to continue dealing with the Lebanese morass.

From Lebanon to the Gaza Strip: IDF Combat Intelligence in Operation Cast Lead (December 2008–January 2009)[1]

Brigadier General (Res.) Dr. Daniel Asher

Former Senior Officer of IDI and Historian of the Israeli Combat Intelligence

Introduction

The IDF was severely criticized after the Second Lebanon War for the way it engaged Hezbollah in south Lebanon. The shortcomings in force preparation and application were analyzed, and field intelligence before and after the fighting was studied. Lessons were learned, two years passed, and no effort was spared to train the troops, especially the ground forces, for combat on various fronts, with an eye to Hamas in the Gaza Strip. A comparison of the two events – the Second Lebanon War (summer 2006) and Operation Cast Lead in the Gaza Strip (December 2008–January 2009) – is admittedly difficult. Nevertheless, this article examines the progress made in combat intelligence in the two and a half years between the campaigns, and the way IDF preparations came to fruition in Gaza during the three weeks of fighting in the winter of 2008–2009.

---

1. Parts of this article were published in the journal *Israel Intelligence and Commemoration Center*, no. 53, April 2009.

Lessons Learned from Lebanon

The IDF learned its lessons from the fighting in the Second Lebanon War and introduced the necessary changes between 2006 and 2008. Concern over a renewed flare-up, most likely against Hamas in Gaza, led the IDF and its intelligence branch, especially combat intelligence, to make changes in force building, battle organization and operational planning. The IDF adapted itself to the combat conditions of the twenty-first century, with an emphasis on counter-guerilla warfare in a flat urban environment such as the Gaza Strip. In addition to doctrinal changes, the new force was based on regular infantry and armored brigades operating as combat teams. IDF planners realized that infantry and armor would be needed regardless of the fighting scenario, with combat engineers, artillery and intelligence-gathering units working with them as a unified offensive support body.

The need for cooperation went beyond the traditional fighting frameworks and extended to the air force, navy and military intelligence. Close cooperation with the ISA (Israel's equivalent of the FBI) was established. The ISA honed its ability to produce positive intelligence (in addition to its main task, preventative intelligence) and learned to translate raw data into clearly defined objectives and target banks for the operational forces. During Operation Cast Lead, the ISA gave the combat units its full support and accompanied them into the battle zone. ISA operators sat in the same war rooms as unit commanders and conveyed intelligence and warnings in real time to the forces on the ground.

The areas of field intelligence's responsibility, besides collecting, processing and circulating information, were and remain primarily the ground situation and the enemy. After the data are analyzed, intelligence officers can indicate expected threats to the fighting forces. That means identifying the enemy's location and deployment, his probable methods of operation, the firepower of the forward combat ranks and spotting and confirming enemy targets vulnerable to aircraft and artillery.

The foray into Lebanon taught the army the importance of preparation and training in two main areas: field and combat information collection. A comprehensive analysis of enemy territory and the transfer of the processed information to the operational forces are the *sine qua non* of a successful mission. It is obvious that combat intelligence gathering cannot rely solely on special force units or on those operating from the border, but must be based on the organic ability of the forward fighting ranks. Those lessons were not entirely put into practice in Lebanon, thus organizational and technological changes were made in Israel's southern command, the Gaza division, and the intelligence units tasked with assisting the fighting. The innovations enabled a more effective use of the intelligence sources by cutting through much of the traditional red tape.

Expanding the Roles of Field Intelligence

The main task of field intelligence – at all levels, from regional command to the last of the grunts – is to provide the forces with the information necessary for maneuvering, assistance and support. Intelligence officers at the field level operate from divisional, brigade and battalion headquarters. Prior to battle they are permanent fixtures at command headquarters because they are involved in every facet of battle procedure, and during the battle they deal with every phase of its direction. They process the information for immediate assessment, and assist the commander and his staff in drawing up and implementing an operational plan. Besides being senior partners in staff work, combat intelligence officers are also required to ensure that information reaches the troops before the battle and is integrated into their preparations and operational capability.

Another important lesson learned in the war in Lebanon was the need to supply the command and divisional levels with targets, a task that also extended downward. Brigade and battalion intelligence officers, as well as their information-gathering units, had to find and confirm targets in both open and built-up areas. The targets were attacked from the air and with regional command and divisional fire (in Gaza the latter two were identical) and with firepower from the advanced combat units.

The Nature of the Fighting in Gaza

The IDF has had a history in the Gaza Strip ever since the UN carved it into being in November 1947. Israeli forces fought in Gaza before and during the Egyptian army invasion, and especially at the end of the War of Independence in 1948 and early 1949. The IDF first captured the strip in the 1956 Sinai Campaign but was forced to withdraw. It recaptured it in the Six-Day War in 1967. From then until the disengagement in 2005, the IDF occupied the Gaza Strip and became intimately familiar with its human and geographical terrain. Hamas's takeover of the strip after the disengagement and the intensification of its military activity against Israel, particularly in the form of rocket and mortar shell fire, compelled Israel to respond and reenter the Gaza combat zone.

The strip's narrow area, flat terrain, refugee camps, built-up areas, roads and open spaces were all clearly mapped, studied and used as precision tools for planning, control and cooperation. The underground environment in Gaza – bunkers and tunnel networks – and the use of IEDs (improvised explosive devices) were new challenges for Israeli intelligence, which is continually upgrading its sensory and spotting capabilities and its skill in processing incoming data to neutralize threats.

Most information in the Gaza Strip was collected prior to Operation Cast Lead from the security fence in the east and north, the Mediterranean in the west and the sky overhead, and the situation did not change during the fighting. The deep incursion into Gaza shortened the target range and enabled weapons to be employed along the contact lines.

Hamas, an amorphous enemy that took control of the Gaza Strip and built itself into companies, battalions and brigades, was not, as one intelligence officer in the southern command put it, a "fearsome dragon," but one of Israel's weakest enemies. Its army was established only in the last two years. Its geographic proximity to Israel and Israel's intimate knowledge of the population, which is Hamas's human reservoir, along with Israel's ability to access information, enabled IDF intelligence to construct a highly accurate picture of the Islamic organization's strength, organization, combat doctrine and probable modus operandi.

On December 27, 2008, in response to a massive barrage of rocket fire initiated by Hamas and other groups with the objective of changing the region's security situation, the IDF launched Operation Cast Lead. From its inception until January 3, 2009, three hundred targets were attacked by Israeli aircraft, including training camps, command posts, military facilities, storerooms and weapons-manufacturing sites. Tunnels used to smuggle weapons under the Egyptian border were also hit, as were the homes of senior Hamas members and civilian homes that had been converted into munitions workshops, storage dumps and launch bases. Surprised by the intensity and dimensions of the Israeli response, Hamas suffered a major setback but managed to recover after the initial shock. It fired more than 350 rockets and 140 mortar shells into Israel, including rockets with ranges of forty kilometers (twenty-five miles) that landed in the southern Israeli cities of Beersheba, Kiryat Gat, Yavne, and Ashdod. To halt the rocket fire, the IDF launched a ground attack that ended on January 18. The cease-fire went into effect on January 21, and Israel withdrew all of its military forces.

Hamas had a defense plan against the Israeli ground offensive but failed to implement it. The plan was based on adapting the modus operandi in each sector to the special nature of the area. IDF firepower caught the enemy unawares, forcing him to redesign his fighting patterns of tactical warfare (which aimed to take IDF hostages and to cause as many casualties as possible). The only plan that Hamas managed to carry out was to attack Israeli ground forces and densely populated areas inside Israel with rocket and mortar shell fire; during the course of the war the number of launchings steadily declined.

Organizing Combat Intelligence

The southern command and the Gaza division were the main formations involved in preparing and transferring intelligence updates to the fighting forces before and during the operation. Intelligence branches in the southern command and Gaza division brigades also participated. Most of the work was carried out on the ground. Various elements studied Hamas's defense plans, located objectives and targets, and made plans for joint operations, which were constantly revised even during the campaign to respond to the changing situation on the ground. The evaluation of photographs and diverse overhead observation devices enabled a precise analysis of events on the battlefield.

Studying Hamas led to the writing of intelligence officer "notebooks" of relatively low security classification, making it possible for the material to be circulated quickly and integrated into all fighting levels. The fresh information was fed into operational plans and had a significant impact on the training program prior to the campaign.

The intensive preparations, especially at the divisional level; the drafting and strengthening of plans for daily security and emergency situations; and the cooperation between the air force, navy, ISA and intelligence made it possible to compose a picture of the enemy's situation. It also provided a picture of his rocket launchings, the ability to destroy them, target acquisition, tracking of objectives until the attack, etc.

The preparations included training exercises and battle procedure. Mechanized systems were added, making it possible to create various assets, such as information circulated to the lower levels, computerized target banks and even digitalized operational diaries. The interface between the command and control systems at the fighting level allowed for a continuous flow of intelligence to the forces, the simultaneous reception of updated reports from the lines of contact and the data's integration into the overall intelligence picture.

The presence of intelligence officers and their aides side by side with the commanders and inside the war rooms and mobile field headquarters made a continuous update of intelligence possible for the operation. Intelligence officers worked inside the combat zone, especially at the command and division levels. ISA operators and wiretappers worked in conjunction with the regular forces to shorten the distance between the sources and target processing, and to deal immediately with problems that arose unexpectedly in the course of the operation.

The integration of experienced reservists into intelligence platoons, especially in the divisions and brigades, and having reconnaissance officers function as information-collecting officers, greatly improved the quality of the work. Working relations were overhauled and an open dialogue was instituted at the three levels – divisional, brigade and battalion – which in the past had been particularly short-circuited, and which now contributed to the sharp resolution of the intelligence picture. However, as in the past, communications frequencies did not operate as expected, mainly because of security measures. Furthermore, some of the information that passed through computerized systems failed to reach all of the units. An alternative, time-tested system quickly solved the problem: a messenger service, that is, liaison officers who scurried between units.

Combat Intelligence Gathering

During the Second Lebanon War reconnaissance units at the divisional, brigade and battalion levels made a poor showing in intelligence gathering. Consequently, one lesson learned was to prepare them, along with general staff intelligence gathering, for the assignments they would probably be tasked with if fighting broke out in the Gaza Strip. The preparations during the two years between the campaigns encompassed all intelligence units and included reorganization and training:

- The southern command's combat intelligence collection battalion focused on the Gaza division's missions. There were new devices, such as observation balloons and mobile and stationary ground-based, electronic-optic systems that operated from positions near the fence. In addition, a battalion was also set up for mobile missions deep inside enemy territory. Regular and heavy-vehicle lookouts were trained to work with brigade combat teams. The mobile lookout forces had considerable success in identifying terrorists and directing helicopters, gunboats, tanks, snipers and Gil-type Spike missile launchers to their targets. The lookouts also directed combat engineers to enemy tunnels, and terrorist ambushes and explosive charges were neutralized. Stationary ground-based lookouts specialized in coordinating operations with forces that crossed the line into the Gaza Strip, such as special force teams carrying out deep penetrations. The lookout deployments on the border had the added advantage of "see and fire." During the war one of the female lookouts used her equipment to destroy a suspicious enemy force.

- Besides reconnaissance companies, infantry brigades also received companies specially trained in observation. Those fully equipped troops trained for the Gaza scenario and became an organic part of combat procedure and operational plans, supplying the units with up-to-date reports of the operation. Most battalions did not send their reconnaissance platoons on intelligence-collecting missions. In fact, most of the recon troops were not even called up, while others were given regular combat duties. Some of the reconnaissance platoons, including those that had been integrated into the ORBAT (order of battle), reinforced the lookouts and strengthened the processing of data collected by the fighting units, so that a quick and comprehensive intelligence picture was possible. However, as noted, combat activity took precedence over field intelligence activity, and intelligence binoculars were not employed to the maximum. It became increasingly clear that the data collected on the contact lines contributed to the compilation of a very high-quality intelligence picture.

- UAVs (unmanned aerial vehicles) were used with the forward forces for the first time. Their deployment on the front, along with the advantage of overhead visual devices, improved beyond belief the quality of intelligence that was received in real time. Their integration into the traditional intelligence deployments at the higher levels created continuity and angles of vision that primarily benefited the forces at the front. The deciphering performed by the general staff's visual unit supplied the fighters and field headquarters with invaluable input. All of the innovations contributed to the reception and transmission of accurate updates of ground events.

The Gaza operation was the general staff collection's finest hour. The agents were deployed in the field, adapted themselves to the needs of the theater of operations, channeled information at various resolutions and contributed to the overall intelligence picture, especially of the targets being attacked. Monitoring and spotting were of special significance, since the forces' needs had to be dealt with simultaneously at both the strategic and tactical levels. Monitoring and spotting concentrated mainly on targets: their acquisition, confirmation and elimination. The valuable experience accumulated before the operation, the no-effort-spared technological preparations and training, and the joint exercises by the fighting forces all came together in Operation Cast Lead. Prisoner interrogation was mobilized and worked alongside the units on the ground. The interrogators advanced with the ground forces to gain information in real time. Some interrogators remained in the rear to complete the questioning of prisoners (only two hundred of whom reached the detention camps). Captured documents and technical equipment collected by the penetrating forces were handed over to headquarters, where they were processed to gain understanding of enemy plans, and the ISA worked wonders with the material. The force's joint operations training proved itself by its rapid, smooth performance, which led to the elimination of scores of enemy targets in an exceedingly short time.

Terrain Research

After years of setbacks in all areas of terrain intelligence, the time had come to restore it to its former place at the center of intelligence activity. The relatively limited field of the Gaza Strip, which was mostly sandy with expanding urban centers (and diminishing agricultural areas) facilitated research and preparations. The southern command intelligence units obtained the necessary backing from the collection and research divisions of the general staff and Gaza division. They received geological and geomorphological analyses, studies of defenses and terrain navigability, and updated reports on the new dimension of underground networks.

Modern photographic and sensing equipment was integrated into intelligence gathering and (with the help of modern systems for information processing, preserving and circulating) enabled vital material to reach the forces. The field units were provided with an abundance of updated aids suited to the nature of their activity, and infantry and armor received detailed (sometimes overly detailed) intelligence reports. Other forces directly involved in the fighting, such as the air force and navy, received an even greater amount of intelligence material. The terrain layers in the information systems were continuously updated during the operation, and all of the incoming data were processed and then circulated to the units. In that way the processed intelligence found its way to the lone vehicle in the field and the lowest-level tactical unit.

There were practically no cases in which the forces on the contact lines were caught by surprise by new and unexpected findings. Any such information was immediately relayed to the field elements in the division and southern command where it was reprocessed.

Conclusion

This article was based on preliminary findings, and it admittedly lacks the perspective of time. We all realize that Operation Cast Lead, the campaign in Gaza, was unique. The intensive preparations at the command, divisional and crew level, at branch headquarters and in the general staff units, were far different, apparently for the better, from those that could be expected in an all-out war on a broad front against fully equipped armies. Be that as it may, the relative failure of many IDF deployments, including field intelligence, in the Second Lebanon War led to positive changes. The enormous effort made to discover weak spots and shortcomings led to far-reaching improvements, which were adapted specifically to the Gaza theater of operations. The troops underwent training in real scenarios and proved that proper preparation would yield the desired results.

The in-depth involvement of the different headquarters – the intelligence branch and land forces' field intelligence headquarters – and the willingness to cooperate with the intelligence headquarters of the air force, navy and ISA, had no parallel in the IDF and yielded excellent results on the ground. Many different deployments prepared for the task and, excluding a relatively few areas that still require improvement, the entire intelligence division functioned as a well-oiled machine with almost no slipups.

Combat intelligence can be said to have proved itself in trial by fire. Similar preparations, perhaps different in scope, are needed for other fighting arenas. The effort must be undertaken with an awareness of particular needs. The search for the best solutions must continue. As the head of IDF field intelligence Brigadier General Ariel Karo says, "Work hard and you'll reach your goal."

Intelligence Challenges in

the Palestinian Arena

Colonel (Res.) Dr. Ephraim Lavie
Former Head of the Palestinian Arena of Production and Analysis Division of IDI

Introduction

In July 2004 the United States Senate Select Committee on Intelligence issued a report on the war in Iraq. The committee's assessment was that the justification for the war, which was to stop Saddam Hussein before he could use his weapons of mass destruction or before they found their way to Al-Qaeda and could be used against the United States, was incorrect. According to the report, the American intelligence evaluations that helped the president construct his case for the war were faulty. They determined that Saddam Hussein's regime was developing WMDs and had stockpiles of chemical and biological weapons. Thus, based on incorrect intelligence and faulty evaluations, the president and Congress sent the United States Army to war.

In March 2004 the report of the [Steinitz] Committee for the Examination of the Intelligence Services Following the War in Iraq was issued in Jerusalem. It had been established by a subcommittee of the Knesset's Security and Foreign Affairs Committee to oversee the secret services, and it determined that Israeli intelligence was a weak reed for the country's decision makers to lean on. According to the report, the intelligence services did not give unequivocal indications regarding Iraq's non-conventional weapons capabilities or about the surface-to-surface missiles and launchers positioned there, and the heads of Israeli intelligence exhibited too much self-confidence regarding the intelligence evaluations they presented. Those evaluations led the Israeli government to vainly take a series of extremely expensive active and passive defensive steps in preparation for an attack of non-conventional weapons.

The case of the war in Iraq reflects the complex intelligence challenge facing the intelligence community in presenting a reliable intelligence evaluation to the decision makers about the enemy's military capabilities and the intentions of its leaders. The decision makers must have those evaluations to determine security and foreign policy and to make decisions that are vital for the state, such as going to war and preparing the home front for an attack, which costs a great deal of money and potentially costs lives. The challenge is no less difficult and complex when intelligence is required to present reliable evaluations about an enemy in the midst of what it perceives as the struggle for national liberation and undergoing revolutionary changes in order to become a country, especially when there are strong opposition forces at work that want to continue the armed struggle and sabotage a peace agreement. That was the situation Israeli intelligence found itself in when, after the mutual recognition between Israel and the PLO after decades of armed conflict, the two sides signed a declaration of principles in September 1993.

With the signing and on the eve of the establishment of Palestinian self-rule in the summer of 1994, Israel Defense Intelligence began making preparations for covering the Palestinian arena. The Palestinian Authority was founded on PLO institutions and units of the Palestinian Liberation Army (PLA) with an infrastructure of civilian institutions established and operated under Israeli rule. The Palestinian Authority set up political institutions (a government, a legislative council and a judiciary system), a security system (police, army and intelligence units) and an economic system. It controlled most of the population in the

West Bank and in the Gaza Strip, and conducted relations with foreign countries and international organizations.

The Israeli intelligence community organized itself for intelligence collection and analysis to present the decision makers with a full, integrated assessment, enabling them to formulate foreign and security policy regarding the Palestinians. Military intelligence's working assumption was that political, military, security-related, civilian and economic events in the Palestinian Authority had to be monitored. The Palestinian organizations opposing the peace process and wanting to preserve the embers of an armed campaign would also have to be monitored, especially Hamas, which constructed its own institutions and represented them as an alternative to the Palestinian Authority. The political negotiations for the final status arrangement, which were supposed to begin in the summer of 1997, necessitated assessments of the positions and intentions of the Palestinian leadership.

Military intelligence was responsible for providing information ranging from the Palestinian political situation to its military situation. That included civilian and semi-military factors, such as the regime's stability (What would happen if Arafat were to disappear from the scene?) and its economic and social conditions. IDI and its analysis units were at the heart of a sensitive peace process (one that caused dissension within Israeli society) with an entity in the process of changing from a national liberation movement to a country.

Within a few years military intelligence developed collection and analysis capabilities for the Palestinian arena. However, in the absence of a comprehensive intelligence authority, for the most part the response to the challenge was only partial. A proper response was given to ongoing political challenges, such as following the positions of the Palestinian leadership concerning the implementation of the interim agreements and negotiations for the final status arrangement. On the other hand, the monitoring of long-term processes was limited, and it led to surprises and the development of fixed concepts.[1]

This article will deal with the question of comprehensive intelligence responsibility and its implications for the Palestinian arena. It will analyze three challenges: intelligence support for the peace process; the interaction between senior intelligence officers and the decision makers; and socio-cultural production and analysis.

Comprehensive Intelligence Responsibility

During the first five years of the Palestinian Authority (1994–1998), the work was divided between IDI and the ISA, and defined by an agreement (called the Magna Carta), which was authorized at the political level. Deliberations regarding the agreement were based on the proposition that the Palestinian Authority was not to be designated as a target country. IDI's conspicuous weaknesses at that time were in collecting and analyzing information about Fatah-Tanzim, the Palestinian intelligence services and Palestinian society. Regardless of their importance, because they had the potential to influence the political and security situations, for the most part Fatah-Tanzim and the intelligence services were left to the ISA. Research into Palestinian society and monitoring changes in public opinion as they developed were carried out by IDI's production and analysis division, based primarily on reports prepared by the Israeli Civil Administration of the West Bank and Gaza Strip.

IDI and the ISA had joint responsibility for early warning. In 1998 there was a growing fear that if the peace process negotiations stalled, the Palestinians would unilaterally proclaim a Palestinian state, engendering a strategic crisis that would develop into a security threat for

---

1. The tendency that characterizes military intelligence research, to deal with developments in their immediate context and avoid strategic analyses for predicting long- and middle-term processes, limits the ability to indicate potential security and political dangers that develop slowly.

Israel. That posed a serious challenge for IDI, and its director wanted to amend the Magna Carta to make it more realistic. In preparation for a declaration, the Palestinian Authority reinforced its civil and military systems, making it necessary for IDI to accept comprehensive responsibility for intelligence assessment.

To realize that responsibility and to develop the appropriate collection and analysis capabilities to cover the gaps that had opened, IDI needed time and resources, to say nothing of settling its differences with the ISA, which opposed designating the Palestinian Authority as a target country.

The ISA's position was that while in general IDI was responsible for the Palestinian issue because it covered the Palestinian security forces, in other areas there was "parallel intelligence responsibility," and those areas included politics as it related to evaluating Arafat's policies and maneuvers. The ISA claimed that the decision makers had responsibility for that particular issue, and that they had the authority to choose the assessment of either one of the organizations.

The ISA leadership demanded the exclusive collection and analysis of material dealing with the prevention of Palestinian terrorism as well as intelligence responsibility for Fatah-Tanzim. It demanded the right, alongside IDI, to provide early warning of the development of armed confrontations or popular civil disturbances.

IDI was troubled by the Palestinian situation. The situation in the field of collection and research of the Palestinian arena was IDI's undoing. Although it wanted overall intelligence responsibility, its ability to follow the internal processes in Palestinian society under self-rule and to give early warning of the development of public disturbances and mass demonstrations was limited. IDI headquarters could also not ensure itself that the ISA would act with full transparency and cooperate in a way that would enable it to warn of developing confrontations. In addition, it was impossible, for professional reasons, to shift the responsibility for analyzing Palestinian society to the Israeli Civil Administration of the

West Bank and Gaza Strip. Thus, I am of the opinion that in real-time situations between Israel and the Palestinians, IDI did not provide the decision makers with early warnings and suitable assessments.

Intelligence Accompanying the Peace Process

As the body responsible for national assessment, IDI had the sensitive, complex mission of monitoring and analyzing the entire political process with the Arabs. Highly professional collection and analysis capabilities were necessary for dealing with the sensitive national issues and intensive friction with the senior political level. The intelligence provided to accompany political negotiations usually includes the following:

- A designated, integrative collection intelligence community system (IDI, the ISA and the Mossad) deployed within the country and directed by the collection division.
- A senior intelligence officer from the production and analysis division who accompanies the Israel negotiator and an intelligence officer who supports the intercommunity team.
- Ongoing analysis support for the accompanying intelligence officer as well as all the intelligence community's analysts.

By their nature and because of their dynamics, negotiations necessitate ongoing intelligence assessment of the issues under discussion and the changes in the adversary's position and tactics. That type of intelligence work, in which the accompanying intelligence officer is on the scene and enjoys intelligence backup, has many advantages. It makes it possible to direct and focus the work of the collection and analysis systems and to create a full, integrated intelligence analysis of events as they happen and of intelligence material. In that way the officer can faithfully brief the relevant agents (the head of the Israeli delegation to the negotiations, the IDI heads and other relevant intelligence personnel) at any given moment. At the same time, the role is sensitive and demands that the officer be extremely scrupulous in following field security rules in using material and distance himself from personal involvement in the process itself.

From September 1999 to January 2001, the head of the IDI's production and analysis division provided intelligence accompaniment for the political negotiations with the Palestinians. While intelligence was intensively used, there were situations in which the Israeli negotiators lacked understanding of the other side's positions and maneuvers. For example, when the Palestinians agreed to hold brainstorming sessions, what they really wanted was to test Israel's flexibility in the final status arrangement issues. To that end, during the sessions they hinted at their own possible flexibility, for instance their willingness – in principle – to discuss the settlement blocks in the Gaza Strip and West Bank. Israel interpreted the hints as practical flexibility and a breakthrough, while in fact, they did not reflect a departure from the basic principle of the full recognition of Palestinian rights to all the territory conquered in the 1967 Six-Day War (i.e., 100 percent) as a precondition.

In cases such as this, which generally arose because issues were considered from the Israeli point of view, the intelligence officer had to explain the error to the negotiators and point out that the development had to be understood from the Palestinian point of view and according to the Palestinian concept of negotiating. According to that concept, no issue was agreed upon as long as Israel did not accept the basis for the negotiations, which as far as the Palestinians were concerned were the legitimate international decisions concerning the Arab-Israel conflict. On the other hand, the intelligence officer also had to identify instances in which the Palestinians showed genuine flexibility and indicate them to the negotiators.

Interaction between the Intelligence Officer and the Decision Makers

There are various dilemmas involved in intelligence work with the decision makers, dilemmas which are especially sensitive when dealing with important political assessments like the Palestinian issue.

Sometimes the assessment of the IDI head or its production and analysis division differs from that of one of the division's units. That will only happen when the facts of two assessments are identical in every respect, neither can be refuted and both are possible. Extreme care must be used to prevent bias, misreading of the adversary's positions resulting from Israel's political views and distance from involvement in political and ideological discourse. In addition, professional research criteria must be strictly adhered to. A biased or mistaken assessment is liable to prove true, since the course of action taken by the decision makers based on the assessment may actualize it (the self-fulfilling prophecy).

When there are two possible assessments, a senior intelligence officer has various options depending on the circumstances. For example, in one case he may recognize his inability to make a decision and present both assessments to the decision makers as equal, and the decision makers, on whose shoulders all responsibility rests, will decide according to their own lights. In another case, he may suggest whichever assessment seems more reasonable, noting that the opinions of the analysts differ, and present his own opinion.

Regarding the absence of a political arrangement with the Palestinians and the outbreak of the violent confrontations in September 2000 (which began the so-called second intifada), military intelligence had two different assessments. One was expressed in documents issued by the production and analysis division, to the effect that the intifada was an expression of the cumulative frustrations of Palestinian society with the Palestinian Authority's internal policies and the peace process. According to that assessment, Arafat used the underground swell to stop internal criticism and force more flexibility from Israel during the negotiations, and he expected the confrontation to cause the internationalization of the conflict as an alternative to the stalled peace process. The other assessment, expressed orally by the heads of the production and analysis division, was that Arafat had rejected Israel's offers and initiated a military confrontation, which he had planned as part of a strategic plot to overcome Israel through the so-called "right of return" and the Palestinians' demographic advantage. The latter assessment was considered credible by the decision makers and the ranking military. It became the main consensus in defining the confrontation with the Palestinians[2] and has provided intelligence support for the government's policies and the IDF in recent years in dealing with the Palestinians. It is my best professional opinion that the first assessment was better grounded, and it is possible that the assessment that was adopted deprived the decision makers, at least formally, of a variety of options for determining policy.

Another challenge posed for military intelligence by both the decision makers and the situation in the Palestinian arena had to do with the question of whether it was correct to involve the production and analysis division (as an appointed professional factor) in the public diplomacy effort of the government (as an elected body) in the fight against Palestinian terrorism, or to leave it as an objective professional body whose only role was to analyze and evaluate the adversary. For the IDI heads and the production and analysis division, participation

---

2. That concept was nurtured, in my opinion, and became a dogma until new information was powerless to change it. For example, despite the independence of the terrorist elements that operated with the support of external factors (Hezbollah and Iran), according to the assessment Arafat controlled the forces operating on the ground (increasing or decreasing the level of violence as he pleased, and with the ability to stop it entirely), a corollary of which being that if Arafat disappeared the problem would be solved. That contributed to personalizing and oversimplifying the conflict, as though the entire problem focused on a leader.

in the public diplomacy effort was clearly in the national interest and an integral part of the fight on terrorism. Sources within the division coined the expression "intelligence for incrimination" and issued open, anti-Arafat anti–Palestinian Authority documents, presenting the confrontation not in terms of a national conflict but rather as "official Palestinian terrorism" whose objectives were ideological and absolute (implementing the "theory of stages" and the establishment of "greater Palestine"). The policy benefitted Israel's public diplomacy, and military intelligence continued it. However, it held inherent dangers for professional analysis failures despite the fact that it was kept in proportion and employed carefully.[3] The IDI revision, or "devil's advocate" department, warned of violating the principle of keeping intelligence and public diplomacy separate.

Societal and Cultural Intelligence Challenges

Palestinian society has been an important factor in the political and security developments in the Israeli-Palestinian conflict over the past two decades (the first intifada, support for the Oslo process, the second intifada, Hamas's rise to power), and it is a target of the utmost importance for intelligence coverage and monitoring. However, studying long-term societal and cultural processes necessitates organizational and professional formats of intelligence work different from those used in dealing with short-term, current issues.[4]

---

3. The dangers from adopting the approach are serious and present conditions for professional analysis failures, such as biasing intelligence to justify a concept, stubborn adherence to a concept coordinated to policy and ignoring the need for frequent examination of information to verify its veracity.

4. Long-term study and monitoring of social issues necessitates wide coverage of the open sources of Palestinian information, such as websites, day-to-day information disseminated by the political powers that be, the local press, and official and private radio and television stations.

In the years after the establishment of the Palestinian Authority, IDI did not have collection capabilities for Palestinian society, and
analysis was based on reports from officers in the Israeli Civil Administration of the West Bank and Gaza Strip, who were not intelligence
professionals. Analyses of Palestinian society were not recognized and
did not receive an independent position alongside the ongoing research
of political and security issues, damaging the division's ability to follow
grassroots processes for early warnings of public disturbances and mass
demonstrations. For the most part, emphasis was put on the Palestinian
Authority leadership and its security services, monitoring the implementation of the interim agreements and preparing for negotiating the
final status agreement. Arafat was in the forefront of the production
and analysis division's reports as the only factor dictating developments
in the Palestinian arena. The contribution of the public and opposition
to the events seemed marginal and insignificant.

In my opinion, with which others may disagree, when the Al-
Aqsa intifada (the second intifada) began in September 2000 as a series
of spontaneous popular eruptions, the production and analysis division
did not recognize it for what it was because of the lack of in-depth social
and cultural research tools. The division did not assess the consequences
of the hard line taken by the IDF and the pressure it had exerted on the
Palestinian population and security services, most of which did not participate in the confrontation. It had not warned of the Palestinians' rage
and desire for revenge, which culminated in an unprecedented wave
of suicide bombing terrorism (which included the secular sectors), its
justifications and increase.

The failure to understand the causes and motives of the Palestinian population led to the production and analysis division's disappoint-
ment with its quantifying analysis tools, especially the public opinion

polls it used for research purposes.[5] A later attempt to adopt qualitative research tools for social research was unsuccessful, because given the antagonistic nature of Palestinian society[6] they could not be employed. The constraints of social research require that the structure of Palestinian society be studied in depth along with the changes of the past decades to identify social, cultural and political trends. The historical context of the conflict should also be studied for purposes of analysis and explanations for events that occur within it, such as the about-face of the regime, and social behavior, such as support for the violent confrontation or for the peace process.

---

5.   Public opinion polls are an accepted tool for analyzing the views of the general public. However, in the absence of firm information, the production and analysis division developed unrealistic expectations concerning the capabilities of such tools to function properly under the conditions prevalent in the Palestinian Authority at the time. Polls can be relevant and provide an idea of what will happen only if they are held in a democratic environment, that is, without fear of reprisal.

6.   The desire to use qualifying rather than quantifying research tools indicated that the researchers did not understand the nature of either. Unlike ordinary intelligence work (focused, pointed, immediate and short-term), a principle of social research is that it requires both types of tools, which complement one another while based on the same information. As a rule, it is always desirable to use both to verify findings and conclusions.

Difficulties and Advantages of

Intelligence in the Palestinian Arena

Brigadier General (Res.) Shalom Harari
Former Advisor on Arab Affairs for the Coordinator
of the Gaza Strip, Judea and Samaria

Background

For thirty years, both as part of the security establishment and as an academic, I have been studying political, societal, religious, economic and cultural Palestinian processes, especially in the Gaza Strip, Judea and Samaria.

This short article will present fifteen factors that in my opinion are unique with regard to intelligence collection and analysis in the Israeli-Palestinian conflict. They usually present difficulties, but they sometimes make intelligence work easier, as opposed to arenas like Syria, Libya and Lebanon. I will also endeavor to explain why those factors are more pronounced and salient in the Palestinian arena.

Because of the limited amount of space I will deal only with those I find personally compelling. They will not be discussed in order of importance, and emphasis will be placed on their political-societal-economic dimensions without relation to hostile terrorist activity.

Influential Elements

The geographic division of the intelligence target: Unlike other arenas, where the populace is concentrated in a space clearly defined by borders, the Palestinian people are divided into several interconnected areas covered by various intelligence factors. They are as follows:

- East Jerusalem (which was the main arena of political activity until 2000) is covered by the ISA and the Israel Police Department.
- Gaza City and the Gaza Strip are covered by the ISA, southern command intelligence and the production and analysis division of IDI.
- Judea and Samaria are covered by the ISA, central command intelligence and the IDI's production and analysis division.
- The political subversion of Arab Israeli extremists who identify themselves as Palestinians is covered by the ISA (counterterrorism) and the Israeli police department.
- The prisoners' movement inside Israeli jails is covered by intelligence officers, the penal service and the ISA. Although the movement is relatively small (11,000 members), it has a great deal of political clout.
- Palestinians living abroad in Arab countries are covered by IDI and the Mossad; those in North and South America and Europe, primarily by the Mossad.

Moreover, there is an unhealthy division of responsibility for the overall national evaluation of the Palestinian scene. When the Oslo Accords were signed, responsibility for intelligence was divided between the ISA and IDI, one answerable to the prime minister's office and the other to the chief of staff and the defense minister (although, theoretically, there is a clear division of responsibilities in the Magna Carta). To worsen the confusion, there are advisory panels covering Palestinian society and economy. Their collection and analysis role deals mainly with the coordination activities in the Gaza Strip, Judea and Samaria, without formal, binding responsibility.

The Palestinians do not operate only beyond the borders of the State of Israel but within or very close to them: inside Israeli cities and smaller communities and in some government institutions, such as university campuses, the Arabic and Hebrew press, political parties, etc. Thus any intelligence activity in those fields is liable to become politically explosive within Israel.[1]

The Palestinians use many channels to maintain formal and informal bilateral relations with Israel's economy, culture and politics. Needless to say, since the disengagement from the Gaza Strip in 2005 there has been a drastic reduction in its relations with Israel. In terms of intelligence, on the one hand it makes collection easier, and on the other, it makes analysis more difficult.

The Palestinian-Israeli conflict is different from the conflict with Syria or Lebanon. From the Palestinian point of view it is a total conflict and embraces all areas, including the economy, culture, society, the media and the "strong police forces" of twelve "national security battalions" and the "preventive intelligence units," which are equipped with light machine guns and rifles. In terms of intelligence, many fields have to be covered that in the Arab countries are today partially covered at best, and the Palestinian coverage has to be broader and deeper.

To a great degree, and especially in the Gaza Strip, Judea and Samaria, the Palestinians view themselves as having enlisted in the "struggle," politically, economically and socially. Almost everything is considered a "national institution," whether a municipality, campus or hospital, the press, the electric company or the health services, and Israeli intelligence has to cover them all.

---

1.   There are a quarter of a million Arabs who live in East Jerusalem, have dual citizenship and can vote in the Jerusalem municipal elections. There are 1.5 million Arabs in the Gaza Strip and 2 million in Judea and Samaria, many of whom come to Israel every day to work or for other reasons, and many who are connected to Israeli Arab citizens by marriage.

We are witnesses to a process of many years' duration that is changing the conflict from national to Islamic-religious, and meeting the challenge of analyzing the Palestinians' Islamic ideology is vital because of their geographical proximity to the State of Israel.

The great involvement of the Palestinian "target" in internal Israeli politics is liable to bias analysis in favor of hidden (or overt) political preferences and lead to an unreliable and unbalanced intelligence review. In addition, the political echelons have a tendency to manipulate intelligence material relating to Palestinians, and Palestinian terrorism has already toppled Israeli governments more than twice. For example, a few days before the elections to the Israeli Parliament in 1988, Palestinian terrorists attacked a bus with Molotov cocktails, burning a mother and her three children to death. According to expert pollsters, the event had a very strong influence on floating votes and changed the slant of the elections.

A large part of the conflict is expressed by viewing the Palestinians as waging a war of metaphors and media against Israel, that is, creating a great many simulations which are either totally or partially fictitious. They include the image of the brutal "Nazi" Israeli, the beast, causing suffering and wreaking destruction for the poor, innocent Palestinian. The Israeli intelligence worker must have a clear, authentic picture without making light of the images and metaphors, which have their own power to motivate.

The political schisms among the various Palestinian factions (the PLO on one side and the Islamists on the other), vast and growing ever larger, and the schisms dividing the clans, which are also political and military (there are dozens of separate militias), all make it very difficult for the intelligence analyst to read the sociopolitical map correctly and to understand the complex interactions between the Palestinian factions and splinter groups.

On the surface the situation would seem to be similar in Lebanon or Iraq, but there is an essential difference: the divided political map of the Palestinians sits within Israel itself, or if not within, at least in its backyard, and every terrorist operative with an explosive belt can influence the course of political events in Israel.

There is a tendency to run after the "urgent" at the expense of the "important." For example, at least from 1967 until the Oslo Accords, the ISA led collection and analysis in the internal arena (Judea and Samaria, the Gaza Strip district, East Jerusalem and Arab-Israeli extremists). Its two main tasks were to cover and prevent hostile terrorist activities and, less well-known, to prevent subversion. The affair of the "lead poisoning" blood libel in Judea and Samaria in 1983, which caused mass rioting (much like the outbreak of the first intifada) led the defense minister, on the authority of the ISA director, to clarify the term "coverage of subversion." The ISA was also given responsibility for intelligence about riots and rock-throwing because they were an important byproduct of subversion. However, in effect the ISA had to turn most of its resources and attention to hostile terrorist activities, and only some of its efforts could be invested in collecting, analyzing and preventing subversion.

It was unclear who the adversary was, especially after the Oslo process began. Were the Palestinians the enemy, and if so, who among them were and who weren't, who more and who less? That also influenced the speed at which Israeli intelligence organized for collection and analysis (the well-known struggles between the ISA and IDI over the Magna Carta, which divided the spheres of influence in intelligence work). The fact that only in recent years have the ISA and IDI opened special divisions to deal with Palestinian society and economy (that is, twenty-five to thirty years after they initiated Palestinian intelligence work) is a good example of the pre-Oslo lack of their internalization of the social-economic-political struggle being waged against us.

In addition, everyone, but *everyone*, has a full understanding of the situation. Every Israeli citizen considers himself an expert on the Palestinian issue, because it is "in our backyard," or as the average Israeli always says, "You're telling me what goes on in the West Bank? I know, my gardener comes from there, my garage mechanic is from Abu Dis, and I sell to a Palestinian businessman in Wadi Joz…" And if that is what the Israeli civilian says, the Israeli politician says the following to the intelligence agent: "I know better than you because I talked to my aide yesterday…" To put it mildly, the intelligence analyst working with the Palestinian issue does not have an easy life.

There has been an increase in the Israeli-Palestinian "peace industry" (from Track 2,[2] which by now has become Track 2002), which also makes a great commotion and sometimes supplies the intelligence network with disinformation. In addition, foreign intelligence factors have intervened in Palestinian politics in support of one side or other (Fatah or Hamas) and in mediating between Israel and the Palestinians. Egyptian intelligence (General Omar Suleiman) has been active, as have Jordanian intelligence and Western agencies, especially the CIA, all adding to Israel's collection and analysis problems.

The recent armed conflict with the Palestinians has been a low-intensity conflict and has continued on a daily basis for several years, while with the Arab countries conflicts are generally relatively short. In intelligence terms, covering it requires many resources invested for years and more patience for collection and analysis than required for covering the conflict with the Arab countries.

Factors Making the Job Easier

Some of the factors noted above bring the difficulties into relief. But some of them also make the job easier, and those fall into two main categories.

- Collection: The fact that "they live with us and we live with them" makes it possible for a system to exist – including

---

2.   Track 2 refers to informal discussions held alongside formal "closed" meetings held by the government in Israel and abroad.

SIGINT, VISINT and HUMINT – which provides more windows for collecting intelligence than in any other arena.

- Analysis: Analysts can have direct access to the subject studied. The analysts themselves, in their offices in Tel Aviv or Jerusalem, have access to almost all the subjects in the area under consideration (although the window into the Gaza Strip was closed with the disengagement); that is, it is easy for them to meet with Palestinian public figures and politicians through open, formal connections.

Conclusion

The intelligence mission of dealing with the Palestinians is unique and seemingly strange. On the plus side, the depth of collection, its particular nature, capabilities and potential are unlike those in any other intelligence arena. On the minus side, in terms of analysis the situation is more problematic because of the nature of the Palestinian issue: there is no single intelligence body with overall responsibility, and the difficulties inherent in splitting the target, that is, the Palestinian people, make analysis complex.

Consequently, in my opinion special emphasis should be placed on reinforcing analysis, especially the following:

- Deepening and reinforcing the integration and dialogue between the analysts in the various intelligence branches, although some steps have already been taken in that direction.
- Integrating into the ISA and IDI staffs more analysts who served in the civilian administration or other organizations in the field and had direct experience with the Palestinians.
- Employing more analysts with a better command of Arabic, especially the ability to read texts, to better understand the vast amounts of open source material found in the Palestinian press, on television and on the Internet. That is the best tool for understanding Palestinian cultural and societal processes.

With all due respect to the IDF unit that translates Arabic materials and the remarkable work it does, there is no substitute for reading material in the original.

Dilemmas and Challenges for the Israel Intelligence Community in Fighting Terrorism

Dr. Boaz Ganor

Head of the Institute for Counterterrorist Warfare at the
Herzliya Center for Interdisciplinary Studies

Introduction

At a time when many analysts disagree about the effectiveness of various counterterrorism measures, one thing they do agree on is the supreme importance of intelligence activity in preventing attacks. Shabtai Shavit, director general of the Mossad from 1989 to 1996, said that good intelligence was more than half the solution, and the better the intelligence, the further it would be possible to reduce or limit the military means used to fight terrorism.[1] This article will discuss a few of the intelligence dilemmas and challenges, and will begin with the first pillar of intelligence: collection.

Collection

Collecting intelligence is not only vital but a prelude to almost every counterterrorism activity. No offensive or operative activity, whether ground operation, air strike or targeted killing, can be carried out

---

1. Personal interview with Shabtai Shavit, November 4, 1999.

without reliable, real-time intelligence. Defensive actions are almost Sisyphean tasks because of the unlimited number of potential terrorist targets and the limitations of budget and manpower involved to prevent terrorist attacks. Therefore, early intelligence warnings about planned attacks are vital for the effective use of resources and for positioning security forces at the time and place they are most needed. Intelligence is also a cornerstone of the criminal justice processes employed against terrorists and their accomplices, and is vital in procuring the evidence necessary to convict them in courts of law.

There are various methods available for collecting information about the terrorist organizations, their operatives, structure, deployment, motives and ideologies, relations with one another, policies and other factors, including their modus operandi, future and current plans for attacks, intentions, etc. The various kinds of intelligence include visual intelligence (VISINT), electronic or signals intelligence (SIGINT) and open source intelligence (OSINT), all of which jointly help build the intelligence picture, the overall understanding of the enemy's intentions and capabilities. However, the most important factor in counterterrorism intelligence and the one that will be dealt with here is human intelligence, HUMINT.

HUMINT

In terms of counterterrorism, HUMINT includes intelligence obtained from agents planted within the terrorist organizations, deserters and other operatives recruited from the organizations' operational, political or social structures, and operatives who were captured and detained. Many analysts stress the importance of HUMINT sources in collecting intelligence about the organizations and their plans to carry out attacks. It can be assumed that because the terrorist organizations are secret organizations, their operatives will do their utmost not to expose themselves, and therefore special attention must be paid to obtaining information from human intelligence sources.

However, collecting HUMINT raises problems specific to the terrorism arena. When an intelligence source is part of a terrorist organization, he may find himself required to participate in an illegal action. The demand may be in the nature of an "entrance exam" or "reliability test." The desire to establish the agent's status as an intelligence source in the organization and promoting him in its hierarchy may pose a dilemma for his handlers: What should an agent be permitted to do to strengthen his status within the organization and establish his credibility, and what should be forbidden? Can he be involved in an illegal activity, or even initiate one? For example, in a secret codicil to its official conclusions, the Shamgar Commission, appointed to investigate the assassination of Israeli Prime Minister Yitzhak Rabin, determined that in certain instances the ISA agents committed felonies, thinking that as agents they were not subject to the law. The members of the commission therefore warned the ISA against giving a free hand to intelligence sources on the ground.

In addition to the specific dilemmas involved in HUMINT, intelligence collection for counterterrorism poses general dilemmas as well. Meir Dagan, director of the Mossad, called one of them "the short shelf-life of an intelligence source." He claimed that intelligence concerning a hostile country was preserved and served long-term strategic needs, especially in time of war. That is not true, however, in fighting terrorism. Since in the latter case the objective is preventing a terrorist attack, the intelligence serves daily operative needs.[2] The operative use of intelligence in counterterrorism places the source in danger of exposure. For example, if information is received that a certain terrorist is going attack a certain target, and he is then detained or access to the target is blocked and the target itself has increased security, the organization will know it has been infiltrated and its plans have been exposed. Thus it is

---

2.   Private conversation with Meir Dagan, December 2, 1999.

not surprising that the first thing the terrorist organizations generally do after an attack by an adversary is investigate to find the leak.

A particularly important example is the problematic relationship between Israeli and Palestinian intelligence, formed after the establishment of the Palestinian Authority. The short shelf-life dilemma of the intelligence source has no solution. If there is an immediate need to use the intelligence information to thwart a terrorist attack and save human lives, the question of the intelligence source's shelf-life becomes secondary.

It is possible to protect the source's shelf-life by keeping strictly to the rules of field security and taking operative steps to fool the adversary. For example, when information has been received about a planned terrorist attack, the security around several similar targets in various locations can be upgraded to lessen the fear that protective measures will expose the source. However, in the final analysis, every operative activity based on intelligence places the source in danger.

COMINT

Communications intelligence (COMINT) is the monitoring of telephone conversations (on both land lines and cell phones), fax messages, telegrams and cyber communications. Modern terrorist organizations, which are basically a global social network of operatives that have become a threat to the world, need to maintain communications between the leadership and the operatives. That need provides a convenient *pou sto* for intelligence agencies in collecting vital information about the organizations, their capabilities and intentions to carry out terrorist attacks. The terrorist organizations, aware of possible breaches of security, do everything in their power to limit the use of exposed communications lines and look for alternative ways to communicate (meetings, couriers, dead letter drops) and even encrypt their open communications to make messages seem innocent. Nevertheless,

COMINT is still an important means of collecting information about terrorist organizations.

Technological-Physical Intelligence

Technological intelligence is an important source of terrorist information. It includes fingerprints; blood, hair and tissue samples; clothing; tire tracks; explosives residue and weapons, etc. Forensic techniques are usually used and contribute greatly to acquiring information about the identity of terrorists who carried out an attack and their modus operandi. Immediately after an attack, police and intelligence officers collect all the evidence that can be found at the scene – residue of explosives, nails, shrapnel and ball bearings added to the bombs, remains of explosive belts, backpacks or other containers used to hold the bombs, detonators, batteries, remains of the terrorist, his or her personal belongings, remains of the vehicle if one was used, and so forth. Many terrorist attack cases have been solved through physical evidence that led to the identity of the perpetrators.

OSINT

Open source intelligence (OSINT) includes all the information gleaned from written material, audio and video cassettes and public communication: for example, newspaper articles, advertisements and announcements, media interviews with the senior figures of terrorist organizations, information from radio and television stations that serve the terrorist organizations, its website, indoctrination material published by the terrorists in leaflets, books and other publications, academic studies, freely accessible databases and legal documents distributed in courts. OSINT is usually considered by the intelligence community to be less "prestigious" than other means of intelligence collection, but in dealing with terrorist organizations it is invaluable. Since terrorist organizations make extensive use of the Internet, OSINT can prove useful in exploring their recruitment processes, their fund-raising, IED (improvised explosive devices), cookbooks and terrorist attack modus operandi, changes in organization leadership and ideology, internal and external rivals, operational difficulties and, in certain cases, even in identifying terrorist organization operatives and supporters, and their intentions to carry out attacks.

VISINT

Visual intelligence (VISINT) is intelligence collected by reconnaissance planes, UAVs (unmanned aerial vehicles), reconnaissance balloons and land surveillance. Generally speaking, VISINT can be useful in verifying the information's relevance and timeliness, for example by following a candidate for a targeted killing from his base to the target place. VISINT also provides tactical intelligence about terrorist organization deployment and efforts to carry out an attack through the changes in their operatives' behavior.

Internal Intelligence and Operative Coordination

One of the reasons for the complexity of the war on terrorism is its multidimensional nature, involving many government and administrative apparatuses: ministries, among them defense, the treasury and the Office of the Prime Minister, and various branches of the army, intelligence, the police, customs and immigration, and the banking system, to mention a few. Dealing with terrorism effectively requires that all the apparatuses operate concurrently and coordinate with one another. Such coordination is likely to make the whole greater than the sum of its parts, so that intelligence information can be concentrated and focused to greatest effect. Lack of coordination may lead to a serious waste of resources, destructive competition between the various factors, bureaucracy and, worst of all, ineffective action.

Over the past years Israeli intelligence and the IDF have chalked up impressive achievements because of the cooperation between intelligence and operative activities. Many terrorist attacks have been prevented and many complex operations have been successfully carried out because of reliable, updated intelligence information quickly disseminated to the operative defensive or offensive forces. In that respect the various intelligence and security services have risen above competition, rivalry over authority and personal differences, and have established an effective, perfectly functioning intelligence-operational system.

Yaakov Peri, former ISA director, said that "in the operational field Israel is a world leader in coordination, lack of inter-service rivalries and mutual aid. I am speaking," he said, "about coordination between the Mossad, IDI and the IDF, and all the other services.... The field where problems arise is concerning responsibility – can the ISA really operate agents outside [Israeli territory]? whose responsibility should the Palestinian Authority be? – things like that. In my opinion they do not harm the independence, initiative, intelligence collection and preventive activities of the State of Israel against terrorism."[3] Meir Dagan noted that "the problem is not coordinating intelligence... because there is transparency.... No [branch] hides information. They may adapt things, but the genuine content of the material gets passed along...."[4]

"The Democratic Dilemma" and Intelligence

One of the problems most difficult to deal with in fighting terrorism is the "democratic dilemma": How can a country preserve its liberal values, remain a democracy and still deal effectively with terrorism? The dilemma permeates every facet of the war on terrorism: offense, defense, punitive measures and even the debate of media censorship, but it is far more important in the field of counterterrorism intelligence. It becomes

---

3. Private conversation with Yaakov Peri, December 28, 1999.
4. Private conversation with Meir Dagan, December 2, 1999.

crucial when dealing with methods of interrogating people suspected of involvement in terrorist activity, following suspects, wiretapping and handling intelligence agents. Since terrorists operate underground and in secret, infiltrating their ranks, following them and obtaining evidence of their illegal activities is particularly hard, and sometimes special methods are needed to bring them to justice.

Israel's democratic dilemma regarding wiretapping came to the fore in an argument between operations and the judiciary. An amendment to the wiretapping law passed by the Constitution, Law and Justice Committee of the 27th Knesset in March 1995 determined that the ISA could not wiretap the phone conversations of Muslim clerics in East Jerusalem and within the borders of the State of Israel, including members of Hamas and the Palestinian Islamic Jihad, without authorization from the president of the district court. It also determined that the ISA would have to reveal to a parliamentary committee, composed of the heads of the Foreign Affairs and Defense and Constitution, Law and Justice Committees, the criteria used to determine whose phone could be tapped. The list of apparatuses that needed authorization from the court before they could be tapped was expanded to include mobile phone, fax machines, communications between computers and wireless media.

The late Israeli Prime Minister Yitzhak Rabin disagreed with the sweeping decision, according to which the ISA's wiretapping would be subject to judicial review. His objections were the following: Wiretapping in the interests of national security is essentially different from wiretapping to prevent crime and apprehend criminals. It is a question of obtaining vital, sensitive information that influences people's lives and the chances of achieving peace in the region, and it is only fitting that the authority be the prime minister's, since he is responsible for that type of sensitive matter.

However, the area of intelligence most conspicuous in the democratic counterterrorism dilemma is collecting information through the interrogation of those suspected of involvement in terrorist activities.

The issue of interrogation methods illustrates the dilemma of having to deal, on the one hand, with the possible infringement of the suspect's civil rights, and on the other, the possibility of obtaining information vital to preventing a terrorist attack and saving human lives. The dilemma has been central to Israeli governments and illustrates the delicate and problematic relationship between the government and the enforcement agencies (especially the ISA), and between the legislative body and the judiciary. The government has usually supported the ISA's interrogation methods, and the legislators do not pass laws to anchor the investigative procedures determined by investigation commissions; the judiciary makes it possible for the ISA to continue using its established methods, while repeatedly expressing its dissatisfaction with the absence of relevant legislation.

The difficult issue of interrogating terrorists is best illustrated by Israeli Supreme Court Judgment HCJ 5100/94 Public Committee Against Torture in Israel v. The State of Israel:

"We are aware that this decision does not make it easier to deal with that reality [Israel's difficult security situation]. This is the fate of democracy, as not all means are acceptable to it, and not all methods employed by its enemies are open to it. Sometimes, a democracy must fight with one hand tied behind its back. Nonetheless, it has the upper hand. Preserving the rule of law and recognition of individual liberties constitute an important component of its understanding of security.... We are aware that this decision does not make it easier to deal with that reality.... We are not isolated in an ivory tower. We live the life of this country. We are aware of the harsh reality of terrorism in which we are, at times, immersed. The possibility that this decision will hamper the ability to deal properly with terrorists and terrorism disturbs us. We are, however, judges."[5]

---

5. *Judgments of the Israel Supreme Court: Fighting Terrorism within the Law*,
    http://www.jewishvirtuallibrary.org/jsource/Politics/terrorirm_law.pdf.

The Dilemma of Issuing Warnings
of Planned Terrorist Attacks

One of the most serious dilemmas facing the security services of a country plagued by terrorism is the degree to which the public should be warned about an impending attack. For example, if there is information about the time and place a terrorist organization is planning an attack, should the public be told or should steps be taken to prevent the attack while keeping the public in the dark? Some security agents and decision makers feel it is their public duty to inform civilians when they are in danger. Others add that issuing warnings is necessary for increasing public awareness, which can help prevent planned terrorist attacks. However, it seems that in many cases the decision to issue warnings merely stems from the desire to avoid responsibility should an attack take place and not be criticized after the fact for "hiding information from the public."

On the other hand, there are those who feel that issuing warnings is a serious mistake and plays into the hands of the terrorists. First, it may cause irreparable damage to the intelligence source who reported the information, because the terrorist organization will make every effort to discover the leak. In addition, if the terrorist organizations know that the security services are aware of their plans they may change the time and place. The damage done by revealing planned attacks goes beyond the realm of defensive intelligence; it causes psychological damage and lowers morale. Actually, issuing a warning may have the same influence as an attack, even though it is never carried out, as the level of public tension and fear rise even though nothing has happened. The security services usually have to deal with a very large number of early warnings: for example, in 2002 the Israeli security services reported having warnings of between forty and fifty potential terrorist attacks. Most of the attacks, however, were not carried out.

Who, then, should decide which warnings to issue and which not? Is not selecting certain ones to make public in a way fooling the populace? Moreover, a sophisticated terrorist organization will study the country's policies and may deliberately use them to send false warnings to disrupt the daily lives of ordinary citizens.

Given the above, what policy should be adopted? Should warnings never be made public? Not publicizing them does not in any way obviate the responsibility of the security services to prevent attacks. However, the best rule is to issue warnings only when the public can be given concrete instructions regarding what to do and what not to do in a specific situation: not to participate in a certain activity, not to gather in large groups or go to a certain location, to take certain precautions or anything else that is relevant. When no such instructions can be given, the public should not be informed of the situation.

Conclusion

During its sixty years, the State of Israel has been an example of a democracy forced to cope with an immense and varied terrorist challenge. The threat has forced Israel to develop counterterrorism skills, and especially to develop intelligence capabilities to overcome difficulties and existential dilemmas. In many instances, the experience gained by Israel has turned it into a role model for other countries around the world.

Iran and the Iranian Nuclear Project as a Challenge for Israeli Intelligence

Colonel (Res.) Dr. Ephraim Kam
Former Assistant Director of the IDI Production and Analysis Department

Introduction

The Iranian threat is a key issue on the security agenda, not only of Israel but of other countries as well. Currently the threat is limited, manifested mainly by Iran's involvement in terrorism through its proxy Hezbollah in Lebanon and in the Palestinian arena. Iran's growing arsenal of long-range ballistic missiles, which can reach any target in Israel, give it conventional military capabilities. However, the situation will be completely different if and when Iran acquires nuclear weapons. Because of the enormous implications of the strategic threat Iran poses to Israel, qualitative intelligence about the regime's intentions, policies and current and future capabilities is of great importance. This article will examine the main issues of Iran as an intelligence challenge.

Decision Making in the Iranian Regime

The rise to power of a fundamentalist Islamic regime in Iran created a strategic threat for many countries: namely, its neighbors and other Arab-Muslim countries with moderate regimes, the United States and Europe, but above all, Israel. The threat is multifaceted: First, Iran aspires to regional hegemony and wants to export the model of its Islamic revolution to other Muslim countries. Second, it is involved in terrorism against and the subversion of other regimes and organizations.

And third, it may use its conventional military capabilities against its neighbors and other countries. However, the main threat is still in the future, that is, what its policies will be and what steps it will take if and when it develops nuclear weapons.

Part of the fear of Iran comes from the fact that the Islamic regime, which has ruled Iran since 1979, is unique. It is the only regime in which the top-ranking decision maker is neither a political or military figure nor an elected official representing the public, but a cleric. In addition, ranking below him are clerics or current and former members of the Revolutionary Guards, all of whom think in radical religious-ideological terms.

This situation poses a unique difficulty for the relevant governments and intelligence communities. The central question is what the weight of religious-ideological factors is in Iran's top-level decision-making process. Are decisions made on the basis of profit and loss, by weighing risks and chances in a balanced view of the situation, or are the deciding factors religious imperatives, which must be met even if it means ignoring risks and paying a heavy price?

Over the years there have been examples of both. On the one hand, the Iranian regime does not make the kinds of adventurous moves Saddam Hussein made against his neighbors and, for example, restrained itself from responding to the provocations of the Taliban regime in Afghanistan at the end of the 1990s. On the other, for religious-ideological reasons the Islamic regime decided from its inception to cut the strategic ties the Shah had developed with the United States, and by so doing paid a high military and economic price. The United States and Europe stopped supplying Iran with weapons and other military equipment, and the shortage of arms was one of the main reasons for Iraq's victory in the Iran-Iraq war. In addition, Iran's hostility toward the United States, which began in the early 1990s, has turned America into Iran's most formidable enemy. Which consideration will be decisive in the future is an open question. Moreover, according to conventional wisdom,

Iran's security concept is defensive-deterrent, not offensive. That gives rise to two other questions: Is Iran pragmatic and careful as an outcome of its current military weakness? And will that change when Iran develops its military capabilities? The answers to those questions will be critically important if and when Iran becomes a nuclear power.

There is another difficulty: the Iranian decision-making process is not well-known or understood, and one reason is because the regime is closed and conceals its internal workings. It is clear that the spiritual leader, currently Ali Khamenei, is the senior decision maker. However, is he involved in every important decision? What weight do other members and powerful figures of the regime's upper echelons have? Does Khamenei have the final say or are matters decided by vote? And in recent years, what weight does the Iranian president, Mahmoud Ahmadinejad, have in making decisions relating to security and foreign affairs? What is the role of the Revolutionary Guards in the decision-making process, taking into account their growing military, political and economic power? In terms of intelligence, the problem is the difficulty in infiltrating the inner circles and acquiring information about the decision-making process, to say nothing of concrete information about the decisions themselves.

The Iranian Nuclear Issue: The Difficulties of Intelligence

Iran's striving to achieve nuclear arms raises a series of questions whose answers depend on collective qualitative intelligence information. First, is Iran really endeavoring to acquire nuclear weapons, or, as it claims, is its nuclear program meant for peaceful civilian purposes? The answer seems very simple: almost all those dealing with the issue in Israel, the United States and Europe agree today that Iran is determined to acquire nuclear weapons. However, other countries have their doubts, and while all International Atomic Energy Agency reports have criticized Iran's conduct and raised doubts as to the peaceful aims of the Iranian nuclear project, the agency has yet to say specifically that Iran seeks to develop nuclear arms. It has also been mentioned that the best intelligence communities in the world, the American, the British and the Israeli, were wrong in their 2003 assessment of Iraq's program of mass weapons of destruction, and that therefore the possibility cannot be ruled out that they are wrong again regarding the Iranian nuclear issue.

The problem for intelligence lies in the assumption that Iran seeks nuclear weapons. There is no incontrovertible intelligence proving that Iran is in fact developing such weapons, but the assumption is based on a reasonable analysis of Iran's nuclear conduct and on the claim that certain nuclear sites and activities cannot be civilian and can only be military. It is also based on the claim, correct in and of itself, that Iran is hiding a significant part of its nuclear activities and consistently lying about them to conceal a military program. However reasonable the assumptions may be, there is no hard evidence to that effect, and theoretically they may prove to be wrong, as were the assumptions concerning Iraq's conventional weapons of mass destruction.

Second, for years intelligence communities have dealt with the time frame required by Iran to acquire nuclear weapons. The Israeli and American intelligence communities agree that by mid-2010 Iran had the amount of low-enriched uranium sufficient for at least two nuclear bombs, if upgraded into highly enriched uranium. Both communities agree that technically Iran could produce its first bomb by 2011. Yet both were wrong in the past. During the first half of the 1990s both claimed that Iran would have nuclear weapons within five to eight years, that is, by 2000 at the latest. That did not happen, and no one can claim with certainty that the current hypothetical timetable is correct. The problem is the lack of reliable information about the progress of Iran's nuclear program, including the possibility that some of the activities are carried out in secret locations unknown to intelligence, and the lack of information about technical problems that have to be dealt with now or in the future. In such a situation, a timetable can only be constructed on hypotheses that may be proved either correct or incorrect.

Third is the most important question: Can Iran be stopped before it acquires nuclear weapons? Two methods of stopping it present themselves, political-economic pressure and military action, and both have intelligence aspects. Using political tools to convince Iran to halt its nuclear program would mean finding its weaknesses and discovering how sensitive the regime is to economic pressure and sanctions, and so far experience has proved that to be far from simple.

A military action targeting Iran's nuclear installations would require much more significant intelligence input. It would require acquiring precise, reliable information about the nuclear sites, their physical and technical specifications, their shields and defenses and the activities taking place inside, in a situation in which the critical sites are sunk deep into the earth and protected by a thick layer of concrete. Without such information a military action would be impossible. It would mean discovering whether there were other, unknown sites, and it would require data about other potentially influential factors, such as the deployment of American troops in the Gulf area and Iraq and meteorological conditions. A full intelligence picture would include an evaluation of Iran's capability to respond to a military action against both Jewish-Israeli targets and American targets, an evaluation of Iran's ability to repair the damage to its nuclear installations and to recover its nuclear program, and a comprehensive evaluation of the intelligence aspects of the risks and chances involved in the operation.

Fourth, regarding the future, what will Iran's nuclear policies be if and when it acquires nuclear weapons? There are two aspects. One concerns how far along the program is and how much of it Iran will expose when it does have the technology. Will Iran decide to manufacture nuclear weapons, or prefer to develop the capability to manufacture them and then, to forestall international pressure and sanctions, stop and wait for the right moment to charge toward the bomb? Will it prefer opacity to transparency, even when the weapons are operative? Will it announce it has weapons, and will the announcement reflect the truth? Will it test them? Each possibility has a different important significance for Israel, and each necessitates a comprehensive intelligence assessment as quickly as possible.

The other aspect is even more important. Will Iran use its nuclear weapons to attack Israel? It is hard to imagine that intelligence communities will be capable of acquiring solid, unambiguous information about Iran's intention to use – or not use – nuclear weapons against Israel. To acquire such intelligence it would be necessary to infiltrate the inner circles of the senior decision makers in Tehran, an extremely difficult task. There have been important breakthroughs in the various types of intelligence collection, including ELINT (electronic intelligence), VISINT (visual intelligence) and OSINT (open source intelligence). However, information about Iran's strategic decisions regarding the use of nuclear weapons apparently will not pass through those channels. In effect, the main way to acquire solid intelligence is likely to be through high-ranking human sources, but those are expected to be quite rare.

In the absence of hard information, Israeli and other intelligence communities will apparently have to rely on various indicators, as is usual in identifying enemy intentions regarding conventional warfare. However, identifying a nuclear attack by early warning indicators is complex and very difficult. The number of participants in the attack will be small and the preparations for it secret and carried out in underground installations. Unlike preparations for conventional warfare, there will be very few external signs that can be used for early warning. Even when such signs exist – for example, reports about Iranian preparations to absorb an Israeli response – they may be interpreted as regular Iranian defense procedures unrelated to offensive measures. It will also be difficult to differentiate between missiles with nuclear warheads and those with conventional warheads, between planes carrying regular bombs and those carrying nuclear bombs. And while it is true that Iranian missiles launched at Israel will be immediately identified, the warning before an attack will be short. Finally, experience with nuclear attacks is insufficient to define and identify early warning indicators.

Other Difficulties Involved in Evaluating Iran's Future Nuclear Policies

Today there is neither substantial information nor any sign indicating Iran's future nuclear policy for the very simple reason that Iran denies developing nuclear weapons and does not release any information about its future nuclear plans. Strategic assessments often prove to be wrong, especially when they are not supported by facts and evidence. In addition, Iran is distant and has no common border with Israel. That makes it difficult to collect intelligence about Iranian nuclear activity using HUMINT or VISINT. Also Iran has had years to perfect its techniques of concealment and fraud, particularly in the nuclear field, but also in the fields of terrorism and subversion, making it more difficult to acquire reliable information about its nuclear activity and links to terrorism.

If Iran does acquire nuclear weapons, an intelligence effort will have to be made to answer other questions, for example:

- Even if Iran does not initially intend to use its nuclear weapons, what will prompt it to change its mind? What are the "red lines" whose crossing will convince it to use them?
- Will Iran become more aggressive toward Israel, for example by encouraging Hezbollah to expand its activity against Israel, or by supporting it in a confrontation with Israel?
- Will Iran ensure that Syria has a nuclear umbrella, overt or concealed, should it become entangled in difficulties during a broad confrontation with Israel?

- Will Iran export nuclear technology to other countries, particularly Syria? Will it provide terrorist organizations such as Hezbollah with nuclear weapons?
- Will Iran be willing to talk to Israel, even indirectly, to determine rules of engagement and "red lines" regarding nuclear activities, in order to prevent the deterioration of a situation which even Iran does not want?

The existence of nuclear weapons in Iranian hands will be a security problem of new dimensions for Israel and other countries, and Israel will need to reorganize its intelligence effort to cope with it. The situation will be made somewhat easier by the fact that today there is broad awareness of the threat Iran poses, leading to international intelligence cooperation on the issue of Iran's nuclear threat. How to identify and evaluate suspicious nuclear activity is also better understood today. In addition, the International Atomic Energy Agency, despite criticism directed at it for not specifically defining Iran as seeking nuclear arms, plays an important role in providing information about Iran's nuclear sites and activity.

A Final Word

One last comment: the significance of the Iranian threat, including its nuclear threat, will alter if and when the Iranian regime changes and becomes relatively more moderate, even if it does possess nuclear arms. An Iran with a moderate regime will alter the strategic environment not only of Israel but of other countries as well. Such a change is within the realm of possibility because a large part of the Iranian populace is already seeking a more moderate regime, one that will make greater political and personal freedom possible, improve the country's economy, limit corruption and allow for greater openness to the Western world, particularly the United States. It is therefore important to monitor Iran's internal events and identify signs of a possible shift.

The Role of Intelligence in the
Battle for Hearts and Minds

Colonel (Ret.) Dr. Reuven Erlich

Former Officer in IDI and Current Head of the Meir Amit
Intelligence and Terrorism Information Center at the Israel
Intelligence Heritage and Commemoration Center

Introduction

Terrorism is a central threat to the international community and influences its agenda. The war on terrorism and its sponsors is fought simultaneously on three fronts: on the ground, where the security forces of all threatened countries and societies battle against terrorist operatives; on the political front, where both sides seek the support of regional and international powers; and in the battle for hearts and minds, where both sides use a variety of ways and means to expose their political positions and ideologies to the relevant target audiences in the hope of impressing them and gaining support.

The terrorist organizations fighting Israel, especially Hezbollah and Hamas, invest impressive resources in the battle for hearts and minds, for they are aware of the great importance of this front. The guns and bullets in the battle are virtual: pictures on television, newspaper articles, information (and disinformation) uploaded to the Internet, the Friday sermons in the mosques, radio broadcasts – and at a deeper level, brainwashing and indoctrination. Their short-term and long-term influence on the morale of the target audiences is no less than if real bullets had been used, because for better or worse, these virtual weapons influence the motivation, will power and determination of both sides to continue the long, on-going campaign, despite the difficulties involved.

Students of terrorism agree on the great importance of intelligence in the war on terrorism. Intelligence provides the decision makers and the forces fighting terrorism with information vital to planning policy and waging the war both defensively (counterterrorism intelligence, early warning of planned attacks) and offensively (intelligence for operations against the terrorist organizations). In the past, intelligence support did not play a central role in the battle for hearts and minds, but its importance has increased as that type of battle has become a major factor in counterterrorism.

Why would the Israeli and other intelligence communities take on such a role – providing intelligence for the battle for hearts and minds – considering that it is not a classic role for intelligence? First, because of its information capabilities and relative advantages. It possesses exclusive information about the terrorist organizations, their modus operandi and the countries sponsoring them. The first use of the information, most of it classified, is for the operational needs of fighting terrorism, but if controlled and used intelligently, it can also meet the political and media needs of the battle for hearts and minds.

Intelligence Missions and Clients

How can intelligence support the battle for hearts and minds? There are three main spheres of action:

- Monitoring the efforts made by the terrorist organizations in every aspect of the battle and using collection, research and operational tools, treating it as a legitimate subject for priority intelligence requirements and as an intelligence task. For example, the media empire constructed by the terrorist organizations, encompassing television, radio, the press and the Internet, has to be studied and monitored not only for the battle for hearts and minds but because they are used for logistic and operational purposes (including ideological indoctrination, financing, contacts between operatives and transferring technical know-how).

- Soberly declassifying intelligence information and making it available to individuals and institutions dealing with the battle for hearts and mind in Israel and abroad: that includes the declassification of data regarding terrorist activity, terrorist military infrastructure, funding, brainwashing, anti-Israel incitement and the support the terrorist organizations receive from their sponsors (including the exposure of the sponsor countries and their links to the organizations). The visual material that can serve as the basis for a media war is extremely important and one of the main components in the battle.

- Making a deliberate intelligence collection effort that can serve both political and public diplomacy needs. Public diplomacy often demands intelligence information, including visual material, which is unavailable or whose use is precluded by security restrictions. The understanding of the requirements of the battle for hearts and minds must lead intelligence to make a determined effort at collection and to make the information available to various clients.

Clients for such information are not necessarily the traditional, classic clients of intelligence services. For that reason there have to be communications channels through which information can flow freely, directly or indirectly, to the various institutions participating in the battle. Among them are the Ministry of Foreign Affairs through the embassies abroad, the IDF spokesman, the Israeli and foreign media, think tanks, and Jewish and non-Jewish individuals, NGOs and organizations abroad that may support public diplomacy. Intelligence must also create close mutual relations with groups abroad fighting the battle for hearts and minds, and help them by providing the necessary reliable information.

Difficulties and Problems

It is only natural that the involvement of intelligence in the battle for hearts and minds would give rise to a series of difficulties and problems, which have caused many dilemmas for the intelligence community in recent years. Experience proved the fears were exaggerated and that solutions could be found, among them the following:

- Safeguarding the security of both information and sources: The classic security effort we were all raised on is aimed at concealing information from the enemy to protect sources, the main asset of every intelligence service. In addition, intelligence traditionally refrains from exposing its members and maintaining contact with those who deal with public diplomacy. As a result, the understanding that intelligence information should be declassified as part of the battle for hearts and minds necessitates a conceptual change and the creation of the proper tools and channels to deal with the issue.

- Preventing intelligence from becoming politicized: The working relationship between intelligence and the senior political echelon is by its nature limited to the common interpretation of the situation of the enemy, but intelligence should not participate in shaping policy in such a way that it would become involved in political disagreement. Therefore, because of the potential for such disagreements, intelligence must ensure that the support it gives the battle for hearts and minds will promote national goals on which there is a consensus, and will not serve narrow political agendas or interests.

- Preserving the objectivity of intelligence officers: Dealing with public diplomacy and other aspects of the battle for hearts and minds is liable to deflect intelligence officers' focus and bias them. They may become enamored of their ability to shape the situation, thus damaging their professional considerations and duty to provide those who make and carry out decisions with exact, reliable information. The potential risk can be obviated by creating separate, designated channels and apparatuses for the battle for hearts and minds, fed by intelligence collection and analysis but not belonging to intelligence. At the same time, intelligence analysts should be encouraged to identify opportunities (or risks) in the battle for hearts and minds on a daily basis and on their own initiative to pass on the relevant information.

Israel Intelligence and Soviet Military Involvement in the Middle East

Dr. Dmitry Adamsky
Former Defense and Intelligence Analyst in the IDF and Ministry of Defense

Introduction

How Israeli intelligence met the Soviet challenge is a unique and fascinating chapter in its sixty-year history. This article will examine the collection and analysis of Soviet-related intelligence.

Before the fall of the Soviet empire – even though beginning in the 1980s it had drastically reduced its regional presence – the USSR was perceived as a strategic threat to Israel and as the force multiplier for the Arab militaries. For many years IDF intelligence closely tracked the course of events in the Soviet Union, especially its arms transfers to Middle Eastern countries. After the Six-Day War, important new dimensions were added: operational deployment of the Soviet forces in the area, the embedding of Soviet advisors within the Egyptian and Syrian armies and eventually the Soviet intervention in Israel's wars. Israel Defense Intelligence also studied Soviet policy in the Middle East and Africa and analyzed the relations between the superpowers and their implications for the region.

Soviet Involvement

The Soviet Union always regarded the Middle East as having supreme strategic importance, and its involvement increased from the middle of the 1960s. Its main motives were global, rooted in the dynamics of the

Cold War. The strategic imbalance between the USSR and the United States in general, and the nuclear threat emanating from the American presence in the Mediterranean in particular, motivated the Soviets to seek a counterweight. In the late 1960s the Soviet Union deployed some of its fleet in key locations around the world, and to the greatest extent possible, established bases in Third World ports. The Mediterranean had priority because of the danger that it could serve as a launching pad for a nuclear attack against the Soviet Union.

The Soviet deployment to counter American naval strength in the Mediterranean had immediate consequences for Israel. Symbiotic relations emerged between Moscow and several Middle Eastern regimes, although Socialist-Communist ideology was nothing more than a cover for other, more pragmatic interests. While Moscow sought bases from which it could counter the American threat, the rulers of the region, especially in Syria and Egypt, needed massive amounts of weapons and military advice to confront Israel.

Soviet involvement in Middle Eastern countries grew significantly following the Arab defeat in 1967. Moscow transferred unprecedented quantities of weapons to Egypt and Syria, and sent them Soviet advisors and technicians. Thousands of military advisors assisted the two countries' armies to rehabilitate themselves and plan for the next round of fighting with Israel. Soviet navy and maritime aviation units deployed permanently in both Egypt and Syria, enabling a constant Soviet presence in the Mediterranean Sea. In effect, the USSR realized its regional aspirations by receiving anchoring privileges for its fleet and deploying military units to deal with the United States. The Soviet presence gradually became an important component of overall Arab military might, and thus became an important intelligence target for Israel.

Collection and Analysis of the Soviets: The Establishment of the *Masregah* (Knitting Needle) Unit

Due to the massive Soviet involvement, communications traffic in Russian – conversations between the advisors and with their Egyptian and Syrian colleagues – increased drastically on the Egyptian and Syrian communication networks. There were not enough Russian speakers in the IDF SIGINT unit, and the need to establish an appropriate intelligence response to the Soviet presence in the arena rose. The issue was relatively new even for IDI analysts, who during those years had only begun to develop expertise in international subjects. Given the importance of the issue and due to intelligence hardships, at the end of 1967 Aharon Yariv, head of the IDI, ordered the establishment of an intelligence collection function to deal specifically with the Soviet affairs. Major Tuvia Feinman, who spoke Russian and who until then had worked in the production and analysis division, was appointed to head the project. The new unit was called *Masregah* (Knitting Needle) and later *Nesher* (Eagle), and it was responsible for monitoring regional Soviet activities. Intelligence folklore dubbed the members of the unit "Grechkos," after Andrei Grechko, the Soviet defense minister at the time. The title, introduced by the Arabists who did not accept the "Russians" with any great affection, initially had negative connotations. However, the Grechkos were quickly accepted and later became the backbone of the chain of command and the center of various parts of military intelligence.

The Soviet challenge was technologically, conceptually and doc-trinally different from the ongoing coverage of the Arabs. Unit 848 (today 8200) did not at that time have the capabilities for even basic coverage of the Soviets' communications, not only because it lacked Russian speakers, but because the Soviet communications systems were unfamiliar and well protected. Establishing collection and analysis procedures was also a conceptual-cultural challenge. Soviet operational-tactical behavior and strategic culture were significantly different from those of the Arab countries, and the techniques used for Arab research and analysis were not applicable in the Soviet field.

Those difficulties made it important for Israel to avail itself of NATO's intelligence apparatus, which had closely followed the Warsaw Pact armies. Intelligence organizations in Europe were also interested in assisting, because Israel provided the actual laboratory for studying operational Soviet signals. The first collection team – Major Tuvia Feinman and Captain Ephraim Lapid – left for Europe to study the subject at the end of 1968.

After the unit was established, one of its permanent priority intelligence requirements, in addition to monitoring the Soviet advisors in the region, was locating Soviet forces sent to the region during crises. That was a significant indication of a potential future escalation, and the wire-tappers searched for supporting SIGINT evidence. The methodical monitoring coupled with significant expertise enabled the unit members, unlike American and Israeli analysts, to determine that the Soviet Union was planning to intervene in the 1969–1970 War of Attrition.

The IDI Production and Analysis Division and the Soviet Challenge

Until the Six-Day War IDI did not possess research capabilities sufficient for analyzing Soviet military involvement and policy in the Middle East. In 1966 a superpowers branch was established within the production and analysis division to deal with three issues: the United States and the West, the Soviet Union and the East, and terrorism and other subversive activities. A small group of experts dealt with the superpowers, especially the activities of the American Sixth Fleet and the Soviet Mediterranean squadron. Most of the intelligence material concerning the Soviet fleet came from collaboration with Western intelligence services.

Without its own independent sources, IDI relied primarily on information and evaluations from its foreign colleagues, open media sources and material from the Foreign Ministry (until diplomatic relations were terminated in 1967). At first the Soviet department had no native Russian speakers with first-hand knowledge of Russian culture, literature, traditions and mentality, and there was no formal IDF intelligence training in Sovietology. At the beginning of the 1970s, however, the IDF started to develop a cadre of Sovietologists to meet intelligence needs. Young officers were sent to study the subject at high-ranking American universities and on their return were integrated into the production and analysis division in Soviet issues. Initially, IDI produced good intelligence only about regional military affairs, but as time passed analytic expertise on the Soviet decision-making processes and on Soviet Middle Eastern policy matured.

In addition to operational input, IDI also contributed to the development of Soviet combat doctrine. In the 1960s, when Syria and Egypt began receiving Soviet doctrinal assistance, Israel intelligence recognized, studied and taught the Soviet military doctrine to the IDF commanders. At first the commanders were skeptical, but the intelligence analysts worked hard to make them aware of a comprehensive stand-alone military doctrine. It was widely circulated and penetrated the professional mindset.

The intelligence analysis of Soviet affairs also suffered failures with strategic consequences. In 1969 and 1970 the analysis department failed to warn of Soviet intervention in the War of Attrition, and on the eve of the Yom Kippur War in 1973 the analysts did not correctly interpret the evacuation of the Soviet advisors' families from Egypt. In both cases the information collectors confronted the analysts, hoping to promote an alternative evaluation, which in retrospect turned out to be true.

Within a relatively short time, intelligence experts on Soviet subjects reached a high professional level and their capabilities became equal to those of the Western intelligence services, which for years had dealt with the Soviet Union.

In a few short years, IDI had abandoned its status as apprentice and become a unique source of exclusive information for its Western counterparts, especially in the fields of weaponry, naval, aerial and land doctrines, and Soviet Middle Eastern policy. Expertise in fields so important to the West gave IDI a prominent place in the major league of intelligence services during the Cold War. In the 1980s, analysts from the Soviet units of the IDI's production and analysis division became world leaders on the issue of the USSR in general and Soviet policy in the Middle East in particular.

European countries and the United States wanted to monitor Soviet military capability in the Middle East at close range; consequently, Israel's interests meshed with those of foreign services. From then on, Israel was able not only to provide the Americans with a picture of the strategic situation in the Middle East but also to analyze and define the Soviet threat. That cooperation led to a significant improvement in the IDI's SIGINT capabilities.

Additional vindication of IDI's Soviet achievements came later, when Soviet veterans of Israeli-Arab wars (primarily those who had served on the Egyptian side) described Israeli intelligence's capabilities in extremely complimentary terms. In their memoirs, Soviet policy makers, military, KGB and GRU officers made similar comments, clearly showing that they regarded Israeli intelligence as a genuine specialist and a serious rival.

Section Five

Branches and Components of Israeli Intelligence

Technology in the Service of Intelligence

Colonel (Res.) Shlomo Tirosh
Former Commander of the IDI's Technological Unit

Introduction

On the wall of the commander of the IDI technology unit, above the framed certificates of Israel security prizes won by the unit's teams, there is a poster reading "Knowledge, will and dedication will make the impossible possible." It was the slogan of the late Avraham Arnan when he commanded the unit (1966–1967).

If we add creativity, initiative and resourcefulness to the slogan, it expresses the importance of the human factor more than any other to the astounding development and great contribution of advanced technology. Technology improved and advanced Israel's intelligence activity and was important in the country's economic growth and the welfare of its citizens.

This article examines technology in the service of intelligence. It has brought improvements to all branches of the intelligence community and made them more effective, exact and sophisticated, and space does not allow for a discussion of them all. The focus here will be on collecting intelligence for early warning, which is critical for the security and existence of the State of Israel, and the various improvements that have made technology an important part of Israel's concept of defense.

The Globalization of Terrorism:
The Technological Aspect

Israel's confrontation with its enemies is now global. Groups hostile to Israel and seeking to attack it and its interests can be found all over the world, including in friendly countries and within Israel itself. The conflict in the Middle East, which in the past was limited to Israel and its Arab neighbors, grew in recent years to a conflict with hostile elements, radical Islamic terrorist organizations such as Hamas and Hezbollah, and antagonistic countries far from Israel's borders, such as Iran, all calling for Israel's destruction.

Communications have developed extensively over the past sixty years. There are global wideband networks, satellite communications, vast branching undersea cable systems, mobile personal communications networks, communication between computers and media networks. Especially important is the great revolution in communications systems and the open, easy access to its contents (including classified contents) from almost any place on the globe through the Internet. All of the above have created a giant communications ocean where nexuses of threat can lurk, their communications capable of reaching almost any spot on earth at the speed of light. In the final analysis, striking ranges grow while warning times are reduced. Someone pushes a button in Damascus and a missile is launched toward Beersheba; a pin is pulled in Tehran and a booby-trapped car explodes in front of the Israeli embassy in Buenos Aires.

The Development of Weapons of Mass Destruction and Their Accessibility

Various irregular, unsupervised factors have improved extremist organizations' access to knowledge and nonconventional resources in the realms of nuclear fission and biological and chemical warfare. At the same time, effective oversight has become tenuous, and difficulties have arisen in monitoring and forcing extremist countries and organizations to comply with international norms, increasing the risk of mass casualties. Technological improvements and knowledge can be accessed with relative ease on the Internet and from commercial sources, making it possible to manufacture efficient, small, fairly cheap warheads that can be used to attack long-range targets.

The Intelligence-Technological Confrontation

With the passage of time, intelligence targets have become aware of the nature of Israel's activities and the technological-operational means it uses. The dynamic, on-going struggle to develop and vary systems to counter them, directed and operated by the human brain, is an integral part of the security confrontation.

The initiative and technological advantage have to be in Israeli hands at all times. The period of time required to develop new intelligence systems is long, measured in months and years. Preserving the advantage requires investing effort to predict and recognize the new weapons systems and technological resources that can be expected on the battlefield and as potential threats. It is important to make the effort as early as possible to provide time for finding the appropriate technological solutions and means of dealing with innovations in the arena of confrontation.

Technological Challenges in Intelligence Early Warning

To a great extent, the need for intelligence information dictates the nature of the solutions. I have chosen to present technology's contribution to Israel's development of early warning intelligence systems for war and hostile activities that endanger the state.

The system for warning the country of war and hostile activity has undergone structural and technological changes during the past forty years. These changes were the consequences of geopolitical processes in which Israel was involved, which influenced the threats to Israel and the confrontations in which it was engaged. Some of them were the following:

- The Six-Day War: In the 1960s Israel's borders changed and new warning systems had to be built, specifically for Jordan, Syria and Egypt.
- The Yom Kippur War: In the 1970s the early warning failure and changed borders meant readapting the warning systems.
- The peace agreement with Egypt: In the late 1970s Israel withdrew from Sinai and the border with Egypt reverted to that of 1967 (with the exception of the Gaza Strip), and the warning system had to be changed again.
- The development of international Islamic and Palestinian terrorism: Beginning in the 1970s, Israel had to find ways of warning of terrorist attacks both inside the country and against Israeli and Jewish targets around the world.
- The relentless confrontations and terrorist attacks along the Lebanese border: Beginning in the 1980s (the First Lebanon War) the need arose to establish an early warning system along Israel's northern border.
- Missile attacks and attacks on the Israeli home front: Beginning in the 1990s, the need arose to establish an early warning system for long-range missile, rocket and mortar shell attacks on undefended population centers.

The Technological Aspects of Early Warning

The effectiveness of early warning is measured in terms of the time passed between receipt of the warning and the beginning of the event. This is the case whether the early warning is strategic – such as a warning that war is about to break out or warning of a massive attack launched on the home front – or tactical, such as a terrorist attack. The longer the time, the better the preparations to meet it, its prevention and defense against it will be.

Effectiveness is also measured in terms of clarity, that is, the ability to identify with a high degree of certainty the intention to carry out a hostile attack and the concrete actions that will be taken to realize it, alongside the ability to verify the information (a low level of "noise" and false alarms is unavoidable).

Every activity in the modern world, whether military or civilian, is accompanied by the emission of signals and signs indicating its nature, sort of a trail of electronic fingerprints. An effective intelligence warning system must include a series of rapid steps that will turn the signals into information with intelligence value. The faster the process and the more clear and reliable the product, the more effective the warning.

The technological components of a typical early warning system (in this case, virtual), without defining it or entering into technical specifications, are hi-tech SIGINT (signals intelligence) and VISINT (visual intelligence), which bear most of the early warning collection burden.

Intelligence Target Accessibility and Signal Acquisition

The proximity of the detectors to the targets and good accessibility are vital for early warning. The better the accessibility, the earlier the warning and the longer the time available in which to respond. High-level targets, the upper echelons and decision makers, are usually distanced, protected and concealed. Technological accessibility to the target often serves as a better, less dangerous alternative than military action.

During the first years of the State of Israel, most of its intelligence collection and early warning was based on HUMINT, i.e., intelligence agents and operatives, and on SIGINT technology from the First and Second World Wars that had been used before the establishment of the state.

The agent's human capabilities and resourcefulness, in addition to basic tools like binoculars, a miniature camera, code, radio transmitter – and in the 1950s even simple recording devices – dictated, to a great extent, his or her ability to collect information and the ability of the intelligence community to provide early warnings. The possibilities of approaching a target to collect information were limited. Information was transmitted slowly, the process was complex and involved risks, and sometimes arrived late. Not much of it was evaluated and reached the decision makers, and some of it was inaccurate.

Uri Ilan, who was captured by the Syrians in the 1950s and who committed suicide, and Eli Cohen, who was hanged by the Syrians in the 1960s, are examples of the collection and early warning of those years, and of their limitations.

On December 8, 1954, Uri Ilan and three other soldiers were sent to deal with a phone-tapping device in the Golan Heights, then part of Syria. They were captured by the Syrian army and imprisoned. On January 13, 1955, Uri Ilan hanged himself after being tortured during interrogation. Before he died he hid notes in his clothing, and one between his toes reading "*Lo bagadti*," Hebrew for "I did not betray." His body was returned to Israel the following day. The auto-destruct mechanism failed to detonate, and the device fell into Syrian hands.

Major Eli Cohen was born in Egypt, immigrated to Israel in 1957 and worked as an Arabic translator for IDI. In 1960 he was recruited by the Mossad, trained and sent to Argentina, where he acquired a false identity, becoming a Syrian exile named Camil Amin. At the beginning of 1962 he went to Damascus where he rented an apartment from which he sent radio messages to the Mossad in Tel Aviv. Thanks to his efforts, between 1962–1965 Israel knew of events occurring in the upper political and military echelons of Syria. Early in 1965, as he was sending a transmission, he was captured by the Syrian security forces. Israel made a superhuman effort to save his life, to no avail. Accused of spying for Israel and sentenced to death, he was hanged on May 18, 1965, in the main square of Damascus in the middle of the night.

Operating HUMINT behind enemy lines continues today, but its status and participation in collecting intelligence for early warning purposes, with the concomitant high risks, have been curtailed to a great degree. At the end of the 1960s, and especially after the Yom Kippur

War (1973), the approach changed. The emphasis shifted to early warning systems based on SIGINT and VISINT, which operate on advanced, cutting-edge detection technologies with a variety of stationary, airborne and satellite platforms.

Smart, sensitive SIGINT systems for receiving and acquiring signals with rapid reaction time were developed, enabling high-quality access to targets. They work around the clock and adapt themselves to changes in communications and signals, and are located both in Israel and other locations. In general, the activity is carried out in electronic silence, receiving information but not detectable.

Similar developments were made for VISINT. Powerful electro-optic sensors were developed for all the relevant monitoring spectrums for various ranges, making it possible to detect physical changes within the threat zone and to provide high-quality identification, even with poor visibility, because of advanced imaging techniques for improving picture quality.

VISINT sensors can operate in almost any arena and in all weather conditions. Some of them are operated by humans, others from planes, including unmanned aerial vehicles both large and small, and still others from satellites, which cover the entire face of the globe, at high frequencies.

Search, Identification, Filtering and Classification

Modern acquisition systems operate at all relevant frequencies and in all directions. They comb and receive signals from a variety of frequencies, modulations and strengths. Modern systems are usually equipped with the ability to provide the primary identity of a signal's source, and after it has been filtered and initially classified, it is transferred to the production and analysis division. In the era of the information highway, the initial processes of identification, filtering and classification are necessary to deal with one of the main problems of intelligence: information dissemination. Modern civilization emits a wealth of various types of signals in peacetime, and more so in war. Identification, filtering and classification thus have to be automatic and are computerized. Human intervention focuses primarily on controlling and monitoring the system. Only in exceptional cases is there human intervention in the process itself.

Producing Information and Turning It into Intelligence

Information which has been indentified, filtered and categorized, and then quickly verified (according to other sources, if possible), becomes a report that is circulated to the clients for whom it is relevant and to evaluating bodies. A significant amount of information, especially but not exclusively, comes from ELINT, VISINT and the Internet, and is processed by computers.

Conveying Information

The rapid, exact transfer of information to the final client is necessary for early warning and wartime intelligence because decisions have to be made as quickly as possible, usually within a time frame dictated by events on the ground.

Modern technology and communications make it possible to transfer almost any type of encrypted information in almost unlimited quantities to any place on earth, almost in real time. The Achilles' heel is the human element, that is, the ability to digest the information, interpret it and translate it into a decision.

The lack of appropriate technology was not responsible for the fact that relevant information was not transmitted to some of the fighting units during the Second Lebanon War. Human failure in the chain of information management was responsible: the intelligence was not provided to the correct client in the correct location at the correct time.

Tailoring Intelligence Systems

Modern intelligence systems cannot be found on shelves in stores. They have to be tailored to the target, their operational conditions and the system for accessing them. Those used by the State of Israel today are designed by the Israeli intelligence community, intelligence clients, operatives, engineers and scientists. Those systems that are developed and constructed by commercial companies are supported by project directors and technical teams dealing with the development of their smart components and systems integrations. Systems intended to solve special problems of accessibility and required to operate under special conditions are developed and constructed within the technological units. As far as technical reliability and duration of use are concerned, the structure of the systems is very reliable and they can operate for many years; they include various backup options and energy supplies that will last their entire lives.

Intelligence and Technological Achievements

It has already been noted that only intelligence failures become known. Successes are never mentioned, and the fruits are plucked in secret. Only infrequently is the curtain pulled aside, and even then, only after decades when the incident has historical value or serves to preserve the legacy. With no other way of measuring success and achievement, one can only note the dozens of times technological teams in intelligence units have won the Eliahu Golomb Israel Defense Prize, named for the founder of the Haganah and presented by the President of the State of Israel for the development of technological systems and solutions which proved themselves under operational conditions and contributed to national security. The intelligence units have won the prize more than any other body in the country. Many teams have also won the Colonel Uzi Yairi Memorial Award for Creative Thinking, but the content of their thinking cannot be revealed.

The Israeli intelligence community has shown it has better capabilities than its adversaries. Israel works hard to preserve its edge, because intelligence superiority is an important factor in the strength of its defense.

The Human Factor

The Israeli intelligence community, which deals with the development of technological and operational ways and means, is blessed with Israel's best men and women of science and technology. In its ranks serve the best engineers and scientists produced by the country's academic institutions, most of them after additional academic training abroad and experience in advanced industry. The best of the academic community serve in the reserves or as consultants to the intelligence community, and are available at all times.

The fields required for technology in the service of intelligence are many and include mathematics, physics, chemistry, biology, botany, zoology, astronomy, computers, mechanics, materials and more. As previously noted, the heart of intelligence is people, with their knowledge, will, dedication, creativity, initiative and resourcefulness, who make the impossible possible.

An Important Addendum

The human contribution to intelligence does not end with the country's defense. Former members of the technological units are the most important moving force behind the amazing development of the hi-tech industry and startup companies, which now number in the thousands and lead Israel's economic growth. The skills and knowledge they acquired in the service of intelligence have been used to make important contributions to Israel and its society.

SIGINT in the Service of Intelligence

Brigadier General (Res.) Hanan Geffen
Former Commander of the IDI's SIGINT Unit (Unit 8200)

SIGINT – intelligence derived from communications, electronic, and foreign instrumentation signals – has been a unique source of intelligence for more than forty years. Its ability to follow targets simultaneously in far-distant locations is what makes it possible to create a dynamic picture of adversaries.

After the Yom Kippur War, SIGINT became a synonym for early warning, providing information to compensate for Israel's lack of strategic depth. In recent years it has acquired the ability to give focused tactical warning, especially in the Palestinian arena.

SIGINT has come a long way from the modest corner it occupied during Israel's early years. The SIGINT unit, which at first only occasionally supported military and political activity, although its achievements were surprising, developed into a body that participated in important security processes and the operational activity of the IDF and security services, both routinely and in times of emergency. During the sixty years since the establishment of the State of Israel, SIGINT has undergone many changes and even revolutions, if not in its methods then in its results. Changes in the SIGINT unit were usually caused by external events that gave birth to new intelligence requirements or exposed conspicuous weakness in the unit. The need for and ability to change are evolving components of its DNA, and it can function even as changes occur. The ability to innovate is one reason why the former members of Unit 8200 who have entered the civilian and industrial sectors are known as creative, visionary initiators.

Despite its impressive long-term achievements, however, SIGINT's abilities waned in one important field. The unit's founders were fluent in Arabic, had intimate knowledge of the culture of the Arab countries and fully understood the nuances accompanying the adversaries' discourse and dialects. The generations that followed worked hard to maintain the level, a Sisyphean struggle for those born in the Hebrew-speaking State of Israel.

The Duality of SIGINT

SIGINT in Israel gained its extraordinary capabilities by virtue of its long-term incorporation of two important disciplines: technology and intelligence. The personnel, education and mindsets of the two are different, and their combination is the secret of SIGINT's success.

The great leap forward in technology in the past thirty years, the changes in communications systems and their place in daily life, opened new worlds of opportunity for SIGINT personnel. The technological creativity that characterized Unit 8200 and its partners in the intelligence community enabled the SIGINT staff to reach distant goals. However, the connection between technology and intelligence is not self-evident, and necessitates an ongoing dialogue between them.

History and Development of SIGINT

The War of Independence (1948) to the Six-Day War (1967)
During these years, the unit functioned as a COMINT (communications intelligence, intelligence between people) unit, keeping a low profile while it accompanied political and military activity, such as reprisals. The unit was one of the first in IDI to learn the lessons of the great intelligence surprise in February 1960, when the Egypt army entered the Sinai Peninsula (Operation Rotem). However, the accomplishment that won world renown was the interception of a conversation between Egypt's Gamal Abdel Nasser and Jordan's King Hussein on the second

day of the Six-Day War. It was a crowning achievement and revealed SIGINT's capabilities and its place in the intelligence community.

The War of Attrition (1969–1970) and the Yom Kippur War (1973)

The unit was enlarged, new bases were built on captured land, technological and conceptual changes were made, and for the first time, because of the Soviet presence in the Middle East, the unit found itself confronting the communications system of a superpower. The new field was an invitation to technological and intelligence cooperation with friendly intelligence services around the world. New areas of operation were also developed, such as a system for dealing with Soviet communications and an ELINT (electronic intelligence) system, making 8200 a full SIGINT unit that incorporated COMINT and ELINT.

The Years after the Yom Kippur War (1973)

Implementing the lessons learned from the failure to warn of the Yom Kippur War, the unit was reorganized, expanded and made more professional. Formal theoretical material was written and procedures were updated to emphasize early warning. It was more clearly understood that maintaining SIGINT capabilities for early warning also necessitated investing in training the staff. Selection was improved and early locating of candidates was broadened. Professional training was increased, service courses were planned and a large budget was invested in equipment and infrastructure.

After the Peace Agreement with Egypt (1978)

As part of the new deployment and with the evacuation of its bases in Sinai, the unit received cutting-edge technology and learned innovative collection systems that advanced its capabilities. Teams of unit operatives studied abroad, learning how to conduct complex projects, assimilate a system and continue developing it. Various aspects of the unit were radically altered, and we enjoy the results to this day.

The Global War on Terrorism

The terrorism in the Gaza Strip, Judea, Samaria and around the world, which has become one of Israeli intelligence's main objectives, required SIGINT to adapt itself to new, complex missions. The First Lebanon War (1982) and Israel's protracted stay in the country provided the unit with the challenge of dealing with tactical targets and even necessitated a closer connection with clients in the field. The September 11, 2001, attack on the World Trade Center in New York increased intelligence cooperation with friendly countries that wanted to learn from the unit's experience and high professional level.

In the past three decades SIGINT, like other intelligence community systems, has had to deal with threats to Israel's existence, and has continually been in the process of improving its capabilities in that respect.

After the Oslo Accords (1993–1995)

SIGINT deployed for the new situation in the Gaza Strip, Judea and Samaria beyond the ISA's ongoing basic coverage. In addition, intensive collaboration was established between the ISA and Unit 8200, which proved fertile. Many of the unit's personnel were transferred to dealing with the new target at the expense of their traditional roles. Differences of opinion accompanied the process as to the resources to be invested in the war on terrorism, in view of the need to maintain early warning capabilities for the Arab armies. Fighting terrorism in the Gaza Strip, Judea and Samaria brought new methods for providing intelligence directly to the forces fighting on the ground.

SIGINT Branches

Radio

For the most part, before the Six-Day War the unit was made up of a hard core of native Arabic speakers, but as the years passed their numbers declined. Until the end of the 1980s the unit gave pre-recruitment courses in radio transmissions to reinforce the language abilities of potential security-force soldiers whose parents spoke Arabic and who had heard it at home. However, eventually that reservoir dried up as well. In view of the growing need and the lack of suitable candidates, new selection and training methods were developed, which made it possible to train soldiers for the necessary tasks within a short time. The role of wireless operator, which during the first years meant listening, understanding and translating at the same time, was later divided into three separate roles.

Processing

After the Yom Kippur War processing was both compartmentalized and professionalized. The members of the unit improved their ability to process and analyze the adversary, and became active partners in intelligence production and analysis. For language translation and analysis, a foundation of modern, comprehensive, professional lexicons was painstakingly constructed. Using the tools provided, the unit managed to acquire some of the knowledge and language sensitivity that characterized the founding generation. Today that knowledge belongs to the entire intelligence community, and preserves the high quality of the SIGINT product.

Technology and Computers

Over the years the members of the unit's technological staff contributed their innovations and high operational capabilities. From the beginning they searched for shortcuts, technology and new ways and means. Generations of soldiers whose enlistment was deferred until they finished their studies, graduating from the Technion (the Israel Institute of Technology) and other technological institutions, brought with them new information and a fresh point of view. Once they were demobilized they took their experience and readiness to innovate into civilian life. Many aspects of technology that are in common use today, such as Internet search engines, were used by the unit many years ago.

The primary mission of the technological unit in 8200 is to be fully competent at all time, despite the fact that it is complex, constantly expanding and spread over all of Israel.

Securing Sources

SIGINT's greatest limitation is its sensitivity, because the incautious use of information is liable to have destructive results. For example, exposing the conversation between the president of Egypt and the king of Jordan to the general public to refute Nasser's claims did long-term damage to the state. Secrets that were leaked from interrogations of our prisoners in the Yom Kippur War toppled important systems many years later. Operational activities as well, based on intelligence information, are liable to expose to the adversary the extent of our knowledge. The daily war on terrorism constantly wears out information sources and makes it necessary to find new ones.

Although most of those dealing with SIGINT are young men and women soldiers in the conscript army, whose short service exposes them to sensitive, secret information, the unit's secrets are not revealed. The turnover is great, enlarging the number of people with knowledge of the secrets, but the unit's internal code and the soldiers' effective training have made them understand how great the responsibility is which rests on their shoulders, an understanding that accompanies them for the rest of their lives. The unit's soldiers, even the lowest ranks, understand the importance of not revealing what they know to the media. Sometimes, because of the limitations imposed by the censors, they discover that other units have won the laurels, but they learn to dismiss the ordinary human need for praise. In that respect they are perhaps different from other Israelis.

HUMINT in the Service of Intelligence

Shmuel Goren

Former Head of the HUMINT Units of IDI and the Mossad

HUMINT in the Bible

Human intelligence, or HUMINT, is as old as mankind. That can easily be seen in the story of the conquest of Israel after the exodus from Egypt, where Moses was the first person to employ spies. He chose twelve leaders and sent them to spy out the land, telling them to "see the land and what it is, and the people who dwell therein, whether they be strong or weak, few or many. And what the land is that they dwell in, whether it be good or bad; and what cities they be that they dwell in, whether in tents, or in strongholds. And what the land is, whether it be fat or lean, whether there be wood therein, or not..."(Numbers 13:18–20). They returned with the fruit of the land, "one cluster of grapes, and they bore it between them, two upon a staff" (Numbers 13:23). Not by chance is that the insignia of one of the collection units today.

Later, Joshua, who had the practical mission of conquering Jericho, sent "two men to spy secretly, saying, 'Go view the land, even Jericho...'" (Joshua 2:1). The two went to Jericho to the house of Rahab, who sheltered them and gave them information, becoming the first collaborator in history. In both instances we can see HUMINT in action, even as it is used today: determining intelligence priorities, location, recruitment, dispatch, investigation and report.

HUMINT in Israeli Intelligence

During the first years of the state, intelligence, especially HUMINT, was based on the legacy of the Haganah's intelligence service and other groups that operated before Israel was established. As the years passed, the need to deal with various wars and continuing terrorism made it necessary to construct a culture of information collection unique to Israeli intelligence, and part of it was HUMINT. Its task has been to provide immediate intelligence on a daily basis, in situations fraught with tension and in the ongoing struggle against terrorism.

The physical proximity of the enemy, constant tension and ever-changing circumstances created the necessity for continuous intelligence activity, as detailed as possible, for routine collection, along with the most effective exploitation of technological developments adapted to the demands of varied coverage. In Israel's sixty years, HUMINT has become part of its intelligence deployment and an important partner in all its battles, and even unique in certain fields. The late Major General Aharon Yariv, who was IDI head, said "HUMINT is queen of the intelligence battlefield."

It would be a mistake to fix an order of priorities for collection. Each branch covers certain fields, sometimes even exclusively, and that includes HUMINT. Cooperation between various branches of the intelligence community is necessary for the performance of its missions.

HUMINT on the Israeli Collection Coverage Map

Examples abound of the role played by HUMINT on the coverage map. Before the Yom Kippur War warnings were given, and during the battles in the Sinai Peninsula vital information was received from a HUMINT agent. As a result, the general staff and southern command changed the IDF's combat tactics, inflicting grave losses on the enemy and vastly improving the situation on the front.

Throughout the history of the State of Israel, HUMINT has been a vital tool in the fight against terrorism, both in Israel and abroad. The fight could not be fought without it, whether in exposing and preventing planned terrorist attacks, or in various other types of prevention. There were several instances in which serious terrorist activities involving El Al planes and Israeli ships and installations were prevented. Some of them were made public, but fortunately most of them were not.

Unfortunately, there have also been several instances in which intelligence and HUMINT were unsuccessful: Munich, Argentina, Sinai, and terrorism on both sides of the Green Line. All those cases have made it critical to study and learn the necessary lessons.

HUMINT in the World Today

According to foreign sources, American and European intelligence have recently realized the importance of HUMINT, especially in the war on terrorism. It can be assumed that two of the case studies were Saddam Hussein and Osama bin Laden:

- After Baghdad fell in April 2003, Saddam Hussein escaped and hid in a cave. Although technological and other efforts were made to find him, he was finally exposed and detained in December 2003, following a HUMINT report.
- Osama bin Laden was number one on the wanted list since the September 11, 2001, attacks. Enormous efforts were invested in searching for him, and without a doubt HUMINT assisted in successfully locating him.

What Does It Take to Be a Case Officer?

The basic requirements for HUMINT have not undergone fundamental changes. The HUMINT case officer needs an ability for pretense, careful thought and improvisation. He – or she – must be composed, reliable, creative and above all, have a talent for exploiting potential and chance occurrences. The case officer must be discrete and know how to keep secrets, unfortunately a quality not found in great abundance today. Intelligence personnel, including senior members of the community, must know that secret activities should not be discussed with the media. Doing so sets a bad personal example and damages national security. Intelligence personnel should remember that the sensitive information to which they are privy is a national deposit that they should keep to themselves, and not use it in any way.

The Current Situation and a Look to the Future

Technological development and changes in and additions to intelligence priorities all make it vital to adapt HUMINT's structure and work force to new circumstances. For example, new places and targets have appeared on the intelligence map, new languages and technologies must be learned and combat doctrine has to be updated.

The intelligence system and HUMINT within it know how to exploit the developments, changes and new circumstances and to formulate the necessary tools and find the manpower. Lessons are learned from mishaps, and they do occur. Those who serve in the HUMINT system are very carefully chosen, know how to deal with challenges and have impressive achievements. We can all be proud of them.

If an agent is to be handled effectively, there is no way of avoiding both personal and security risks to the case officer, especially if the agent deals with terrorism. To our great sorrow, over the years a number of case officers have been killed during Israel Security Agency operations, both in Israel and abroad. This short article is dedicated to their memory.

The Unique Nature of HUMINT

Avner Barnea
Former Senior ISA Member

What Is HUMINT?

HUMINT, human intelligence, is the oldest secret collection activity in history. It is variously defined, but is generally considered a category of intelligence derived from information collected and provided by human sources. It is set apart from other forms of intelligence by the agent's ability to penetrate the decision-making center of an enemy or adversary, whether at various levels of the political and/or military upper echelons of a country or a terrorist organization, or even the nerve center of a terrorist squad, and to bring back information about their intentions along with personal insights.

The basic principles of HUMINT are the following:

- A human source is handled and communicated with secretly.
- A continuing personal connection exists between the intelligence agent and the human source, and it is developed to improve the source's access to sensitive information while guarding his safety.
- Regular meetings are held between handler and source. While information may be transmitted by various clandestine means, meetings still have to be periodically held.
- Since some of the sources are hostile to the country handling them, it is particularly important to conduct regular loyalty and reliability checks.

This article deals with HUMINT as defined above (and not with agents operating behind enemy lines or in target countries, such as Eli Cohen in Syria), and its aim is to present the HUMINT aspect of Israeli intelligence, and its unique nature and challenges. We will begin, however, with a short survey of HUMINT in modern times.

HUMINT in Modern Times

HUMINT in modern times can be divided into four major periods:

World War I and Formalization

At the beginning of the twentieth century, intelligence activity became legitimized. Professional organizations were founded and a distinction was made between diplomacy and intelligence. In 1909 the British established its Secret Service Bureau, which became the Directorate of Military Intelligence Section 6 (MI6) when World War I broke out. MI6 fixed professional working procedures, such as training its members and recruiting and handling agents.

World War I provided the impetus that turned HUMINT into a formal institution, and the process continued after the armistice. During that period HUMINT made a major contribution, especially in military matters. The Yishuv (the Jewish settlement in the Land of Israel before the establishment of the state) was involved in the British war effort when Nili (a pro-British Jewish espionage organization) provided information about Turkish military forces.

After the war intelligence dealt with a broader range of topics, not only military and combat information but internal political, economic and strategic issues, and the distinction between military and civilian intelligence organizations became more defined. At that point disciplines were established for the main activities of intelligence collection: analysis, evaluation and circulation to relevant parties, including upper government echelons.

World War II as a Turning Point

During World War II there was an enormous amount of HUMINT activity, and there are many classic examples that entered intelligence history. They include the Red Orchestra, a network of agents deployed throughout most of Europe, run by Soviet intelligence and providing excellent military intelligence as well as information about Hitler's intentions. It was headed by Leopold Trepper, who died in Jerusalem in 1982. Other examples include Britain's double agents, who helped fool the Germans about the time and place of the Allied invasion of Europe; the network headed by Richard Sorge, a German correspondent stationed in Japan who worked for Soviet intelligence in the Far East for many years and reported the German invasion of Russia; and the activities of the American OSS (Office of Strategic Services) throughout Europe, including running sources inside Nazi Germany. One of the greatest intelligence successes was the British cracking of the codes generated by the German Enigma machine, which began with information provided to British intelligence by a Polish agent.

The extensive use of HUMINT also exposed its fundamental problems. For example, an agent known as "Cicero," the personal servant of the British ambassador to Ankara, was run by a diplomat in the German embassy. In 1943 Cicero delivered information about military operations the Allies were about to undertake against the Germans, including the planned invasion of Normandy. The Germans failed to make use of the information because they suspected it was false.

The Cold War

Toward the end of and after World War II, the Soviet Union was informed of the nuclear secrets of the United States, shortening the time it needed to develop its own nuclear weapon. That was the result of the efforts of agents who believed in Communist ideology and who had been recruited by Russia. One of the best assets of Soviet intelligence was Kim Philby, a member of the British intelligence community who defected to the Soviet Union in 1963.

At the end of World War II it was obvious that in view of the limitations of human agents, especially in closed, suspicious countries, efforts had to be invested in developing capabilities to complement HUMINT, especially new technological tools. The confrontation during the Cold War was a symmetrical competition between political superpowers that invested enormous resources in technological intelligence to gain an advantage over one another.

In 1947 the American CIA was established, directed by Allen Dulles, a great believer in HUMINT. However, the United States was disappointed by HUMINT's capabilities when in 1962 the first information about Soviet intentions to station long-range missiles in Cuba came from pictures taken by an over-flight and not from agents inside the country. One of the CIA's low points was in the 1970s, when its director, Admiral Stansfield Turner, decided to make drastic cuts in the agency's HUMINT investment and fired most of the employees who had specialized in Soviet intelligence. The United States would need years to recover from the consequences.

The Collapse of the Soviet Union and the
Era of the Twin Towers Terrorism

The collapse of the Soviet Union at the beginning of the 1990s and the terrorist attacks of September 11, 2001, were turning points. Without making light of the importance of technological intelligence, there was an increase in the relative importance of HUMINT to confront radical Islamic terrorist organizations deployed over the face of the globe, belonging to no country, closed, compartmentalized and concealed.

HUMINT in Israeli Intelligence

Most of the intelligence activity before the establishment of the state was HUMINT. The members of Shai and the Palmach's Arab division ran agents within the Arab population to discover plans to attack the Yishuv. The activity was made possible by the free passage existing through the area, knowledge of Arabic and Arab culture and the agents' skills. After the establishment of the state new intelligence frameworks were devised. As far as HUMINT was concerned, with slight changes, the framework has remained the same for sixty years: Israel Defense Intelligence is responsible for activity beyond the borders of the State of Israel (by means of what is known today as Unit 504), the Israel Security Agency is responsible for preventive intelligence within the borders of the state and the Mossad is responsible for activity abroad.

Difficulties and Challenges

In general, Israel's HUMINT has to cope with a series of difficulties and challenges, some of them characteristic of intelligence services in general, some of them unique to Israel.

- A multitude of threats: While many other countries have only one main enemy, Israel faces a variety of threats from several countries, near and far, and from terrorist organizations. That necessitates a broad HUMINT deployment, early warning of war (which is at the center of intelligence priorities), and focusing on HUMINT capable of penetrating the planning ranks, both tactical and strategic, of all the countries and organizations threatening the state.

- Target enemy countries that are closed to Israel: There are many countries that can deploy their HUMINT resources through diplomatic missions in the target country, but that is a luxury unavailable to Israel. Isolation and the difficulties of operating in Arab countries led Israel to adopt global intelligence tactics, establishing bases in third countries from which the Mossad could work in enemy territory.

- Recruitment problems: The hostility toward Israel of the citizens of the target countries make it difficult to recruit and run sources. The conditions in those countries endanger lives, demand a high level of awareness and necessitate the development of tools to examine the motives of potential agents and their readiness to cooperate. There were cases of agents who betrayed and even harmed their handlers, both in Israel and abroad. In 1972 in Madrid, Mossad agent Baruch Cohen was shot by his Palestinian handler. In 1981 a Palestinian agent killed Moshe Golan, his ISA handler. There were also sources who carried out terrorist attacks in Israel to save their reputations and those of their families.

- Danger and rehabilitation: The danger to agents, should they be exposed, requires a serious investment in preserving the secrecy of the connections. When there is no personal connection with an agent, evaluating his reliability and the risk he might pose to Israeli security becomes difficult. His cover story has to be creative, and the right opportunity to get potential and active agents out of target countries has to be exploited. Agents who worked for Israel and were exposed were executed or sentenced to particularly long prison terms. Priority is devoted to rehabilitating sources in Israel or other locations.

- The short geographical distances: As far as the Palestinians are concerned, the geographical distance and control of the territory are great advantages, but at the same time present a problem in that the operative use of intelligence information risks exposing the agent. For example, if after a source has provided information about a potential attack roadblocks are set up and concrete warnings are given, the terrorist organization will understand that its plans have been leaked and will conduct an internal investigation, which might expose the source.

Sources of Strength

- Close cooperation among HUMINT branches: As opposed to many other countries, there is no intense rivalry between the various intelligence branches. For example, in 1967 Israeli intelligence blindsided Egypt, leading to the IDF's swift victory in the Six-Day War. The operation was conducted by an ISA agent in collaboration with IDI. The agent was an Egyptian citizen who had been given the identity of an Egyptian-born Jew and planted in Israel by Egyptian intelligence. After his exposure he was turned and for many years worked as a double agent in the service of Israel. He convinced the Egyptians that the Israeli air force was not deployed for a preventive attack against the Egyptian air force, paving the way for Israel's surprise attack, which destroyed the Egyptians planes on the ground on the morning of June 6, 1967.

- Sacrifice and involvement with the target: Since the Six-Day War and with the growth of Palestinian terrorism, the ISA has moved to the forefront of the counterterrorism struggle. From its inception, HUMINT was the ISA's most important asset. Control over the territories, the family connections between Israeli Arabs and Arabs living on the other side of the Green Line and their entrance into Israeli territory aided in recruiting and running live sources, leading to the prevention of a large number of terrorist attacks both in Israel and abroad. The increase in Palestinian terrorism, deployed for action only a short distance from Israel (especially at the end of the 1990s), led to an improvement in operating HUMINT and close collaboration between intelligence branches and IDF units to effect the immediate prevention of attacks in Israel. One of Israel's conspicuous advantages in fighting Palestinian terrorism is that the agent is usually in an area controlled by Israel or very close to it, even if he leaves for target countries for short periods of time. That facilitates contact with him and aid in case of a security danger. The care for agents even after they are no longer active is a fundamental principle which has been preserved for years.

- Success: Israeli intelligence successes have enhanced its reputation and reinforced its deterrent capabilities, making it difficult to take action against it. That makes its agents feel secure, helps in recruiting and running agents and in initiating contacts with the residents of target countries. One example is a top-level Egyptian who of his own volition volunteered to act as an agent in 1969. He provided excellent strategic information about Egypt, including a detailed early warning in 1973 of the Egyptian intentions fourteen hours before the attack, and a general warning more than twenty-four hours before that.

- The high quality of the handlers: Throughout the years, all the organizations – the ISA, the Mossad and IDI – have devoted a great deal of attention to ensuring the high quality of the handlers who run the agents. They are highly motivated and receive intensive training in the language, society and culture of enemy countries, as well as in various intelligence fields.

- Cooperation with other countries: Israel's experience, especially in intelligence warfare against terrorism, has contributed to solidifying relations with friendly intelligence services, especially since the increase of international Islamic terrorism. Those relations also contribute to joint HUMINT operations.

Conclusion

Israel's intelligence collection has become more difficult and complex than in the past. Some of the most important targets are closed both ideologically and physically, geographically distant, compartmentalized, closely supervised, demonstratively unyielding and deterringly cruel.

During its sixty years as a state and even before, Israeli intelligence gained a great amount of experience in HUMINT. However, there were periods when it did not receive the priority it should have from some of the intelligence branches. In 2004 the Knesset's Foreign Affairs and Defense Committee appointed a committee to examine intelligence following the war in Iraq. Its mandate was to make recommendations following the failure of the intelligence community to correctly evaluate the presence of Iraq's surface-to-surface missiles and nonconventional weapons in the months before the war. The committee issued a report, one section of which noted that the war in Iraq had shown that despite the technological breakthroughs of the previous ten years and the impressive developments in communications, computerization, electro-optics and space, which gave espionage services effective tools to carry out the work of collection, it was clear that technology was not the most essential element and could not provide a full collection response. The committee found that in the ten years preceding the war, much attention and many resources had been invested in developing and exploiting new means and methods possibly at the expense of quality human intelligence.

One Last Remark

High-quality HUMINT has no replacement. Even today it is important and is well integrated into technological information sources for the sake of achieving national goals.

For further information see:

- Aldrich, Richard J. *British Intelligence, Strategy and the Cold War, 1945–51*. New York: Routledge, 1992.
- Goodman, Allan E. and Bruce D. Berkowitz. *The Need to Know: The Report of the Twentieth Century Fund Task Force Report on Covert Action and American Democracy*. New York: Twentieth Century Fund Press, 1992.

- Richelson, J. *The US Intelligence Community*. Boulder, CO: Westview Press, 2007.
- Richelson, J. *A Century of Spies: Intelligence in the Twentieth Century*. New York: Oxford University Press, 1997.
- Shulsky, A. and G. Schmitt. *Silent Warfare: Understanding the World of Intelligence*. Dulles, VA: Potomac Books, Inc., 2002.
- Wright, Peter. *Spycatcher: The Autobiography of a Senior Intelligence Officer*. Toronto: Stoddart Publishing, 1987.
- https://www.cia.gov/library/center-for-the-study-of-intelligence/kent-csi/subjectII.htm
- http://www.fas.org/irp/threat/khobar_af/part2ae.htm
- http://usmilitary.about.com/od/glossarytermsh/g/h2941.htm
- http://mosad.gov.il/About/Dictionary.aspx
- http://www.mi6.gov.uk/output/Page59.html
- http://www.nationalarchives.gov.uk
- http://www.shabak.gov.il
- https://www.cia.gov

OSINT in the Service of Intelligence

Colonel Shay Shabtai
Senior IDI Officer

Introduction: From Poetry Anthologies to Computer Files

Israeli poet Haim Guri tells the following story:

> In December 1977 I visited Egypt for the first time with a delega-
> tion of Israeli correspondents who went to Cairo after Sadat came
> to Jerusalem. I met the famous Egyptian painter Dr. El-Hussein
> Fawzi,[1] and we talked about the Israeli-Egyptian wars. He said
> that the Egyptian attack on Israel in 1948 was a historic crime,
> and then he said something I will never forget. He said, "In the
> Six-Day War you humiliated us. Our wives scorned us, our chil-
> dren mocked us. If Israeli intelligence had read the Egyptian po-
> etry written after '67, it would have known that October '73 was
> unavoidable." Every good intelligence officer has to read poetry,
> and ours didn't....[2]

In other words, an intelligence officer has to understand the culture of
the target country. A thorough understanding of the intentions and

---

1. El-Hussein Fawzi, 1905–1999, was known in Egypt and the Middle East for
    his pioneering work in the field of journalistic graphic arts and for designing
    some of Nobel Prize winner Nagib Mahfouz's books.

2. Interview by Shiri Levari, "Intelligence Officer Must Read Poetry," *Ha'aretz*,
    October 1, 2006.

even actions of an adversary does not come only from monitoring his modus operandi. It is also necessary to monitor the cultural, social and ideological norms of his environment. That is a recurring motif in analyses of almost all Israel's main intelligence failures, and manifested itself as a severe blow after the failure of intelligence to warn of the Yom Kippur War in 1973; for example, knowledge of the extraordinary instruction given to the Egyptian army to eat during the Ramadan fast did not clearly tip the scales in favor of a warning.

However, the poet was making another point. He was expressing his hope that a careful examination of overt, easily accessible enemy information would make it possible for intelligence analysts to uncover the enemy's hidden intentions, including a strategic surprise attack kept secret within the limited circle of decision makers.

That aspiration, which in the 1970s seemed impossible to realize, now seems closer than ever. In the past several decades the world has undergone an information revolution. It was based on technological breakthroughs that made it instantly possible to create and absorb information, to transmit and store it. Today the world overflows with enormous quantities of information that anyone with a computer can access from anywhere in the world, regardless of geographical borders and physical distance.

The change in the political climate in the two decades since the end of the Cold War has also had its influence. Only countries that are technologically backward or politically closed (North Korea, for example) are not connected to the Internet, but they pay a high economic, societal and political price for it, which turns their chosen isolation into weakness.

Our adversaries – Al-Qaeda, Iran and its terrorist network, terrorist and guerilla organizations, the crime and drug barons – expose themselves, either deliberately or of necessity, on the Internet. In addition, oppressive, dictatorial regimes find it hard to silence protest when the protestors use information technology. Videos are shot in the street using cell phones and are uploaded directly onto the Internet and become public property. They define the protests against the government and make it possible to see what is happening behind the closed doors of such regimes; for example, the video documenting the death of Neda Sultan became the symbol of the Green Movement in Iran.

This article will deal with the integration of information from open sources into intelligence work and will describe five circles in which open, easily available information is part of constructing the intelligence picture. It will also analyze the advantages and limitations of open source intelligence (OSINT), show how Israeli intelligence deals with it and try to predict OSINT's future.

The Definition of OSINT and the Concept of the Five Spheres

The world we live in takes us ever closer to the poet's vision that intelligence will penetrate the enemy's secrets through the use of open source information. During the Cold War it required tens and even hundreds of thousands of "James Bonds" around the world to fill gaps in intelligence; today, a large part of these gaps can be filled using the Internet. Using readily available information for intelligence purposes is known as open source intelligence, or OSINT.

What exactly is OSINT? According to current definitions:[3]

- It is the management of intelligence collection, translation, processing, production and analysis of information which is publicly available at the relevant time and as a response to the priority intelligence requirements of the intelligence client.

---

3. Including the Wikipedia definition of OSINT; Richard A. Best, Jr. and Alfred Cumming, *Open Source Intelligence (OSINT): Issues for Congress*, CRS Report for Congress, Congressional Research Service, December 5, 2007; and Robert David Steele, "Open Source Intelligence," in Loch Johnson, ed., *Handbook of Intelligence Studies* (New York: Routledge, 2007), ch. 10, pp. 129–47.

- It requires an investment of resources (there are fees for some access), of working time (for mining data, sometimes in far-flung areas of the public space) and sometimes even of collection efforts (purchasing publications in the target countries).
- It is based on a deep awareness of the enemy's culture and an understanding of the overt information, making it possible to locate information and give a primary evaluation based on an analysis of the sources.

Today OSINT is part of the general intelligence effort in five circles (from outer to inner):

- The story: A survey of the major developments in the public sphere.
- Behind the story: Information that makes it possible to analyze the intentions of the object under consideration and explain its actions.
- What cannot be concealed: Some information the enemy would prefer to keep to itself but which cannot be hidden because of political, societal and business reasons.
- What was leaked: The increase in the number of information channels enlarges the ability of the individual to expose and transmit, deliberately or not, information considered classified by his government or organization.
- Penetrating secrets: Within OSINT it is possible to find the leads necessary for developing other collection sources.

The Outer Circle: The Story

OSINT asks: Based on immediate media exposure, what's going on – what's new? Most of the time the information is based on and influenced by what has been made public in open sources.

The decision maker for whom the intelligence agencies work has to know what the day's agenda is. Intelligence experts estimate that between 80 and 90 percent of the information the decision maker needs is OSINT.[4] Crises – whether security, political, economic or even strategic – are the result of media headlines. In many instances, a development that a decision maker might choose to ignore if it remained secret, demands a response simply because it has been made public.

In such a case, the analysis of an issue as reflected in the media is a large part of intelligence work. In addition, the profusion of OSINT reports exposes the analysts to information that was unavailable to them previously because they were not physically present at the event, and it enables them to crosscheck various sources and arrive at an intelligence picture that faithfully represents the situation on the ground.

Today, anyone entering the command post of an army currently engaged in operational activity will see a television screen broadcasting updates from one of the international news channels or Internet stations. Often such sources provide the first exposure of important events as they occur in real time.

OSINT is important for constructing a comprehensive picture for the following reasons:

- The butterfly effect: Today the political, military and security picture provided by intelligence to the decision makers is influenced by other developments, especially economic (e.g., the main developments of the global financial crisis) and those occurring around the world (e.g., earthquakes that prompt large military assistance operations). The main channel for relevant information in those areas is OSINT.

- Broad scan: One of the tasks of intelligence today is to conduct a broad scan of the international arena to identify changes that might influence the relevant political and security picture. The changes may relate to military confrontations and terrorist

---

4. *Open Source Intelligence (OSINT): Issues for Congress*, p. 4.

activities (e.g., a new type of terrorist activity that might be copied by other organizations), the international approach to strategic and political issues (e.g., the political-legal approach to accusations of war crimes) or the development of new geostrategic conditions (e.g., détente between world powers or the development of new sources of energy).

- Monitoring fundamental changes: OSINT becomes particularly important when fundamental changes occur in the existing order (e.g. velvet revolutions, in which the general public brings about political change through open, non-violent protest). In such a situation covert sources of intelligence, SIGINT and HUMINT, lose their relevance because of their focus on the leaders of the previous order. Some of the new order comes into being through the media, and it is necessary to scan the media in depth to map the new elements of power.

- Open diplomacy: A significant amount of the activity of political and public systems takes place in the media through the transmission of messages between the sides. The messages can be verbal (e.g., official statements made by North Korea, which are considered relatively reliable) or practical (e.g., a unilateral decision to publicize advances in military technology or the holding of military exercises). A considerable amount of diplomatic fencing is explicitly public (e.g., the deliberations and resolutions of the UN Security Council and the reports of the International Atomic Energy Agency). A central part of today's military confrontations revolves around public diplomacy and open psychological warfare in the battle for the hearts and minds of the local population, as well as regional and international public opinion.

The Second Circle: Behind the Story

Another intelligence task is to understand the story behind the story. A considerable amount of the effort behind clandestine missions is devoted to discovering and interpreting the intentions of the enemy's decision makers. Quite a few hair-raising intelligence affairs are related to constructing and handling intelligence sources located deep within the enemy leadership.

OSINT makes it possible to find an indirect route to that inner domain. A serious reading of the leaders' public speeches and interviews can sometimes reveal their mindsets as well as can high-quality intelligence sources. Regardless of how good the means of collection are, it is impossible to acquire information about things a leader might not tell even his closest advisors, but they may slip out in an interview, especially if the questions have not been rehearsed.

Speaking publicly before his own people, a leader projects his worldview and ideology to gain support, at least the support of those loyal to him. In general, it is possible to learn what his intentions are, how he views the challenges and difficulties facing him and what the disagreements, achievements and internal arguments are in the upper echelons of the regime or organization. Thus, often a leader's true intentions can be discerned, at least those that are declared.

Examples are the speeches made by Egyptian President Anwar Sadat before the Yom Kippur War in 1973, in which he publicly stated that he intended, finally, to carry out an attack on Israel; the speeches of Saddam Hussein before the First Gulf War in 1991, in which he said he meant to attack Israel with missiles; and the public statements of Hezbollah leader Hassan Nasrallah throughout 2005, the year preceding the Second Lebanon War, regarding his intention to abduct IDF soldiers.

OSINT also makes it possible to view the leader in action and judge his health and mindset, and to identify his body language, especially when he is speaking publicly about sensitive issues. The ability to see the other side also provides an insight into the relative forces within the enemy's upper echelon, a method used by Western intelligence agencies every May 1 as they examined the arrangement of the Soviet leadership reviewing the military parade from the Kremlin walls. Today in Iran the relations among the heads of the regime can be calculated from their appearance or non-appearance and the seating arrangements during events (e.g., the absence of Akbar Hashemi Rafsanjani at many official functions in the second half of 2009).

OSINT has a conspicuous advantage in analyzing the stability of regimes, as it makes it possible to delve deeply into social trends, expose the societal, political and cultural movements that support or oppose a regime, and to evaluate their relative strengths and weaknesses vis-à-vis the monopoly of power in the regime's hands.

One of the historical problems in evaluating the stability of a regime has been that information received by Western intelligence communities is usually based on relations with the regime, for example, Iran before the Islamic revolution. The Shah's intelligence services broadcast messages of stability and a decrease in the strength of the opposition at a time when the West already sensed that something important was happening in the Shah's family. In the era of the information revolution, accessibility to open sources gives external intelligence communities the capability to monitor the calming messages usually emanating from a regime's security apparatuses.

The exposure to movies, poetry and literature of the target provides another level of understanding. One obvious example is watching or reading about Iranian cinema, which makes it easier to understand some of the main features of Iranian society. Another example is the book *The Yacoubian Building* by the Egyptian writer Alaa al-Aswany, which early on pointed the way to the strengthening of Egypt's democratic opposition between 2000 and 2005.

In some cases, internal and external public opinion surveys can be useful for sensing the general way the winds are blowing, even if reservations should be had about their reliability. Notable in the Arab world are the surveys of Zogby International and of Khalil Shaqaqi in the Palestinian arena. As to their reliability and validity, and regarding their integration into the intelligence picture, there are very serious differences of professional opinion. But their results indicate, at least, the general trends of the societies they examine.

Another valuable open source is the tourist guide book. Such books provide an enormous amount of information about the country, its society, culture and economy, making it easier to understand ongoing intelligence information. For example, tips for using public transportation reveal information about the road system.

An important way to understand the story behind the story is reading academic studies conducted about the subject or having indirect access to leading academics in the field. Using open channels to collect the PhD theses of the most important scholars or to conduct on-going dialogues with them enables intelligence analysts to enrich the discussion with insights that are hard to acquire only from reading intelligence information.

For example, in 1977 Professor Bernard Lewis met senior members of Israeli military intelligence after a visit to Egypt and told them that President Sadat was ready for peace. That was at odds with Israeli intelligence evaluations at the time, but those evaluations were proved false a number of months later when Sadat visited Israel, launching the peace process between the two countries. Another example of academic evaluation that influenced intelligence deployment was that of Professor Asher Susser, who, in discussions about the American involvement in Iraq in 2003, said that the non-Arab forces in the Middle East – that is, Iran and Turkey – were getting stronger at the expense of the Arab world.

The Third Circle: What Cannot Be Concealed

There is information in open sources that the various regimes would be very happy to keep to themselves, but are forced to reveal or accept the fact of its disclosure. Such information is extremely valuable for intelligence analysts, and includes the following:

- Commercial information: Large economic bodies, such as corporations that develop and sell weapons, reveal large amounts of information for business purposes, such as the makeup of their holdings, financial balances, deals made and the basic data of the weapons systems they sell. For example, one of the most interesting issues of the Cold War – the identity, number and basic properties of the rivals' weapons systems – is today at least partially accessible to anyone following international arms market publications.

- Information officially released to the public as part of transparency: The governments of countries wishing to join international markets release a large amount of information for economic reasons or to increase the degree of transparency. Thus, for example, the status of existing or planned national projects can be determined; tenders are issued, including those related to security; and macro-economic data that is relatively reliable can be obtained.

- Information about transportation routes: Hauling and conveyance, especially by air and sea, is done fairly openly today. Open data about sea lanes and air routes can be followed to identify areas of potentially suspicious activity carried out by illegal elements (rogue states, terrorist organizations and crime networks) and to focus on firm intelligence sources. An example would be using accessible databases of information about the identity and formation of suspicious naval vessels to serve operational activity.

- Academic information: Academic research networks can be used to collect information about the target countries, such as Iran or Iraq under Saddam Hussein. Some of the legitimate academic research carried out in the target countries by local and visiting scholars may indicate the enemy's hidden research and development intentions. Research workers and institutions have no choice but to reveal a large part of their activity to receive the academic accreditation necessary for financial and other compensation.

- Geographic information: Geographic information systems and satellite photos (Google Earth, sites selling satellite images) can be accessed, revealing much relevant information to intelligence analysts and saving time and resources. In some instances, what is not revealed (the "black holes") in the databases hints at intelligence of much greater value.

- Terrorist networks: Because of the international pressure on terrorist organizations and the increasing difficulties had by terrorist operatives in moving freely between countries, the organizations have been forced to transfer some of their activity to the Internet. By doing so they have gained many advantages, among them exposure, links and flexibility. However, their activity in cyberspace also exposes them and their supporters to governmental monitoring. Their websites can reveal intentions and, more importantly, their modus operandi and potential supporters.

The Fourth Circle: What Was Leaked

In the 1990s a large military exercise was held in one of the Arab countries. Israeli intelligence officers had questions and could not agree on an evaluation. Some of the answers were found in information accidentally exposed during a televised interview with one of the senior officers of the army involved.

Mistakes in securing information occur even in regimes that are strict about secrecy. The more channels there are for possible exposure, the greater the chances of information leaks. The desire for praise and recognition is a strong motivating factor. People want to boast of their achievements even if they cannot fully publicize them, and that opens a window for intelligence organizations to find valuable information through OSINT – information governments would rather not have revealed.

In the past decade social networking has exploded onto the Internet: chat groups, Facebook, Twitter, P2P (peer-to-peer) file sharing. The networks are open to all and censoring their traffic is difficult. A close examination of text messages, pictures and the networks connecting people reveals extremely valuable information to intelligence bodies.

Unquestionably, in some instances the Internet serves as a platform for illegal activity. Sometimes extremist Islamist chat rooms are used to contact terrorist networks. Terrorist organizations also use the Internet to send coded messages to their operatives. The combination of deep intelligence penetration and a scan of open sources may reveal their intentions. Information produced in such a way from OSINT may serve both as a lead to other intelligence capabilities and as the foundation for publicly exposing the illegitimate activities of countries and organizations ("name and shame").

The Fifth Circle: Penetrating Secrets

By itself OSINT cannot penetrate the enemy's hidden domains systematically or over time. As noted, it can profit from the enemy's security slipups, but in general it depends upon chance. For a long-term, stable penetration of the enemy's innermost secrets, clandestine intelligence capabilities are necessary, such as SIGINT, HUMINT and VISINT. Nevertheless, OSINT can provide many leads for constructing such capabilities, including the following:

- Personal information: Addresses, telephone numbers and email addresses of individuals in the intelligence crosshairs. The information is available in open databases which are so broad and extensive it is difficult to hide the details.

- Operational intelligence: OSINT can be used to put an operation into action. It is not by chance that since the Second Lebanon War, Hezbollah head Hassan Nasrallah has not appeared at his organization's public rallies. He knows that knowledge of a rally whose time and place have been advertised is liable to be the starting point for operational and intelligence measures against him.
- Classified zone breach by open source manipulation: OSINT can be manipulated to create a lead for intelligence collection or access to operations. For example, the young man who uses a chat room to express his desire to participate in an extremist activity can be invited to a meeting. The distance between cyberspace and physical action can be made very short indeed.

Clandestine intelligence channels contribute their share to OSINT collection. A HUMINT source or collaboration between intelligence organizations is a means of acquiring open source material in the target country, from a flyer distributed in a mosque to books in a store. Clandestine sources, including SIGINT, create leads to valuable Internet sites later covered by overt intelligence organizations.

A Reality Check for OSINT
Potentially, implementing the five circles of OSINT has both advantages and disadvantages. Among the advantages are the following:
- It is a vast, easily accessible reservoir of human information. It contains much relevant information that has only to be mined.
- OSINT covers the entire globe and a tremendous number of issues. For that reason it is well-suited to meet the needs of intelligence because, as opposed to focused clandestine collection, it makes it possible to scan and identify new topics.

- It is relatively cheap and far less dangerous than other forms of intelligence collection. Even if a fee is charged to subscribe to databases, the amount is negligible compared to the costs of technical investments in SIGINT and VISINT, or of mounting a HUMINT operation.

- There are many OSINT sources, some of which, at least, work at cross purposes, making it possible to compare and cross-reference them to increase the reliability of the intelligence picture obtained.

- OSINT is also the enemy's operational platform, and as opposed to the Cold War, both sides use the same information network. For a variety of reasons, the subjects being investigated are exposed, whether out of commercial necessity, operational necessity or desire.

- In the end, almost everything is publicly revealed, even the greatest secrets. The only question is when and how relevant the information is at the time of exposure. Thus, for example, a large amount of secret diplomatic and political information becomes public property in a matter of hours, days or weeks.

- Analyzing information located through OSINT is easier because it has been subjected to fewer security restrictions. Raw and even processed material can be disseminated through civilian systems, and more important, it is easier to outsource information gathering and processing.

- OSINT information can be used without restrictions or the danger of exposing sensitive sources. As a result OSINT is an important component of public diplomacy.

OSINT's disadvantages are as follows:

- The amount of information is enormous, demanding the implementation of systems for mining, filtering, focusing and processing so that intelligence officers do not drown in irrelevant information.

- Cyberspace is open to manipulation and fraud, as opposed to clandestine channels regarded as secure by the rivals, where they think they can communicate more openly. That increases the challenge of verification and cross-referencing.
- In cyberspace it is impossible to systematically find information about the enemy's most sensitive secrets. A country or organization that regularly hides a project or an existing capability may succeed in keeping it from leaking into open sources for years. A considerable amount of the intelligence regarding such fields is the result of the secret collection by the intelligence community. For example, much of the important information made public in international reports about Iran's nuclear program is based on sensitive intelligence collected by the Western intelligence communities and released for publication.
- Intelligence has lost its monopoly over information. The decision makers and their aides are exposed to open sources, and it is difficult to update them with new information before they have been personally exposed to it. The intelligence communities are faced with the great challenge of competing for the attention of the decision makers in providing the most accurate and professional intelligence pictures and analyses when they have already been exposed to a storm of open information about the issue under discussion.
- Intelligence clients do not expect intelligence officers to deal with OSINT but rather to use resources that will bring them the enemy's secrets. Sometimes they find it hard to understand that correctly monitoring and analyzing all the information, including OSINT, to construct an exact intelligence picture is a central part of intelligence work. For that reason,

the funds allotted for OSINT may never be received because they may have been reallotted to reinforce clandestine collection activities.

- Inefficiency is a drawback. The fact that anyone with a computer can access the Internet, and that almost every intelligence officer has one, means that the same searches are being carried out in many places. Only deep interorganizational coordination can make the search more efficient.

- The information explosion has increased the problem of language and translation. During the Cold War only one professional translator was needed to read *Pravda* every day to understand what the Soviet regime wanted its citizens and rivals to know. Today dozens of language experts are needed to monitor information that may or may not be relevant.

- There are legal problems resulting from copyright laws. Most of them are resolved by indicating that the problematic material is meant for internal consumption only.

OSINT's Influence on Israeli Intelligence

In Israel the OSINT effort has existed since the establishment of the intelligence community. Collecting information from open sources was part of the intelligence picture before the establishment of the state. It reached its peak with the establishment of a special unit for collecting OSINT called Hatzav. However, during the past decade the unit was disbanded, and OSINT collection was distributed among other units.

In the author's opinion, behind the decision was the weighing of the advantages and disadvantages of OSINT. It can be seen that the two external circles (the story and behind the story) carry a wealth of relevant information, but to enjoy its advantages it has to be properly mined and processed. For the three internal circles, OSINT loses some of its advantages, but with a concentrated collection effort supported by an operational effort, valuable information can be acquired.

Unlike other intelligence communities and commercial groups, which can invest huge resources in mining relevant data, the Israeli intelligence community is very small and has to perform great feats with few resources. Therefore, in Israel OSINT is regarded as an integral part of constructing an intelligence picture based on clandestine collection methods, and it emphasizes the three inner circles, which focus on searching for open information about the secret world of the enemy.

In addition, methods were developed for collection and analysis to use limited means to acquire high-quality information about the second circle, the story behind the story. The first circle, in which OSINT covers the story, is dealt with today by Israeli intelligence in a limited way and covers only open sources considered the most valuable to the overall intelligence assessment.

In contrast to the Israeli intelligence community in the past two decades, dealing with the first circle has become the province of many intelligence agencies as well as many private groups around the globe. The American intelligence community, for example, established a national OSINT center.

A Look to the Future and Conclusion

Looking toward the future, the world of open sources will only grow. As a result of technological developments, OSINT potential will continue to multiply at a whirlwind pace, with the parallel growth of intelligence relevance.

An examination of the five circles of OSINT, based on advantages and disadvantages, provides a number of possible directions for development:

- Expanding the development of the relevant mechanized data mining and automatic translation tools and promoting and extending OSINT disciplines: The more computerized methods are developed for coping with the information explosion, extracting relevant, necessary information and translating it (at a level that only has to be checked by humans), the more valuable OSINT will become for the intelligence communities. Such developments will also be problematic, and may flood intelligence networks with information. It will require a revolution in OSINT disciplines, based on academic and other methods for mining data, to utilize the increase in the amounts of material to the fullest, and to focus collection, insofar as is possible, on relevant, reliable, valuable sources.

- Active search: Today it is possible, under camouflage, to operate in the open source sphere to collect relevant information by using methods similar to those used to handle agents. In that way valuable information can be accessed, possibly even within the circles of the enemy's secrets, through open sources. The concept can be called "HUIOSINT," that is HUMINT In OSINT, and it requires theoretical, operational and legal development.

- Outsourcing: Transferring the production of OSINT to other locations and/or to private enterprises based on cheap manpower and fast communications. For example, it can be transferred to Asia, where manpower is relatively cheap and workers can be trained in the target language and in English.

- International cooperation to deal with the amount of information: Every intelligence community in the West has independent OSINT production capabilities. The creation of a joint community, through the identification and correct use of the strengths of each component, will make it possible to utilize OSINT more thoroughly and in all likelihood more accurately. Intelligence cooperation in OSINT production can be the first step in uniting the intelligence communities with both bi- and multilateral agreements.

- Sharing OSINT information with the public: A controlled release of OSINT produced by national collection agencies will enrich public discourse in the Western countries and make it more relevant. The intelligence communities will profit because it will enrich the academic research nourishing them. In addition, disseminating information will also be a source of income for the OSINT community, which constantly complains of a lack of funds.

In conclusion, today we stand before the realization of Haim Guri's vision. From one intelligence agent reading one book of poetry, we see large sectors of the intelligence communities around the world dealing with constructing better intelligence assessment based on OSINT and an exploitation of the information revolution, which makes it possible to enjoy much greater relevant information than in the past.

VISINT in Israeli Intelligence

Brigadier General Eli Pollak

Commander of the Combat Collection Corps, formerly VISINT Commander of IDI

This article surveys VISINT, or visual intelligence, as part of intelligence collection in Israel. VISINT includes collection on land, in the air and, in recent decades, in space as well. The information is collected by ground patrols and observation posts that photograph the area and by video recordings, and in the air by reconnaissance planes and UAVs (unmanned aerial vehicles). There are also planes fitted with special cameras for a sub-classification called IMINT, or imagery intelligence, which deals with aerial photographs taken by surveillance planes or satellites, and provides simulated information based on sensors.

Such activities are carried out when there are gaps in the information needed by intelligence groups, and their products are not only important but sometimes unique. It reveals the actions of the enemy and presents an intelligence picture allowing decision makers at all levels to view the situation on the ground with their own eyes in planning critical moves.

History: The Development of the Visual Field

Ground Collection

Collecting VISINT on the ground is as old as history. Twice in the Bible, Moses and Joshua send men to inspect the land and collect intelligence. Moses sends twelve spies to the Promised Land, one from each tribe, and tells them "to see the land" (Numbers 13:18), and their reports leave the Israelites in the desert for many years. Joshua "sent...two men to spy secretly, saying, 'Go view the land, even Jericho'" (Joshua 2:1). The ability to investigate the desired area, collect information, see for themselves and report back took considerable effort, along with the HUMINT investment, the same as is carried out by all intelligence bodies in every army in the world.

The technical advances of the twentieth century enabled collection agencies to work around the clock and further afield to provide documentation with still and video cameras and thus improve the decision-making process.

Aerial Intelligence Collection: Balloons and Planes

Until the eighteenth century, observations were carried out without technological equipment. At the end of the century, during the wars following the French revolution, hot air balloons were used to locate the enemy. In the nineteenth century their use extended to various armies in America and Europe. Telescopes were put to military purposes at the end of the nineteenth century. Planes were developed in the early decades of the twentieth century and were used for reconnaissance missions. Intelligence photographs were taken for the first time in 1919 during the Balkan War, and during World War I the French, British and Germans flew light planes to locate and photograph enemy forces. During World War II aerial photographs and their decipherment became VISINT's most important mission.

In the 1950s Lockheed developed the U-2 jet plane, designed as a reconnaissance aircraft. With the founding of the state, Israel operated reconnaissance planes called Mosquitoes to collect intelligence from battle sectors. The use of warplanes for reconnaissance has increased over the years, and in every era they have been a platform capable of carrying advanced cameras for intelligence collection. Technological developments make it possible to photograph targets at greater and greater distances, with improved quality under difficult weather conditions, part of today's response to surface-to-surface missiles.

UAVs: Unmanned Aerial Vehicles

The Americans began using UAVs at the beginning of the 1960s, but they were unsuccessful in Vietnam and the army decided they were impractical. At the beginning of the 1970s an Israeli officer developed the prototype for a miniature UAV. Israel used them in operations in the First Lebanon War (1982) and has since become a world leader in their manufacture and operation. Today there are UAVs of various sizes for a variety of uses. Some are as small as a light plane and some reach the size of fighter aircraft and carry sophisticated intelligence systems. Today most are used for intelligence reconnaissance purposes, such as aerial photography and monitoring targets. They can photograph from lower altitudes than manned planes, are cheaper to operate and of course do not endanger the lives of pilots.

Satellites

Satellites were first launched into space at the end of the 1950s and led to a VISINT revolution. Their greatest advantage is that it is extremely difficult to shoot them down, but no less important is the fact that they can continuously cover the desired target. There are a number of types of satellites, differing in orbit and altitude. One is a satellite that orbits the Earth and passes over a specific area once every 90–120 minutes. Another reaches an altitude of between 2,000 and 36,000 kilometers (1,240 to 22,370 miles) and orbits the earth between once every two hours and once every twelve hours.

Israel's activity in space began in the 1980s, and it has launched a small number of satellites into space. Most of the military satellites were launched with a mechanism locally developed and manufactured. The first military reconnaissance satellite was launched in 1995, and since then a number of electro-optic and one radar satellite have been put into space. Satellites enable Israel to collect information about targets hundreds and thousands of miles away without risk to men or equipment.

The ability to monitor developments in distant locations has improved the country's evaluation and early warning capabilities.

The Advantages of the Visual World

The ability to see what the enemy is doing enables military and security intelligence to follow processes, carry out evaluations, make decisions and attack precisely. The most prominent advantages are the following:

- Being able to see the enemy's exact location in the photographed terrain cell makes it possible to track enemy troop deployment and changes in fortifications, obstacles or camouflage. A continuous monitoring of the enemy and his movements makes it possible to evaluate his intentions and indicate the implementation of a possible plan. Even when the enemy engages in clandestine activity while maintaining radio silence, VISINT can overcome gaps in intelligence.

- Continuous, long-term coverage makes it possible to monitor activity over a period of time, such as construction, fortification and changes in deployment. Existing technology makes it possible to monitor a large terrain cell at short, specific time intervals for an exact evaluation. When the focus of intelligence interest is small – a single object, a person, a car – it may be monitored over a long period of time using UAVs and with ground collection.

- Exact mapping is one of the most important revolutions caused by VISINT. Being able to take high-resolution photographs and anchor the photographed objects in their real locations on the ground makes it possible to pinpoint them. At the same time, guided missiles have been developed, and the more exact the weaponry becomes, the greater are the demands made on collection elements to acquire and provide more exact targets.

- The transition to attacking with exact weapons allows the attacker to hit his targets, but the superiority of those weapons has increased the need to monitor the results of an attack and to ensure that the desired outcome was in fact achieved. VISINT ensures the most accurate evaluation possible of the percentage of direct hits and the physical state of the enemy after an attack; thus the decision makers can be presented with recommendations for the continuation of operational activities. The opening moves of the Second Lebanon War (2006) and Operation Cast Lead in the Gaza Strip (December 2008–January 2009), based on attacking pre-determined targets, were carried out extremely well. After two minutes of exact attacks, the decision makers waited for aerial videos and photographs to be analyzed (and for other sources of intelligence) to evaluate the damage and discover whether the desired results had been obtained.

- The concept of field security as practiced in Israel is integrated into the concept of overall operational activities on the country's borders. A continuous visual "collection screen" was constructed along the borders with an emphasis on the most important areas. It was to achieve non-stop coverage combined with certain technological capabilities, providing a complementary synergy between various elements, for example, day and night visual aids with radar. That made it possible to locate the enemy and prevent his activities even when there was no previous intelligence available. Many terrorist attacks in the Gaza Strip that began without early intelligence warning were successfully prevented thanks to the concepts of ongoing security and awareness, and to the professional conduct of the individuals involved.

- Given the changing nature of the conflict Israel is engaged in, it is not always clear whether someone is an enemy or a civilian.

From fighting a national enemy whose army was distinguished by its uniforms, equipment, location and ethical code regarding the use of the civilian population on both sides of the struggle, after 2000 Israel has had to engage an enemy who lives within the civilian population and uses it for its own purposes, sometimes as a place to hide and sometimes as human shields. That requires the IDF to be very careful in deciding to attack, especially from the air. Current VISINT capabilities make it possible to obtain information about the location of a target, its distance and civilian components – residential dwellings, institutions and sensitive sites. Thus the decision makers and those responsible for firepower can suit the type of weaponry to the target and estimate the strength of the strike. The deeper the enemy penetrates into the urban landscape – for instance during the ground fighting of Operation Cast Lead in the Gaza Strip in January 2009 – the more decisions must be based on updated, exact VISINT.

- Dealing with VISINT requires professional, skilled manpower. Professionalism and specialization in its various fields produce the high-quality intelligence received from the various VISINT systems. Israeli intelligence invests a great deal in human resources, training and teaching professional knowledge. Women are involved as well, and the ground observation sites along Israel's borders are staffed by women soldiers in the conscript army. For example, they are the soldiers who locate the attempts made by various terrorist networks in the Gaza Strip to infiltrate into Israeli territory.

The Disadvantages of the Visual World

Alongside VISINT's advantages and strengths there are disadvantages that restrict collection and intelligence analysis. The main ones are the following:

- Collection agents see only what their sensors have received, i.e., only the undisguised part of the enemy's array, and not the elements the enemy has chosen to hide.
- The ability to see further and deeper has been made possible thanks to airborne and satellite collection systems that cover the points of interest around the clock. However, they have many limitations, one of which is the fact that a satellite is positioned over the object only once every 90 minutes.
- It may be difficult to understand the enemy's plans or intentions, and the ability to provide a broad picture is limited. Deployment, movement, construction or any other activity identified by one of the sensors indicates activity; however, activity that has been indentified without complementary intelligence does not necessarily penetrate enemy intentions. Certainly, recognition of the enemy's intentions enables VISINT to either strengthen or disprove evaluations regarding the realization of their plans.
- Using UAVs makes it possible to follow objects, a significant advantage – but with the important potential disadvantage of an extremely narrow field of vision. The picture that identifies specific elements in detail cannot cover a broad terrain cell.
- One of VISINT's greatest limitations is the weather, which influences the capabilities of optical, electro-optic and thermal collection. Electro-optic and thermal capabilities, which under normal weather conditions can be used for continuous collection, are restricted both in operation and coverage when the weather is bad. To compensate, radar is used on the ground, in the air and in space, since its capabilities make continuous collection possible regardless of the weather.
- Using broad coverage to find small, isolated items is expensive. The coverage possibilities and the desire to collect VISINT even without additional information make the amount

of raw photographed information – especially satellite and reconnaissance plane photographs – very large. Some evaluators are of the opinion that it is a waste of resources to take a large number of photographs and accumulate material. However, experts in the field know that the information stockpiled is valuable for intelligence purposes. Often it is used months or years later to fill in the gaps when information is received about a specific area or subject.

- There is an enormous amount of material, and it needs to be used effectively. Recent years have brought VISINT to the point passed by SIGINT several decades ago. The amount of photographed and stored information, along with a limited amount of manpower, made it clear that tools were needed to assist in filtering, labeling and retrieving the information. In addition, there was a need for the analysts working in the field to specialize in integrating capabilities and means in other fields.

What the Enemy Does about VISINT

Israel's VISINT is not hidden from enemy eyes. It has been made public in various ways, causing enemy countries and relevant enemy organizations to conceal their actions in order to prevent Israel intelligence from acquiring information.

The main methods for avoiding Israeli VISINT capabilities are the following:

- The world under ground: The enemy blinds VISINT eyes by putting important elements below the visual surface. This has the advantages of both concealment and protection. The enemy usually chooses to hide his command sites, missile stores and launches, and ammunition bunkers. The information made public about the secret site near the Iranian city of Qom revealed Iran's intention to construct a hidden site that would be part of its nuclear program. The Second Lebanon War and

Operation Cast Lead in the Gaza Strip exposed a large number of underground sites from which Hezbollah and Hamas fired rockets and their operatives emerged to fight, and which were also used for concealing various types of weapons.

- The enemy also uses camouflage and deception: Since antiquity, armies have camouflaged their fighters or weapons as civilian. In the Second Lebanon War the Israeli air force struck a long-range rocket-launcher camouflaged as a civilian semitrailer. In the fighting in the Gaza Strip in Operation Cast Lead, large numbers of weapons were uncovered in civilian dwellings, but of far greater significance was the disclosure of heavy weapons in mosques, schools and public institutions. Camouflage can be anything from simple nets to buildings constructed to appear completely civilian while having only military purposes, all of which are intended to overcome ongoing VISINT.

- Simulations of various types of weapons are used to flood the battlefield with targets. The most famous incident occurred during the war in Kosovo, where NATO forces attacked from the air. After the war it became evident that the number of genuine targets attacked was significantly smaller than assessments during the operation.

- Densely populated civilian areas are used to hide weapons and ammunition and as firing points. The IDF's last two military engagements, in Lebanon and in the Gaza Strip, exposed some of the enemy's methods for dealing with Israel's military and intelligence superiority by dispersing weapons to every location. In that way Hezbollah deliberately hid its vast military infrastructure within the civilian population, including rockets to attack Israeli population centers. Hezbollah cynically used the Lebanese civilian population, which supported it and served it as human shields.

- Enemy forces are dispersed into isolated components. In the past, a significant intelligence effort was invested in locating enemy masses: troop concentrations, reserves and firepower. Today the enemy decentralizes its forces throughout the width and breadth of all the terrain cells under its control. That is possible because the types of autonomous weapons the enemy currently possesses have greater range and are more accurate than in the past. Thus the number of intelligence challenges has risen dramatically, and VISINT has been forced to comb large terrain cells to find the proverbial needle in the haystack. In addition, the enemy saturates the ground with targets, meaning that some would remain in place throughout the fighting.
- VISINT, from lowly field glasses to the satellite in the sky, looks for signs by which to identify an object to decide if it is military or civilian. Identification is based on parameters such as resolution, range, color, characteristic structure and location. The enemy's transition to low-signature activity is characterized by small squads firing anti-tank and anti-aircraft weapons and launching mortar shells and rockets, which challenge VISINT capabilities. Locating a rocket that has been positioned in a large orchard in advance, or an anti-tank squad observing a main road and changing its position often, is a significant challenge, and one which VISINT seeks to meet.

What Is VISINT's Place in the Future?

A simple answer might be to look at the special effects in movies and television, but the truth is somewhat different.

- Map coordinates can be improved to strike enemy weapons more accurately. In addition, an improvement in accurate support systems will make communicating easier among the various forces, especially collection, maneuvers and attack.

- Pictures can be used as a common language. The ability to photograph and transmit pictures from a sensor to an attack system, and vice versa, will make collaboration possible without the need for human intervention. The capability of a team to transmit the picture of a target as detected by the systems already exists. However, the innovation will be an exact picture received by the end user from the necessary angle.

- IMINT will become a dominant element. Beyond the increase in the use of radar for all forms of collection, the general evaluation is that the use of hyperspectral imaging[1] will increase, which will make it possible to receive multi-colored images (using more than 180 colors, some of which are invisible to the human eye) for every pixel in a picture. It can be used to receive unique chemical-physical information about a specific area, for example, an experimental field can be examined and knowledge can be gained about the materials used on it without having to be present or have samples.

- There will be automated systems for seeking and locating changes, enabling the VISINT analyst to deal with deciphering and assessing information, relieving him of the need to examine a terrain cell and locate changes. Computerized VISINT is continually advancing in both academia and the security sector, and will eventually provide the intelligence analyst with an

---

1. Hyperspectral imaging increases human viewing capabilities. A hyperspectral camera can translate tiny changes in the wave lengths emitted by various bodies into pictures allowing exceptional findings to be identified. It senses signals from afar without physical examination and deciphers them with computerized tools. The camera is especially sensitive to wave lengths and is able to decipher and translate them to a kind of colored map to indicate changes and exceptional situations.

automated system to scan the territory and identify and mark changes by comparing previous photographs.

- Larger areas will be covered at higher resolution and with capabilities to transmit the raw material more quickly for better decipherment and mapping. That will enable intelligence officers to become more effective in influencing battles in real time.

- Unmanned aerial vehicles will be available for every use. Technological developments will create new systems which will put them into every fighting framework, from company to division. Thus at every fighting level it will be possible to see the enemy on the other side of the hill and to open roads, close firing circles and control forces, all of it automated and independent.

- In the final analysis, each component is only one part of the entire VISINT picture. Only a system that can include all the information from the sensors, and compare, unite and complement it, can provide a more complete result. A system to fuse or merge data that will be able to integrate all the various sensors, along with experienced analysts, will give the full picture.

Conclusion

The enemies the State of Israel faces today chose an asymmetric form of battle. They draw the IDF from its position of strength to locations on the enemy's turf, fighting according to rules of engagement that prevent the IDF from exploiting its capabilities to the fullest. VISINT, as one of its strong points, has been forced to cope with new challenges posed by an enemy operating in a civilian environment, beneath the ground and keeping a low signature. Looking both to the past and the future, VISINT has a sufficient number of tools for dealing with those challenges and to find solutions for the problems they pose – and to be an important partner in providing the intelligence necessary for every operation.

However, the VISINT world is not alone on the battlefield. Only the combined, coordinated work of HUMINT, SIGINT and VISINT will provide the best intelligence picture.

Counterintelligence

Colonel (Res.) Dr. Barak Ben-Zur
Former Senior IDI and ISA Officer

Introduction

One of the main fields of counterintelligence is fighting espionage and subversion. Stories of espionage are immensely popular – the tales of spies who penetrated the highest levels of government and of the exposure of traitors. The public is always interested in people who, motivated by greed, the desire for high living, frustration with lack of advancement or some other strong emotion – or even ideology – have renounced loyalty to country, friends and sometimes even family and passed state secrets to a hostile adversary.

Experience has shown that a certain discomfort is felt when a spy is exposed, especially by members of the government, the army and whatever facility he worked for. His directors and associates wonder how he could have betrayed them after they promoted him and trusted him, and how they could not have noticed in time.

However, some of the discomfort seems to be aimed at the counterintelligence branch that hunts for spies. At least during the first stages of an investigation, the highest offices in ministries, facilities or headquarters seem to display a certain lack of warmth, a hesitation to cooperate. That increases with the depth of the spy's penetration and seniority of his position. That was how the country's leadership reacted when Israel Beer, a high-ranking officer in the IDF and a trusted aide in the Ministry of Defense, was exposed as a Soviet spy. The prime minister did not particularly like the enthusiasm of Mossad director Isser Harel.

His own close advisors at the time, including Israeli president Shimon Peres, the late Yitzhak Rabin and long-time Jerusalem mayor Teddy Kollek, hinted to Harel to drop the affair, or at least to deal with it discretely. The staff of the Technion, Israel's technical university, reacted in a similar fashion when Professor Kurt Sita was arrested in June 1960 and charged with spying for the Soviet Union. His colleagues could not credit the accusations and even tried to attend the trial as observers to make sure he was treated fairly. Sometimes the betrayal itself, even after it has been exposed, remains a well-kept secret for years.

Affairs of espionage and the books written by case officers provide a fairly good picture of how spies are recruited: prospective candidates are constantly searched for (although some of them volunteer directly to foreign intelligence services). Sometimes the process is complex and tortuous, and after the first contact a long, patient process is initiated to gain the potential agent's cooperation. If it develops as desired, the candidate is recruited as an agent. He, or she, is then trained in the rules of tradecraft and equipped with the necessary technology. On the job he is given the means to collect information and transmit it to his case officer. He has only one objective: to transmit the information in its entirety and on time. His security is also jealously guarded so that he may continue as an agent for as long as possible. A spy is alone in the field, but behind the scenes he is the subject of a full team of handlers who direct him and are aware of the risk of his being discovered. Sometimes an agent is given an escape hatch, a back door he can open if his identity is revealed.

One of the most famous examples was the Soviet Union's recruitment of five Cambridge University students in the 1930s. Slowly and with great patience they infiltrated the British government and were directed by the Soviets to key positions in various ministries and departments. In September 1940, John Cairncross became the personal secretary of a minister who was a member of the British Cabinet, giving him access to many highly sensitive documents whose contents he passed on to his Soviet case officers. Donald Maclean infiltrated the British Foreign Office and Guy Burgess the British security service (MI5). Burgess helped recruit the fourth and perhaps most famous member of the ring, Kim Philby,[1] who eventually became head of the British security service's Washington branch and a candidate for the post of director of MI5. The fifth member, Anthony Blunt, infiltrated the British secret service, MI6. Thus Soviet intelligence received continuous reports about Britain's most secret political and security activities.

The State of Israel as an Espionage Target

Since the day of its founding, the State of Israel has been a target for the intelligence services of both friendly and hostile countries. Both have shown interest in its development and its various armaments and technological capabilities. The Soviets were interested in Israel's relations with the West, especially the United States, and in Israel's perceptions of Soviet weapons and the countermeasures developed to thwart them. Regional steps taken by Israel were a permanent target of Soviet intelligence, and a considerable portion of the information collected passed into the hands of the Arab rulers and the heads of their armies.

Several factors make Israel a relatively convenient, easy target for intelligence collection by hostile elements:

- Israel is a country of immigrants from all over the world, paving the way for foreign countries to use former nationals as spies, underlings, couriers and operatives.
- Israel has commercial ties around the globe, making it possible to infiltrate spies as "businessmen."

---

1. In his autobiography, *My Silent War*, Philby tells the story slightly differently.

- Israel is an attractive tourist destination and popular media target.
- Israel attracts religious personnel of all stripes: priests, monks and nuns, and clerics who come to the country for religious work that serves as a cover for intelligence activities. Various academics and aid organizations or foundations also come for longer or shorter periods.

In other words, there is almost no innocent activity an intelligence agent has not used or considered using for collecting information or in the service of an intelligence organization. Israel has always been an excellent base for foreign intelligence services that want to establish networks for collecting information and recruiting and running spies, and that is in addition to the classic espionage carried out by the skilled teams of dozens of operatives who work from the various diplomatic legations.

Israel's short history is full of affairs illustrating the many possible methods for recruiting agents and constructing their cover stories. Some agents did serious damage to the country's security. However, the real harm is in the accumulated extent of espionage. The scope and variety of penetration into Israel's security and scientific establishments presented a picture of a country riddled with Soviet and Soviet satellite spies, making Western countries unwilling to trust Israel with important secrets, lest they be leaked to hostile elements.

Case Studies

Zeev Avni

Zeev Avni worked for the Foreign Ministry and penetrated the heart of Israel's intelligence and foreign relations. Born Wolf Goldstein in Latvia in 1921, he was recruited in Switzerland by Soviet intelligence in 1942. By the time he immigrated to Israel in 1948 he had already been a Soviet spy for six years. After repeatedly applying for a job in the Foreign Ministry, he finally passed the security exam and worked there until April 1956, collecting a great deal of information about Israel's foreign policy and weapons deals, security agreements and political maneuvers, but also about the Mossad and the identity of its operatives abroad. Without a doubt, the process that allowed him to be employed by the ministry was flawed. An agent of Soviet intelligence, he hid his true activities, opinions and motives.

Lozian Levi

Lozian Levi Ignazy Levi ("Levi Levi" to his friends) was a Pole who immigrated to Israel in 1948 after having been recruited by the Soviets in the country of his birth. In Israel he joined an operative unit of the Israel Security Agency, and if there is one place where the more sensitive issues of the ISA are exposed, it is an operative unit. Levi Levi, who had the operative knowledge and daring that are characteristic of such people, methodically collected the names and pictures of ISA operatives, documented special activities and gave it all to his case officers in Polish intelligence, which in turn passed it along to Soviet intelligence. Levi Levi worked for the ISA for more than seven years, from 1950 until August 1957.

One of the factors behind his exposure was the systematic investigation of new immigrants who had security and military backgrounds in their countries of origin. They were a rich source of information about the security establishments in the Soviet Union and the satellite countries, providing details about combat doctrine, arms and the structure of technological development units. Their contribution was considered very valuable, and Israel shared it all, primarily with American intelligence. Information also came from the recruitment or desertion of Soviet intelligence personnel to foreign services. In the case of Levi Levi, a Polish officer who deserted to France reported to the French, and they informed the Israelis.

Marcus Klingberg

Abraham Marcus Klingberg was probably the greatest Soviet intelligence asset recruited in Israel. He worked at the Institute for Biological Research in Ness Ziona in the central part of the country and eventually rose to the position of deputy director. He immigrated to Israel in 1948 and, with his wife, joined the IDF's medical corps, and in October 1956 began working at the institute. According to one version, he was recruited by Soviet intelligence in 1957, and for 18 years provided them with valuable information about the State of Israel's most sensitive secrets in microbiology and chemistry, as well as developments made at the institute itself.

Despite suspicions and security checks throughout his years of employment, the fact that he was a Soviet spy was only revealed in early 1983 after he was incriminated by evidence from the ISA, warranting a full investigation. The fact that they waited as long as they did hints at the restrictions and reservations binding counterterrorism intelligence services in democratic countries. There are limitations on the type of investigation that can be conducted and strict laws about invasion of privacy, sometimes at the price of suspending or even closing an investigation before results have been obtained.

Intelligence Collected by Friendly Countries

Israel is a target for friendly countries as well, including the largest of them, the United States. Some of the collection is visual and some is electronic. Some, the systematic collection on the ground, is carried out by skilled Americans working in the embassy in Tel Aviv and by agents who visit for short periods. The United States wants to know about Israel's capabilities and the results of the decision-making processes in the upper echelons of the government.

Clearly, the ongoing dialogue at various levels between the two sides is the result of Israel's courageous relations with the United States. The fact that there are no clearly specified limits to those relations has blurred the boundaries between what is permitted and what is forbidden, and without a doubt, in some instances the decision to provide information is a local one, made because it seems like the right thing to do.

Intelligence Collected by Hezbollah: Omar al-Heib and Others

Israel is open to the media, making life very easy for the intelligence services of neighboring countries. In recent years it has become apparent that militias and terrorist organizations such as Hezbollah have developed impressive collection capabilities, some based on classic tools such as observation, wiretapping and reading open source information, and others, on invasive intelligence activities, including recruiting agents and dispatching spies, especially as "tourists."

Conspicuous among recruited agents was Omar al-Heib, an IDF lieutenant colonel, whose initial contacts with Hezbollah were felony related. As the relationship progressed and the contacts turned to intelligence, for several months in 2002 he passed valuable information to Hezbollah. He reported on the movements of Major General Gabi Ashkenazi, then head of the northern command, the deployment of combat vehicles along the northern border and other operative topics.

Hezbollah, whose talents and daring are perhaps greater than those of the other intelligence services in the region, had another interesting system for collecting information. They dispatched "lone wolves," intelligence agents who had been trained for long periods of time and for whom convincing cover stories had been invented after they returned from extended stays in Western countries such as Canada and Britain. They generally arrived in Israel as tourists, and even after they were captured, it was impossible to completely fathom the purpose of their missions. They included Fawzi Iyoub, an operative of the organization's terrorist wing abroad, a Canadian citizen who entered Israel in October 2000 on a forged American passport. He stayed in Jerusalem for a while and from there went to Hebron, where he was detained by the Palestinian security services. In June 2002 he was handed over to Israel after the Israeli takeover of the city. Another example was British subject Jihad Shuman. He entered Israel with his own passport and was detained in Jerusalem in 2001, a short time after he arrived in the country.

Conclusion

The law that established the ISA defines its targets and missions and validates its counterterrorism activities. A civilian who seems suspect in any way related to security is liable to find himself scrutinized through databases, interrogations of his friends and relations and an investigation of his possessions before he finds himself hooked up to a polygraph or facing a team of curious, experienced investigators. That anonymous civilian will be subject to a wide variety of checks, observations and analyses.

However, the threats to a country's secrets grow and change constantly, and the challenge to keep them becomes ever more complex. Insight may be gained from the testimony of David Szady, former FBI assistant director of counterintelligence, before the Senate Judiciary Committee in April 2002. He presented to the committee the changes the FBI planned to make in its counterintelligence methods and activities in view of the changes in the nature of the threat. His main topics were globalization, changes in technology and computers, and the immense power they placed in the hands of players who did not represent states. He referred specifically to hacking into databases.

The level and power of computerization as it develops in the private sector, and the great opportunities for communication – the technology and knowhow passing freely to and from every spot on the globe – allow individuals and limited teams to collect information that in the past was the exclusive province of the services of national countries. The increased interfacing between business and politics (employing consultants and experts), the strengthening ties among corporations around the world, and outsourcing production and development have all created a new tempo and breadth for transmitting all types of information from one location to another. The fact that the development capabilities of new technology pass through extremely sensitive fields from governments and governmental systems to the private sector draws a new map of the focal points of knowledge and state secrets. A country's ability to oversee the flow of information and its application has become more complex. The challenge is even more daunting for Israeli counterintelligence because of Israel's special situation, as noted above.

Sources

- Intelligence and Terrorism Information Center website, http://www.terrorism-info.org.il/site/home/default.asp?lang=En
- United States Senate Committee on the Judiciary. "Reforming the FBI in the 21st Century: The Lessons of the Hanssen Espionage Case." 2002.
- The Report of the Royal Commission (RRC). "The Defection of Igor Gouzenko." Laguna Hills, California: Aegean Park Press, 1946.

Air Force Intelligence

Brigadier General Itai Brun
Head of the IDI Production and Analysis Division

Israeli air force intelligence has two functions: it both operates for the air force and is a dominant factor in the national intelligence assessment. That is a result of the Israeli intelligence community's unique structure, in which both air force and naval intelligence also have production and analysis responsibilities. In the case of air force intelligence, the responsibility concerns the enemies' air forces, aerial defense and surface-to-surface missile systems (SSM). The constant tension that exists between the two "hats" worn by air force intelligence shapes its image. The air force hat requires it to focus on precise intelligence for operations (targets and threats), while the national intelligence assessment hat requires broad perspectives and thorough analysis.

The Six-Day War, 1967: Operation Moked

This short article is based on the hypothesis that the patterns of thinking and operations of air force intelligence were shaped by the major events in which it has participated during the past sixty years and the challenges it has faced. Under various names, since the founding of the corps in 1947 as the "aerial service," there has been a body within the Israel Air Force (IAF) whose mission it has been to collect, analyze and circulate intelligence. That is not surprising, because since the inception of air forces at the beginning of the twentieth century, it was clear that there was a strong linkage between knowledge of the enemy and the air force's ability to operate. As early as 1921, Italian theorist Giulio Douhet, who had a great influence on early air force development, wrote that choosing the target was the most important activity of aerial warfare.

In fact, target intelligence is usually considered the main reason for the existence of air force intelligence. The best illustration of that in the IAF's short but very eventful history was Operation Moked, carried out on June 5, 1967, the first day of the Six-Day War. The operation, which destroyed the Egyptian, Jordanian and Syrian air forces while the planes were still on the ground, was based on precise intelligence that had been systematically collected and processed since the plan for Operation Moked was formulated at the end of 1963. The importance of intelligence in the success of the operation was expressed by Air Force Commander General Mordechai Hod, who said, "I think no commander could pray for better intelligence than I had in this war."

As a broad operation to achieve air superiority and defend Israel's skies, Operation Moked best reflected the tremendous threat to the state at the time, i.e., enemy aircraft that could attack deep within Israeli territory. Most of the efforts of the IAF – as well as air force intelligence – focused on the threat and the ways and means to neutralize it. Dealing with the attack aircraft of the Arab countries had challenged air force intelligence from the War of Independence (1948–1949) until the War of Attrition (1967–1970). The latter, largely forgotten war symbolizes to a great extent the fundamental change in the ways the IAF operated and the new challenges facing air force intelligence.

Attacking deep within enemy territory in the War of Attrition frustrated Israel because it forced the IDF to wage a war irrelevant to the foundation of its combat doctrine: transferring the war to enemy territory and a swift, decisive victory. Air force intelligence had to reorganize and emphasize some of the elements that still characterize it: the importance of real-time intelligence and the need for intelligence support for helicopters in special operations. However, more than anything else, the War of Attrition symbolized a new challenge and new threat: surface-to-air missiles (SAMs).

SAM batteries appeared in the Middle East before the Six-Day War, but in view of the types used, their number on the ground and deployment, they were not considered important on the aerial battlefield. During the War of Attrition, especially toward its end, a fundamental change occurred in the Egyptian arena, leading to a loss of planes, including the modern American Phantom F-4 jets, and to extreme uneasiness in the air force. The War of Attrition ended without the IAF's having found a solution to what it called "the missile problem." The problem worsened between 1970 and 1973, with the outbreak of the Yom Kippur War. When the war began, the IAF was confronted with a relatively dense array of missiles, which included 140 mobile and fixed batteries along both the Egyptian and Syrian fronts. Air force intelligence, by then an air force division, focused on them but could not decipher their secrets and made fundamental mistakes in evaluating important components in their operation. In the Yom Kippur War the IAF paid a high price for the gaps in its knowledge.

The Yom Kippur War, 1973: Operation Dougman-5

Air force intelligence has always been a key partner in IDI's early warning efforts because of its production and analysis responsibility for the vital systems of the enemy military. Thus it also bore responsibility for the lack of early warning on the eve of the Yom Kippur War and for the intelligence community leaders' adherence to the incorrect theory, one of whose components was linked directly to air force intelligence responsibility (specifically Egypt's long-range attack capabilities).

However, any contemporary discussion of air force intelligence should start on the second day of the Yom Kippur War, October 7, 1973. That morning the IAF initiated Operation Dougman-5, an attack on the Syrian SAMs in the Golan Heights. The operation, which the IAF had planned and prepared years before, was a total failure. Six planes were shot down, two air crew members were killed and eight captured by the Syrians. Not one SAM battery was located, and for that reason almost no battery was damaged. The trauma caused by Dougman-5 prevented the IAF from attacking SAMs during the war itself, making Ezer Weizman, a former IAF commander, write some years later that "the missiles bent the planes' wings." The lessons learned from the operation are the basis for the structure, mindset and activity of IAF intelligence to this day.

Learning the Lessons of the Yom Kippur War

The failure to deal with the SAMs and the similar failure in close air support focused attention on the lessons of the war. That was true for the IAF in general and its intelligence division in particular. Benny Peled, the air force commander at the time, complained of the lack of updated intelligence on the enemy forces and claimed that if he had had such intelligence, which he said existed, the achievements of the air force would have been completely different. He concluded that the air force responsibility to support the ground forces had to be coordinated with its authority to collect and develop the necessary intelligence to carry out the mission. He demanded full independence for the IAF in developing the targets for its missions. His demand was not fully met, but it did lead to changes in the structure of air force intelligence and improved its communications with intelligence producers in the ground forces. The problem continued to plague the IAF in the following decades and worsened during the 1990s, when the gap grew between the limited responsibility of air force intelligence to search and provide targets (which remained largely in the hands of IDI), and the growing responsibility of the IAF to attack various targets.

One way or another, meeting the challenge of the SAMs demanded a different solution, because there was neither intelligence regarding them nor the capabilities for obtaining it. In retrospect it was clear that the failure of Operation Dougman-5 kick-started the air force's initiative to meet the challenge of SAMs in general and mobile batteries in particular. The process was completed in record time, a mere five years between 1973 and 1978, and changes were made which fashioned the air force's way of thinking about mobile targets, and which have influenced not only the IAF but foreign air forces as well. Understanding that the precondition for coping with SAMs is intelligence, the subject was given top priority, and emphasis was put on shortening the reaction time between locating the target and attacking it (Dougman-5 was based on outdated intelligence supplied by aerial photographs taken in flyovers forty-eight hours before the beginning of the operation). The understandings reached strengthened cooperation between intelligence and operations and created their still-current close working relations.

Of all the changes made, there is one that is usually neglected: one of the main conclusions drawn from the war was that the members of the production and analysis division, the people who routinely study the enemy's weapons, combat doctrine and deployment, have a very important role in time of war. After the war the head of air force intelligence wrote that "production and analysis in wartime have to be operative and tactical, know what the enemy is doing from one moment to the next and have direct information about the IDF and IAF plans regarding the enemy in the air." That conclusion led to the reorganization of air force intelligence, based on the concept that the objective was not the result of a chance meeting of collection means and the enemy force, but the result of an analytical process. The idea was novel, but has served as the basis for coping with mobile targets, both by the air force and other groups in Israel and around the world.

The First Lebanon War, 1982: Operation Artzav-19

The concept in an attack on SAMs is to shorten the reaction time between locating the battery and attacking it, in a series of steps, especially direct communications between the collection assets, and production and analysis. The second half of the 1970s was rife with exercises and tests to implement and improve the concept. The Syrian SAM disposition, on the other hand, was content to rest on its laurels, and assumed that the Yom Kippur War had reflected the superiority of its missiles. That assumption was reinforced when the IAF, because of a combination of politics and weather, did not attack the Syrian batteries in Lebanon during the missile crisis (April 1981, after two Syrian helicopters had been shot down by IAF planes). However, Operation Artzav-19, in which Syrian anti-aircraft missile batteries were attacked on the fourth day of the First Lebanon War (June 19, 1982), proved the concept developed by the IAF to be applicable, and it yielded the unprecedented achievement of destroying the Syrian SAMs along the Lebanese border.

Operation Artzav-19 was named for the 19 targeted SAM batteries. The overwhelming majority of them were destroyed based on exact intelligence furnished by aerial intelligence photographs. Mobile targets were the most important challenge in the 1980s, and the attack during the First Lebanon War signaled an important success in meeting it. That, along with shooting down dozens of Syrian warplanes, in which aerial intelligence also played a critical role, illustrated the IAF's superiority and caused Syrian President Assad, two weeks after the operation, to give his soldiers an order of the day that recognized Israeli aerial supremacy. However, the success also signaled a greater challenge for air force intelligence. The Syrians, realizing Israel's ability to pinpoint its attacks, made a great effort to hide or camouflage all the systems that were potential targets, especially SAMs. Recognizing Israel's overall superiority, the Syrians turned to surface-to-surface missiles (SSMs) as their primary weapons.

SSMs were not new to the Middle East, but were particularly suitable for the world of the early 1990s, as Iraq's Saddam Hussein was one of the first to discern. When the first Gulf War broke out, he launched SSMs at targets in Israel and Saudi Arabia almost until the end of the war. The failure of the American air force to hunt down his rocket launchers illustrates how difficult it is to hit hidden targets. The results were reminiscent of those in Operation Dougman-5: despite intensive aerial efforts, no Iraqi SSM rocket launcher was hit. The lessons of the first Gulf War led to formulating a general doctrine for coping with mobile missile launchers operating deep inside enemy territory.

The Second Lebanon War (2006)

The late 1990s brought the IAF a new, different challenge. Operations Din v'Heshbon (Operation Accountability) (1993) and Invei Za'am (Grapes of Wrath) (1996) in Lebanon illustrated the problems of the intelligence needed to attack Hezbollah's rockets. The Second Lebanon War (July–August 2006) provided an opportunity to meet the challenge of invisible targets. Air force intelligence closely followed Hezbollah's military buildup in south Lebanon. Its combat doctrine, expressed by its leader, Hassan Nasrallah, in March 1999, was that "in guerilla warfare, anyone who cannot defend himself in a confrontation with the enemy can reduce the importance of the air force by hiding targets and not appearing openly…Hezbollah's preventing the enemy from identifying the targets have made it incapable of doing much [damage]."

The typical characteristic of the era of invisible targets is that there is "nothing to attack." While during the Second Lebanon War the IAF did destroy a large number of medium- and long-range rockets, having learned the lessons of the first Gulf War, it did not have the same success with short-range rockets, which are extremely small and mobile. It still does not, as seen by the rockets launched by the Palestinian terrorist organizations at population centers in the western Negev, sometimes sporadically, sometimes on a daily basis, and short-range rockets remain a challenge for the air force intelligence.

Challenges of the Future

The experience accumulated in the past sixty years has shown that the two hats worn by the IAF's intelligence division – operating for both the air force and national intelligence – are together responsible for its strength. They give air force intelligence officers a wide perspective and enable them to provide the air force with solid, precise information.

In recent decades a series of technological, societal and conceptual developments turned the air force into a dominant factor in the effort to win wars. Its ability to penetrate deep into enemy territory improved greatly with the developments in electronic warfare, unmanned stealth aerial vehicles, and its stand-off capabilities. The air force's attack capabilities have been improved by its greater use of precision guided munitions (PGMs) and new collection and surveillance assets as well as command and control systems. Today the air force can carry out long-range attacks on both mobile and fixed targets in difficult meteorological conditions and in complex, threatening arenas. They all demand large amounts of intelligence more exact than ever before, at longer ranges in shorter periods of time.

The invisible targets noted above will become more important in the coming years. Another very important challenge will be battle damage assessment (BDA). On June 5, 1967, two hours after Operation Focus began, Ezer Weizman, then deputy chief of the general staff, called his wife Reuma to tell her that "we won the war." He reached that conclusion after having received reports from the pilots who had attacked the enemy aircraft on the ground and made the logical and relatively simple connection between the success of the attacks and their strategic outcome. However, in recent decades air force intelligence, like other forms of intelligence, has had to deal with the difficulties arising from the fact that evaluating damage assessment has become extremely important, at both tactical and higher levels. The more complex the relationship between air force operations and strategic outcomes becomes, the more problematic evaluating outcomes becomes, especially when the targets are invisible.

Challenges related to non-conventional weapons and long-range threats are beyond the scope of this article. Air force intelligence, like the IAF itself and the entire IDF, has to deal with a broad spectrum of confrontations, including the type of conventional warfare used in wars of the past, as well as a limited but continuing confrontation of the sort conducted with the Palestinians in recent years. At the same time, air force intelligence must develop the capabilities to deal with a possible confrontation with distant enemies, especially Iran.

Naval Intelligence

Captain (Navy Res.) Shlomo Gueta and Captain (Navy Res.) Arie Oren

Formerly Heads of the Production and Analysis
Division of Israel's Naval Intelligence

Introduction

The Israeli Navy has participated in every war fought by the State of Israel in its sixty-year history. In two of them, the Yom Kippur War and the ongoing war on terrorism, the enemy was overcome at sea, to a considerable extent thanks to the activities of naval intelligence. This article will devote a few words to naval intelligence and survey its history.

In the Beginning

Israeli naval intelligence was established on April 20, 1948, with a small number of men, some from the Palyam (the Palmach's sea company) and others from the ranks of the Haganah's Shai – and some (including its first commander) with no knowledge of either intelligence or the sea.

At first naval intelligence had no data about enemy fleets, not even open source information. Shortly before the outbreak of the War of Independence, collecting information about the enemy's local maritime activity was a matter of observation conducted from the shore and by aerial patrols, questioning merchant fleet sailors who had visited ports in Arab countries and, to a certain extent, wiretapping. Naval intelligence undertook independent information collection and recruited and handled agents (for example, a British officer in Cyprus who provided

Israel with its first edition of *Jane's Fighting Ships*, an annual reference book of information about all the world's warships). It also dealt with radio disinformation.

When the battles ended, organizing a naval intelligence branch was begun (Sea Branch 4). The branch, which was housed in the Israeli navy headquarters on Mt. Carmel in Haifa, included departments of research, intelligence collection and field security. A unit for deciphering aerial photographs, an archive, a library (of books about military vessels, shores and ports) and a naval map collection were established.

Work procedures were formalized with production and analysis officers from the intelligence division (including distribution and division of research responsibility), and a working mode was established whereby naval intelligence had two functions: as intelligence for the navy, and as navy intelligence for IDI. While procedures for collection were formalized only in 1953, naval intelligence continued independently; it directly operated collection teams in the ports of Haifa and Tel Aviv, and sent others to collect information in Arab ports and along the coasts of Arab countries.

Naval Production and Analysis Takes on the Arab Fleets

During its first years naval research focused on three main areas: enemy Arab fleets (order of battle, weapons, activity and training, especially with regard to the Egyptian fleet), ports (structure, activity and defenses), and coast lines (landing areas and defenses).

The navy was only marginally active in the Sinai War. It engaged in one prominent naval battle, where it overcame the Egyptian destroyer *Ibrahim Al-Awal*. From the intelligence point of view, the battle was a success, in that naval intelligence headquarters in Haifa received, in real time, a translation of the communications between the destroyer and Egyptian fleet headquarters, intercepting information about activities aboard the ship and its intentions and enabling the Israeli navy to deploy in order to intercept and overcome the ship.

In the early 1950s the Arab fleets were equipped with British and French vessels. But in 1956 the Egyptian fleet (and shortly thereafter, the Syrian fleet as well) began using Russian ships, first destroyers but later others (mine sowers, torpedo boats and landing craft), and toward the end of the decade, submarines, which provided a new threat. Those changes forced naval intelligence collection to acquire, analyze and disseminate information about the new ships and weapons and their combat doctrines.

In the 1960s the Arab fleets significantly increased their military buildup with Russian Komar and Osa missile boats, first in Egypt and then in Syria. Sea-to-sea missiles completely altered the face of the naval arena, forcing naval intelligence to search for detailed technical data that would enable the navy to develop defense systems for its vessels.

As Soviet weaponry reached the Arab fleets, a Soviet flotilla entered the Mediterranean to counterbalance the presence of the American Sixth Fleet. Soviet vessels were based in ports in Egypt and Syria and operated in many areas, including off Israeli shores (in addition to their permanent patrolling reconnaissance vessels). In view of the implications for Israel of a Soviet presence, naval intelligence investigated the activity of the flotilla, partially in cooperation with foreign intelligence services. Naval intelligence also followed the activities of the merchant fleet, which brought weapons from the Soviet Union to the Arab countries, and developed capabilities for identifying the type of equipment transported.

Naval Intelligence Collection

Also important in the 1960s was developing the independent capability to tap Arab fleet communications. Naval intelligence allotted positions and its own manpower to work with IDI's central ELINT (electronic intelligence) unit, and later established wire-tapping squads that participated in navy voyages, both as part of the vessels' defense system during operations and to collect intelligence. Naval intelligence also established its own ELINT team, whose role was to identify and document seaborne, airborne and coastal radar reception.

During the Six-Day War there were no naval battles, and the Israeli navy focused on commando activity in the Arab ports. At the beginning of the War of Attrition the navy sank Egyptian vessels in Port Said, but in October 1967 the Egyptians fired a sea-to-sea Styx missile and sank the Israeli ship *Eilat*. The incident had consequences for intelligence, because information received in Israel, which could have warned the ship, was not transmitted to it. Moreover, the incident forced the navy to improve its intelligence capability in order to be able to cope with missiles possessed by the enemy's navies.

Changes in Naval Intelligence in the 1960s and Intelligence Success in 1973

At the end of the 1960s and the beginning of the 1970s naval intelligence underwent many changes. Extensive naval activity on many fronts necessitated deployment and closer collaboration with IDI, Israeli air force intelligence and the intelligence of the various commands. In 1969, Sea Branch 4 became the naval intelligence division and toward the end of 1972 was transferred from navy headquarters in Haifa to IDI in Tel Aviv.

On the eve of the Yom Kippur War, IDI did not accept the naval intelligence evaluation that Egypt was about to start a war. The Israeli navy, on the other hand, took the warnings seriously, prepared vessels and deployed for war. In the battles, especially those involving missile boats, it became clear how exact the technical information about enemy missiles was. Moreover, the tactical intelligence supplied by the wiretapping teams to the commanders at sea contributed greatly to the navy's successes in the war. Without a doubt, the technical intelligence about the enemy's missiles and the tactical information acquired by naval intelligence about the combat doctrine of the Arab fleets in firing sea-to-sea missiles, that was processed, analyzed and provided to the forces after the sinking of the *Eilat*, contributed to the fact that not one of the fifty Styx missiles fired during the war hit an Israeli ship. When the missile boats returned from battle the flotilla commander said, "The enemy behaved like a textbook exercise."

After Israel's success in neutralizing Soviet sea-to-sea missiles, at the end of the 1970s the Arab fleets acquired modern missile boats equipped with missiles manufactured in the West and equipped with advanced electronic systems, and more use was made of aircraft in open and attack missions over the sea. The changes in the sources and quality of weapons again forced naval intelligence to alter its collection deployment and analysis, since it had to acquire detailed information for technical intelligence production and analysis missions, which could provide the navy's development teams with the data necessary to improve and update the defense systems of Israeli vessels.

Naval Intelligence Expands

At the end of the 1970s, naval intelligence gained additional manpower. This was necessary for the expansion of intelligence evaluation and analysis, in response to the acquisition of Western arms, the build-up of the "second circle" fleet and naval terrorism. There was an increase in the number of intelligence representatives in the navy's bases (following the growth of the navy's combat order) and a deepening of hydrographic research. At the same time, manpower development became formalized in naval intelligence and independent, designated courses were opened at the navy's camp for new recruits (the first courses offered for training intelligence officers).

Naval Intelligence Faces the Terrorist Challenge

At the end of the 1970s naval intelligence was faced with the new challenge of maritime terrorism. At first terrorists infiltrated Israel by sailing directly through the Dead Sea or from south Lebanon (by swimming or using rubber boats), and later by exploiting merchant vessels as mother ships, which lowered them to the sea in smaller craft west of the Israeli coastline. The terrorists conducted several successful attacks, two of which, the 1975 Savoy Hotel attack (which cost the lives of eight Israeli civilians and three soldiers) and the 1978 Coastal Road massacre (in which thirty-eight Israeli civilians were killed, thirteen of them children, and seventy-one were wounded), led to a change in mindset and the creation of a counterterrorism division. In addition, depth of coverage of the Lebanese coast was extended to locate naval activity in the sector.

It was a radical change for naval intelligence. In addition to focusing on the destroyers, missile boats, submarines, helicopters and advanced weapons of the enemy fleets, it had to track camouflaged rubber dinghies, fishing boats and small commercial vessels, both along the Lebanese coast and on the high seas.

The issue of civilian vessels quickly revealed itself as complex, forcing naval intelligence to initiate special information-collecting activities (with the full and fruitful cooperation of the other intelligence community agencies and reserve soldiers who were specialists in the necessary fields).

By the mid-1970s fighting maritime terrorism had become an important component of naval intelligence activity. The navy carried out dozens of counterterrorism operations along the Lebanese coast and was involved in comprehensive IDF operations. In the First Lebanon War, naval intelligence supplied the information necessary for landing operations, shelling the shore and raids. Alongside its many successes in the Lebanese arena, in 1997 Israeli Navy SEALs were ambushed by Hezbollah and twelve were killed, a traumatic incident for naval intelligence.

Since the Coastal Road massacre, naval intelligence has deterred and prevented all terrorist organization attempts to launch attacks from the sea. Two of the more important counterterrorism actions were sinking the bomb-laden *Agius Demetrius* in the Straits of Tiran as it was sailing to the port of Eilat (1978) and sinking the mother ship *Attavi-rus*, which was carrying a twenty-one-man squad of terrorists who were planning to carry out a mass-murder attack in Tel Aviv. To preserve secrecy, the ship had sailed from the far-off Algerian port of Annaba. For identifying the terrorists' plans, tracking them and preventing the attack, naval intelligence as a unit and some of its individual officers won the IDI Director's Prize for Creative Thought. The attack prevented during the early summer of 1990 was the last time terrorists attempted a showcase attack from the sea.

Naval intelligence also located and disrupted the terrorist organizations' maritime activities, locating dozens of various merchant vessels that sailed the eastern basin of the Mediterranean and brought terrorist operatives and weapons to and from Lebanon. Scores of successful Israeli counterterrorism activities that foiled terrorist-organization plans convinced the organizations that they did not have the capabilities to deal with the Israeli navy, which was everywhere all the time, or so it seemed. As one of them graphically put it, "We are afraid to take a shower, because as soon as we turn on the water, Israeli ships show up."

When control of the Gaza Strip was turned over to the Palestinian Authority, naval intelligence took on a new task: preventing arms from being smuggled in from the sea. Its most famous operation was capturing the *Karin-A*, after a long, complex intelligence action, exposing the involvement of Iran and Hezbollah in smuggling weapons to Palestinian terrorists. For its years-long activities in preventing smuggling via the sea, naval intelligence again won the Director's Prize for Creative Thought.

The Second Lebanon War and the Surprise of the C-802 Missile

The Second Lebanon War offered proof of the extent to which classic naval intelligence and terrorism were intertwined. The C-802 missile that hit the Israeli ship *Hanit* was supposed to be possessed only by regular armies, but had nevertheless reached Hezbollah. Despite the fact that naval intelligence had technical information about the missile, the Israeli navy was surprised by its being in the hands of the enemy in the Lebanese arena, and by seeing it hurtling toward the ship.

New Challenges for Intelligence

Needless to say, throughout the years naval intelligence continued fulfilling its classic functions of monitoring the Arab fleets (purchasing and military buildup, various types of weapons, routine activity and training exercises, manpower, port development and coastline defenses) and those of foreign powers sailing in the eastern Mediterranean, and monitoring the changes in those areas that necessitated an intelligence response. It also increased its monitoring of the merchant fleets to provide a response to the war on terrorism and weapons smuggling by sea. In addition, in the 1990s, when the Israeli navy received new submarines, naval intelligence instituted underwater monitoring to provide more comprehensive intelligence.

Conclusion

The advanced technologies finding their way to the Arab fleets and terrorist organizations such as Hezbollah pose a great challenge for naval intelligence and will continue to do so in the coming years. That is, of course, in addition to classic monitoring of the Arab fleets and coping with their continuing efforts to smuggle weapons and carry out maritime attacks. The ongoing process of learning lessons and improving, along with cooperating with other agencies for intelligence collection and analysis, will make it possible for naval intelligence to attain impressive achievements in the future, for as it is written in the Bible (Deuteronomy 30:12–13), "It is not in heaven... Neither is it beyond the sea... But it is very near to you...that you should do it."

Section Six

The Dynamics of Israeli Intelligence Activity

The Mossad

Efraim Halevy
Former Director of the Mossad

A personal note: I served in the Mossad for close to forty years. I entered the Mossad as a junior research analyst, and saw service as a case officer during my first and second tours of duty, more than once under a false flag. I then rose in the ranks to serve as a deputy division chief, twice as a foreign station chief, two terms of five years each as an operational division chief and five years more as deputy head of service. I retired after close to thirty-five years of service, only to be recalled by Prime Minister Netanyahu to lead the Mossad after the abrupt resignation of my predecessor. I served three prime ministers in this post over a four and a half year period. I finally retired from government service after serving for one more year as head of the National Security Council. Obviously those many years of service provided me with insights that no one from the outside could ever hope to obtain; at the same time, of course, I cannot claim objectivity. And yet, perhaps this is a story, of necessity bowing to the exigencies of self-censorship, that may be told from a unique vantage point.

The Beginning

During my tenure as head of the Mossad, from time to time I met with several of my predecessors and former heads of the Security Service. Isser Harel, the legendary head of the Mossad for eleven eventful years (1952–1963), spent time with me and enriched my understanding of the ethos that guided him in the early days of the state; Amos Manor, who led the Security Service for ten years, more or less a contemporary of Harel, spun many a yarn, which always ended with his familiar roar of laughter. One day Amos told me he would never forget the morning he was awakened by a phone call from Yitzhak Navon, Prime Minister Ben-Gurion's chief of staff who later served as Israel's fifth president, ordering him to come in all due haste to see Ben-Gurion. Upon arrival, Navon met Manor on the office steps and told him to proceed alone to see the prime minister. He refused to give Manor any clue as to what it was about. Within minutes Amos was seated across from Ben-Gurion, who told him that Isser Harel had been in that very morning and urged him to appoint Harel to the post of deputy prime minister. Harel had told Ben-Gurion that Israel was about to face grave security threats, and his service at the side of the prime minister was essential to guarantee the survival of the fledgling State of Israel. Harel was not a member of the Knesset and therefore could not be appointed as a cabinet minister (that has since changed) but Ben-Gurion was at a loss how to deal with the unusual demand. Amos reacted calmly and assured the prime minister that all was well. There was no need to take such an extraordinary step.

I met Navon a while ago to confirm the accuracy of the story. He could not recall the incident, but then proceeded to tell me that it made sense and was right for the atmosphere at the time. He said that when Ben-Gurion resigned from office in 1963, Levi Eshkol, his finance minister, chose to assume the twin roles of prime minister and minister of defense. Harel, who had resigned only a few months previously as Mossad chief following a bitter policy dispute with Ben-Gurion, immediately asked to meet his former political master and told him that Eshkol was not qualified to become minister of defense and that Ben-Gurion should see to it that he, Harel, assumed the position. Ben-Gurion declined to intervene.

There is more than one way of looking at those two moves by Isser Harel, the legendary director of the Mossad. The easiest is, of course, to attribute them to hubris or megalomania; but Isser was by no means a man with a disturbed mind or tormented soul. For more than a decade he reigned over both the Mossad and the Israel Security Agency, and he was a highly respected member of the innermost circle controlling and underwriting the destiny of the State of Israel during the first decade of its existence. Those were days when a small population of six hundred thousand Jewish Israelis had to absorb over a million immigrants, most of them destitute survivors of the German Nazi concentration camps, alongside hundreds of thousands of Jews from Arab countries who had left all their worldly goods behind and spent years in temporary dwellings in hastily erected Israeli villages before they could go out and live meaningful lives. And those were the days when Israel, totally isolated in the Middle East following its valiantly fought War of Independence, had to confront all its neighbors, who continued to deny its right to exist.

In such a grave and unprecedented predicament, the citizens of Israel had to place their faith in the leadership, and in its overt and covert capabilities, to do the impossible and guide the nation toward a safe haven. The national military arm – the Israel Defense Forces (the IDF), into which every male and female of a certain age was conscripted – constituted one anchor of security; the secret services, the ISA for internal security and the Mossad for external operations, was the second anchor providing vital protection, early warning, priceless intelligence and extended capabilities unreported and little known. In those circumstances the myth was born – to which the entire nation subscribed – that Israel's capacity to survive and triumph against all odds was based not only on the power embodied in its conventional fighting forces but also on those hidden assets and capabilities that defied normal logic. For the people serving under Harel in those danger-filled days, the Mossad had a mission the likes of which was entrusted to no other intelligence service on earth: to guarantee national survival and well-being, come what may.

The mission was never spelt out in words – neither Harel nor any other person committed it to writing, and it was never alluded to even in Mossad gatherings – but it was in the air, something akin to a spirit guiding the Mossad in its early days and motivating the small band of anonymous officers serving under Harel as they were called upon, time and time again, to carry out clandestine operations, most of which still remain cloaked in secrecy. Harel, who faced many an impossible challenge, was often catapulted into a situation where he was expected to perform wonders with his meager staff, and the burdens his political masters placed on his shoulders led him to believe that the very fate of Israel depended on him. I believe that part of that indescribable aura survives to this very day, both inside the Mossad and within the general public.

The Name "Mossad"

The official name of the Mossad is the Institute for Intelligence and Special Assignments, but in the early '60s the Mossad assumed the English title of the Israel Secret Intelligence Service. I remember the occasion when it became necessary to have an official English name for the Mossad. Those present hastily convened and one of us said, somewhat in jest, that we should take the British SIS and add an I at the beginning; thus the ISIS was born. The name Mossad was taken from the original pre-state arm of the Jewish leadership in British-mandated Palestine, which had organized the waves of illegal Jewish immigrants who attempted, often successfully, to overcome the British naval blockade. In modern-day Hebrew, the word "*mossad*" is used to describe an educational, medical or academic institute or a professional, civilian arm of government, such as the national insurance institute. But the name Mossad has survived because successive governments have striven to perpetuate the myth that what we have is not just a service or an agency or a bureau. "Mossad" conjures up so much more, as does the name "special assignments." During my forty years of service I was often asked to spell out the multitude of sins covered by this appellation and have invariably responded with an elusive smile.

The missions and mandates of the Mossad have been fashioned from its modus operandi. The acid test as to whether a particular situation needs to be handled by the Mossad is determined by the degree of secrecy required.

If intelligence collection abroad needs to be a secretive task, the Mossad must do the job. If a traitor to Israel's cause in the person of Mordechai Va'anunu, for example, has to be brought home for trial clandestinely, it is the Mossad that must act quickly to perform the task. The upshot of this approach is that the Mossad must maintain a high degree of flexibility to be in a position to respond effectively to any challenge that might arise.

The growth of the Mossad over the last sixty-odd years has been incremental both in substance and in scope. In the early 1950s it began primarily as a collection agency operating in foreign lands, "the queen on the international intelligence chessboard," HUMINT as it is now called, but from the outset it became involved in clandestine operations under the heading of "national interest." One such interest has been to rescue Jewish communities in distress, thus the rescue of hundreds of thousands of Jews in Morocco in the 1950s and '60s was a Mossad operation.

HUMINT – the recruitment and running of agents – is the bread and butter of every intelligence service. To this day there is no substitute, technological or otherwise, for the two-legged source of information, and the Mossad has had multiple successes in the field. However, the cloak of secrecy covering the issue of sources and methods – the crown jewels of every service – needs to be preserved at any cost. Here and there the armor created to guard the treasures has been penetrated, but it should be noted that both quantitatively and qualitatively, the number of failures has been surprisingly small.

Liaison

In the late 1950s and early '60s a second aspect of clandestine activity came to the fore, that which is generally known as "liaison." For Israel, liaison carried many levels of significance; it took on the functions normally performed by all intelligence outfits around the world: contact between intelligence services and exchanges of information – sometimes raw and pinpointed and at other times collated – leading to written assessments. There are also meetings between experts, and ultimately, even operational cooperation falls into the area of common interests and necessities.

But for the nascent Israel, surrounded by the unyielding wall of its neighbors, united in hostility, and often internationally isolated in major parts of the world, it was immediately necessary to forge a strategy to overcome the initial disadvantages and to provide successive political masters with an effective political and defense bypass. Clearly the tool had to be clandestine, and the task was therefore assigned to the Mossad, where it was placed in the hands of the liaison division. Due to its critical nature and because it entailed creating and maintaining relationships at the highest level, every director of the Mossad was personally and extensively involved in it.

Two distinct areas were therefore added to the conventional field of liaison. The obvious one was the creation and maintenance of relationships with heads of state and their high-ranking subordinates in those countries where Israel was not allowed to establish normal diplomatic relations. The second was forging relationships with non-state actors who played significant roles in the Middle East.

The liaison function included links with King Hussein of Jordan and King Hassan of Morocco, to mention only two, coupled with large, extended operations like the link forged and fostered with the Kurdish movements in Northern Iraq in the early 1960s and the Christian community in Lebanon in the mid-'70s.

There was also a third area in need of attention. David Ben-Gurion believed that Israel should stretch its hand beyond the tight circle of Arab-state hostility to contact and create meaningful joint commitments and interests with the "outer circle" in the Middle East. Thus the triple informal alliance between Israel, Turkey and Iran under the Shah was born. The outreach to Ethiopia was another aspect of the approach. The Mossad was at the center of the strategy and was thus ordained to play a key role in enabling the state to break out of the regional isolation into which it had been born.

These tips of the iceberg illustrate the extensive and diverse nature of the missions that the Mossad has undertaken over its scores of years. The political and strategic value of its efforts catapulted the Mossad onto center stage time and time again; the cloak of secrecy and assured discretion endeared it as a tool of diplomacy to many a prime minister and gave the state an additional effective arm to pursue clandestine operations and diplomacy as necessities arose. It also automatically propelled successive Mossad directors into the inner circle of prime ministers and gave them an authoritative voice on many of the crucial issues of foreign policy and defense that adorned the weekly agendas of the political masters.

Thus it is no surprise that in the 1970s it was a Mossad director, Major General Yitzhak Hoffi, who was able to use a Moroccan platform to bring together the Israeli foreign minister at that time, Moshe Dayan, and Egyptian Deputy Prime Minister Hassan Tuhami. The first peace treaty between Israel and an Arab-Muslim state, Egypt, was in no small measure the ultimate product of that capability. Years later the Israeli public awoke one morning to the news that Prime Minister Rabin, a few months before his assassination, had paid an overnight visit to Oman, where he had conducted a long talk with its ruler, Sultan Qaboos.

Similarly, Israeli journalists accompanying Prime Minister Rabin on a state visit to China were unhappy to learn that they would spend a few more hours as passengers on the homecoming aircraft because

Rabin would be stopping off in Jakarta to meet the President of Indonesia, the country with the largest Muslim population. Mossad director Shabtai Shavit was the sole senior Israeli figure to accompany Rabin to that historic encounter.

Those relationships were passed on from one Mossad chief to the next and retained their unique value long after normal diplomatic relations were established. The relationship with the Hashemite throne is one such example. Successive heads of the Mossad, Generals Zamir and Hoffi, Nahum Admoni, Shabtai Shavit, Danny Yatom, Efraim Halevy and Meir Dagan, have each played significant roles in the link. In July 2010 Mossad Chief Meir Dagan participated in a meeting between King Abdullah II of Jordan and Prime Minister Netanyahu, and is said to have been influential in ending a yearlong estrangement between the two.

The Moscow Connection

The political role of the Mossad was expanded over the years and embraced contacts at the highest levels of state. One such effort has recently been made public. The Soviet Union severed diplomatic relations with Israel in the wake of the Six-Day War of 1967, when Israel emerged triumphant and, inter alia, assumed control of Egypt's Sinai Peninsula, Syria's Golan Heights and the West Bank of formerly British-mandated Palestine. A few years later Moscow realized that the lack of contact with Jerusalem was detrimental to its interests, and a clandestine link was established, initially run by senior diplomats on the Israel side and Russians who claimed to represent the leadership on the Russian side. When it became clear that the Russian representation included at least one identified KGB officer, Yuri Kotov, who had served in the Soviet Embassy in Israel, the link was passed to the Mossad and for over fifteen years was conducted by it.

The true nature of this contact was revealed by none other than the leading Soviet representative in the talks, who in later years served as Russian prime minister, foreign minister, and director of the SVR, the current successor to the intelligence arm of the former KGB. In a book he published in New York in 2009, entitled *Russia and the Arabs*, Yevgeny Primakov devoted fifty pages to his experiences in the role of representing "the higher level" of Moscow in its contacts with Israel. He recounted his visits to Israel, his secret meetings with Israeli prime ministers and more. His side of the story as he wished to tell it is public; the Israeli version will have to wait. One more tip of an ever-growing iceberg.

The growth of the Mossad and the gradual addition of capabilities and functions was, as already stated, incremental. It was only in the late 1960s that it created a variety of operational and technological arms, and it was only in the mid-'70s after the initially disastrous Yom Kippur War of 1973 that it was mandated by the findings of the judicial Agranat Commission to establish an assessment division. All of those steps were traditionally opposed by other elements within the intelligence community, which zealously fought to preserve their exclusivity and supremacy: the ISA in the operational field, and IDI in the minefield of national assessment.

Today it would be seen as a curiosity, but in the mid-'70s the IDI director forbade the dissemination of Mossad assessments, supposedly to prevent the military analysts from being influenced by the work of their Mossad compatriots. Tension rose even further when the Mossad created a small military assessment unit inside the original division. In my opinion, it took the Mossad almost a quarter of a century to gain true senior-level recognition for its legitimate role in the assessment field.

It was only in the final years of the 1990s that the Mossad established an intelligence division incorporating both assessments and requirements. The process of consolidation and streamlining was continued on the operational side of the "house" during the first decade of the current century.

Deniability

From time to time the presence of its head in one context or another has indicated Mossad involvement. In 1972 the Palestine Liberation Organization attacked the Israeli team at the Munich Olympics. Several sportsmen were taken hostage and as the crisis developed, the Mossad head at the time, Major General Zamir, appeared on the scene as Prime Minister Golda Meir's personal representative. The tragic end of the affair, the murder of eleven sportsmen, cast a shadow on the years to come and moved the Mossad to enter the clandestine war against terrorism, first Palestinian and subsequently against others who followed suit.

In that area, as in many others, the Mossad has been scrupulous in preserving the all-important principle of deniability, a major asset for any state and every government. It transcends the natural desire of so many to exercise the right to know and leaves the media free to speculate, to spin their yarns, more often than not far removed from truth and reality. This is a vital necessity because espionage, although a profession dating back to ancient, nay, biblical times, has never enjoyed a legal or formal status of any kind. An agent who is caught red-handed enjoys no privilege under international law or custom. He is not a prisoner of war and he cannot claim any kind of consideration or protection. Very often a country's insistent disavowal of a captured officer held by a foreign power increases the chances of securing an early release.

Deniability is practiced by almost all intelligence agencies worldwide, and the Mossad is no exception. In many cases it has been a very rewarding approach. It is a sad commentary on the Israeli media that in some cases, journalists' insatiable hunger to aggrandize themselves by exposing Mossad activities has caused enormous damage to national security.

A Clandestine War

Israel's security-war theater has grown geographically and qualitatively over the years. Its adversaries and enemies span the globe from North

Korea in Southeast Asia to the wilds of Latin America, as well as the dark continent of Africa, long known and appreciated. In order to cater to the country's vital security needs, a key requirement has been to develop a long arm, making it possible for it to preserve its vital interests against many a far-off foe. In the 1980s the Mossad launched a decade-long operation to rescue Ethiopian Jews from the hostile regime in Addis Ababa. The operation focused on Sudan, a neighboring country on the receiving end of a massive influx of more than a million refugees. Sudan has always been hostile to Israel, and the test of mounting and conducting a clandestine long-term operation in such a backward and unfriendly terrain, a thousand and more miles away from Israel's southernmost point, was severe. The operation, which saved the lives of many thousands without one loss of the force operating in the field, bears testament to a mere fraction of the Mossad's capabilities.

The Mossad has played vital roles in many operations where other factors have naturally and sometimes deservedly captured the limelight. In the Entebbe rescue operation the IDF landed in the heart of Uganda and released scores of captives being held hostage by Palestinian terrorists who had hijacked a civilian Air France flight. Were it not for the Mossad, the vital intelligence required for the dramatic and successful operation would not have been available, and the IDF plane would not have taken off from Israel. The same applies to the 1981 Israel Air Force attack on the Iraqi nuclear reactor, destroyed before it became operational. Most of the other Mossad contributions to the vital interests of Israel – the more daring ones, the ever more productive ones – will probably see the light of day several generations from now.

Who are the Mossad intelligence officers and where do they come from? During the formative years of the state, the Mossad was able to tap the rich reservoir of thousands of immigrants from Arab countries, who were well versed in Arabic language and customs. There were also the thousands of immigrants from European countries who could easily blend into the roles they had to play as Mossad agents in Europe, which was initially almost the only hunting ground for the Mossad. All that has now changed; the theaters of operation are multiple and the threats are more diverse, sophisticated and difficult to penetrate. The less said about successes in these times, the better.

Given the key role played by the Mossad in so many areas of vital importance to Israel's well being, a reader might assume that somewhere in the statute book provision was made giving this invaluable arm of government legal status. After all, the prime minister and the head of the Mossad are responsible for a multitude of activities, presumably, worldwide. Officers of the Mossad are ordered to expose themselves to dangers and hazards that are unequalled in any other branch of public service. The Mossad is a civilian, not a military, organ of the state. However, discipline among the ranks seems military more than civilian. Shortly after taking office as head of the Mossad, I raised the issue of the Mossad's legal status with the senior political levels. I was met with overt readiness to pass legislation providing for the conditions of the appointment, tenure and retirement of the head and his senior staff. However, I explained that I was seeking legal basis for the substantive orders given and clear legal commitments from the political level to the operatives in the field. At certain meetings I also listed the types of actions undertaken daily by officers operating in foreign countries. Invariably I was met by a wan smile followed by the short observation, "On second thought, we are better off without a law for the Mossad, although there is a law, a very generous and all embracing law, on the statute book for the ISA."

The upshot is that the level of mutual trust and understanding that must be almost religiously preserved in the Mossad surpasses that cultivated by any other arm of government. It creates a special bond between the prime minister, the Mossad chief and the latter's men and women who serve not only under conditions of anonymity but also under conditions of pure trust, devoid of legal coverage. That sacred trust must never be breached by either partner.

The Senior Command

A final word needs to be said about the senior command of the Mossad. The first head, Reuven Shiloah, spent many years in faraway Arab territories getting the lie of the land. He was appointed the first head of the Mossad by Prime Minister David Ben-Gurion and saw it through its formative years. He was succeeded by Isser Harel, who was a key figure in establishing its legend and myth and is best known for capturing Adolf Eichmann, the architect of the Final Solution, Adolf Hitler's plan for the extermination of the Jews. It was one of the Mossad's first long-arm operations, and many have followed. Harel was followed by Major General Meir Amit, who revamped the Mossad and modernized its activities. He represented Israel at the festivities mounted by the Shah of Iran to celebrate the 2500th anniversary of Cyrus, Emperor of the Persians. Amit was followed by Zvi Zamir, a retired army general, who presided over the service for six years, including the Yom Kippur War. In his days a central operational arm was created, and the technological division envisioned by his predecessor was established. The walls of this and other units are adorned with special plaques, each recording the receipt of the top prize for Israel's security by an individual or a team that invented and/or implemented a technologically excellent innovation. The reasons for the awards have never been made public, none of the names of those on whom an award has been conferred has ever been published, and rarely has the Mossad, as such, been cited in public as the recipient of such a distinction.

Major General Yitzhak Hoffi took over from Zamir in 1974 and stayed on the job for eight long, formative years. A quiet and outwardly unassuming officer, he demonstrated a nerve and character of steel and infinite patience, a rare but essential trait in human conduct, and was a born commander.

A year before his departure, Hoffi brought into the service a veteran serving army officer, Major General Yekutiel Adam, and appointed him to head the HUMINT division. He was obviously being groomed to succeed Hoffi, but when the First Lebanon War broke out in 1982 Adam was pressed back into military service and killed in action. In a public tribute, Prime Minister Begin stated openly that Adam had been slated as the next head of the Mossad.

Following that tragic event, the prime minister appointed Nahum Admoni, then deputy head of the service, to lead it. That was a precedent: never before had the appointment of a person from "within" been contemplated. Admoni had risen from the liaison division and served in the past both in Africa and in Europe. As deputy for close to six years, he had an uncanny knowledge of the system and a wide acquaintance with many of the officers in the business. He played a key role in renewing the relationship with the Hashemite royal house, which had been dormant for several years, and successfully commanded many major operations of great value. Moreover, he was the first Mossad head to cultivate a successor from within and thus set the scene for what might have become a rule rather than an exception.

Admoni left after seven years and was succeeded by his deputy, Shabtai Shavit. A veteran officer with much experience in both HUMINT and special operations, Shavit embodied a rare mix of daring and caution and was a leader in the best sense of the word. Under his reign, the Mossad changed its focus from its traditional targets to the growing threat from Iran. Seven years later, in 1996, Shavit left and was succeeded by Major General Danny Yatom, who had been military secretary to assassinated Prime Minister Yitzhak Rabin. His brief term of office, twenty-one months, was cut short by his resignation in the wake of the Mashaal affair, the Mossad's aborted attempt to kill a leading figure in the Hamas movement, a Jordanian citizen, in the heart of Jordan's capital, Amman. A commission of enquiry appointed by Prime Minister Binyamin Netanyahu did not specifically call for his departure, but the incessant public pummeling of the Mossad over the failure was exacerbated by another mishap, which resulted in a veteran Mossad operative's being caught and arrested in Switzerland. Yatom decided to resign and was replaced by the writer of this article, who was recalled from his post as Israel's ambassador to the European Union. I had previously served in the Mossad for close to thirty-five years, lastly as its deputy head for five years under Shabtai Shavit. I served for four and a half years and for obvious reasons will say nothing about that period. I was succeeded by Major General Meir Dagan, who was lauded for his eight-year stint. He was replaced by Tamir Pardo, a most distinguished insider, making him the fourth appointment from within.

Eleven Mossad heads, only four from within the Mossad, as compared to twelve heads, all except one from within, who served in the ISA. What does that say about the Mossad? What significance does that have in relation to the devoted and exceptional band of capable officers who have served in the service for more than sixty years? Of the three Mossad chiefs coming from within, only one was specifically groomed for the mission. Only one Mossad director saw it as his duty to groom a successor.

Looking around the world for comparisons, the findings are mixed. Britain has invariably chosen a person from within for both its intelligence service and the security service, except in a very few cases. In the United States the CIA has usually had a director from outside the service, often a former political figure. In Germany, Italy, Spain and France, there have rarely been promotions from inside.

And yet I cannot escape being disappointed that, whether by intent or coincidence, the position of head of the Mossad has often been viewed as a consolation prize for a distinguished army officer who did not make it to chief of staff. The performance of those chosen, by and large, has been admirable, but surely that is not proof that service in the Mossad should be predicated on the assumption that no one should strive to make it to the top. Given everything noted above, and in view of the superb performance by Mossad officers and the exemplary courage they have often displayed, day in, day out, I think they deserve better on that score.

Vital Intelligence

In this day and age it is increasingly difficult to ensure the secrecy vital to mounting, maintaining and executing the clandestine operations required to preserve and protect the security of a state and its citizens. Every intelligence agency operates under basic rules and fundamental norms, one of which is the preservation of the need-to-know rule. That not only refers to the separation between all those inside the fold and the public at large, but also within the agency itself. Compartmentalization is a basic tool for protecting the crown jewels. That, of course, collides with the public's ever-growing demand to exercise its right to know. By and large, the Mossad has succeeded in raising a shield of secrecy around its most delicate and successful operations, and that in itself, I believe, is an achievement. The downside is that journalists and others, eager to publish and thus make a living, have written books and articles on the Mossad claiming to reveal inside information and quasi-authoritative accounts of one type or another. Much of it has been based on unsubstantiated gossip and is a cross that the Mossad has willingly, if somewhat reluctantly, borne with dignity.

So, in conclusion, where does that leave us? Is the Mossad a myth or reality? Is the emperor naked? Has the Mossad become a power by perpetuating its mythological escapades, or has it become of the victim of these very myths and does it, in reality, fall far short of its legendary image.

On the basis of my forty years in the business, I am convinced that our achievements have outshone the myth. But why take my word for it? Why not demand that I prove my contentions, citing chapter and verse? What is my response to the claim that the Mossad's known and publicised failures stretching over sixty years have exposed the weaknesses of this faithful band? I cannot reply in substance but I can respond by citing statistics, an accepted yardstick in the field of public and academic endeavor. Every time a failure hits the fan and is spread over the front pages of the daily tabloids, the press invariably recalls previous mishaps. They are trotted out to remind the reader that the Mossad is a serial bungler. How many have there been? Five? Ten? Fifteen? In more than sixty years? Even by the most stringent statistical measure, the Mossad and its sister agency, the ISA, are clearly second to none.

Close to fifty years ago, a young Jewish boy was kidnapped by his grandfather because the parents had decided to remove him from his ultra-Orthodox environment to a secular surrounding. Yosseleh Shuchmacher disappeared into thin air and had most probably been smuggled out of the country. Prime Minister Ben-Gurion summoned the head of the Mossad, Isser Harel, and ordered him to find the boy wherever he was and bring him home. Harel, who was also invested with a supervisory role over the ISA, set up a special command post and clandestinely began a worldwide search for the child. The abduction was judged by Ben-Gurion as an act carried out by a specific sector of the population in blatant defiance of the authority of the state and as a strategic threat to its viability.

It became necessary to penetrate the ultra-Orthodox community, and those in the relatively small service at the time who had both a native English-speaking and religious Jewish background were rounded up to pose as ultra-Orthodox Jews and to collect information. As one of them, it was my first introduction to the clandestine world. I never asked at the time why I was to participate in such a mission or what the legal basis for the entire enterprise was. The operation seemed endless, and I operated inside Israel appropriately disguised. Ultimately the Mossad was able to discover the missing boy in a New York apartment, and the FBI was approached and agreed to secure his release and transfer him to Israel. To this day I do not know how it was all ultimately accomplished; I was a very small cog in the wheel. The return of Yosseleh was a feather in the cap of both the Mossad and Isser Harel, and became one of its legends.

A few months ago the family of a former colleague asked me to record a video message of congratulations to be shown at a party celebrating his eightieth birthday. I had known him for more than forty years and from time to time our paths had crossed. The family came over and spoke of the man's tight-lipped secret deportment. One of them told me that the only bit of information they knew about him had to do with his clandestine activity in the Yosseleh affair. Neither he nor I knew till then that we had both been cogs on the same wheel.

Operational Demands
Placed on Intelligence

Brigadier General (Res.) David Tzur
Former IDI Chief of Staff and CEO of the Israel Intelligence
Heritage and Commemoration Center

Introduction

This article deals with the present-day operational challenges faced and met by intelligence, focusing primarily on military intelligence. They are born of changes in regional and global military and strategic environments (which in turn alter the nature of warfare and the relevant threats), important military technological developments (with an emphasis on exact armaments) and a surfeit of information and information warfare.

Changes in the Strategic Environment and the Circle of Threat

After the founding of the State of Israel, the armies of the Arab countries were the main threat to its existence. However, with the changes in Israel's strategic environment over the past few decades, the nature of the threats has changed as well. The new threats are the result of changes both global (the collapse of the Soviet Union, the rise of radical Islam and global Islamic terrorism led by Al-Qaeda) and local, of which three are particularly important: (1) the fact that Israel's peace agreements with Egypt and Jordan and the American occupation of Iraq reduced to a minimum the level of conventional, symmetric confrontation

(confrontation between national armies) and eliminated the eastern front; (2) the new situation created in the Palestinian Authority territories (with the signing of the Oslo Accords, PA security and police forces entered the territories), along with the continuing activity of the traditional nationalist and religious terrorist organizations; and (3) the creation of a northern front, which includes Syria, Iran and its proxy in Lebanon, Hezbollah.

The changes shifted the weight of the threat to the following:

- Local terrorism, including surface-to-surface rockets and suicide bombing attacks. The sources are Palestinian, Lebanese or related to Al-Qaeda.
- Surface-to-surface missiles and non-conventional weapons: Scud missiles centered in Syrian land and long-range Shihab missiles in Iran. There is also an arsenal of biological and chemical warheads that can be fitted to the missiles and Iran's developing nuclear threat.
- Conventional army warfare: a potential threat emanating especially from Syria. However, with the current strategic situation of peace with Egypt and Jordan, the chances of its becoming an actual threat are very low. Only dramatic changes in Egypt and/or Jordan might put a conventional war back on the agenda.
- Border infiltrations, which are increasing, especially along the border with Egypt. Most of the activity centers on drug smuggling, but there is also traffic in women and illegal immigration, all of which pose a threat to Israeli society. In addition, every illegal border crossing is also a potential terrorist activity.

Accordingly it can be said that currently most of the frequently realized threats (terrorism, rocket and mortar shell fire and illegal border crossings) fall within the bounds of asymmetric warfare. That is more complicated and complex than symmetric warfare, in which national armies fight one another, making aggressive use of regular military formations according to recognized international rules. In asymmetric warfare a non-national belligerent force operates differently. First of all, it employs terrorism and guerilla tactics and operates clandestinely in small groups and from within a civilian population, which serves as a shield and hiding place. The group attacks the Israeli civilian population, using for its own ends the ideological restrictions the IDF places on itself, and for the most part the battlefield is urban. The media are a weapon in its arsenal and are exploited to influence public opinion, and the involvement of local and international governmental organizations is common. All of the above make intelligence action far more difficult and challenging.

Basic Demands from Intelligence

Based on what has just been said, the basic demands placed on IDI are the following:

- It must provide all types of military and political early warnings, including of terrorist activity, symmetric warfare, changes in regional and international strategy that are liable to endanger Israel immediately and eventually, and so forth.
- Operational analysis of the territory is the cornerstone of producing tactical intelligence. Asymmetric warfare has new dimensions in that a large part of the fighting takes place in an urban setting, which has special operational significance. There is also an underground dimension, the use of tunnels, which is widespread in Lebanon and the Gaza Strip. An operational ground analysis is also important in symmetric warfare, because it became clear how important the element of maneuvering was after the Second Lebanon War.
- The continual monitoring of threats, as well as existing and potential opportunities, is the basic work of military intelligence, necessitated by the situations of symmetric and asymmetric

warfare, during both battles and lulls in the fighting. Based on the information, intelligence is able to provide the best results in early warning, an update on the enemy, updated objectives, possible scenarios and possible enemy action. A classic example of threat monitoring is the Iranian nuclear program, which was identified by military intelligence when it began and which has been closely followed for years.

- Exact information about various targets is vital. Knowledge of enemy firepower is an important element in warfare and can prevent losses to troops. Considering the technological capabilities of exact ordnance on the one hand, and its high cost on the other, intelligence is required to provide the most exact targets possible in quantities that will produce the most effective results. In addition, given the nature of the confrontation, the mission is even more vital in asymmetric warfare because of the necessity to minimize collateral damage.

- Intelligence in real time and almost real time is also vital. Because relevant, effective decisions regarding events in battle must be made, receiving intelligence in real time or almost real time is critical. That is especially true in asymmetric warfare, particularly regarding targets, because they are relatively small and individual (unlike the troop formations in symmetric warfare), as well as extremely short lived. The best scenario is for information to be relayed directly from sensor to shooter to shorten the circle of action.

- Intelligence superiority and information warfare are also important elements. Intelligence must be superior to the adversary's for understanding the strategic, operative and tactical situation and for turning understanding into an operative advantage leading to victory. That superiority is created on the one hand by better intelligence, and on the other by preventing the adversary from obtaining information about our side. To that end intelligence has to wage information warfare, an effort as important as firepower and maneuvering.

- Information has to be utilized to the fullest in an era when "the information cup runneth over." The amount of information pouring into the various collection systems, especially open source information, is enormous, now far more than in the past. The challenge of intelligence filtering systems is to separate the wheat from the chaff and strain out firm, relevant intelligence from all the information collected.

The Response

To meet the aforementioned challenges, an intelligence system has to based on the following:

Within the Range of Pure Intelligence

- Information and knowledge collaboration inside the organization, between the branches of the organization (the intelligence community) and internationally (foreign relations) is vital for success.
- Centralization coupled with decentralization makes it possible to bring independent collection to the operative and tactical level, while also making it possible to profit from regional strategic collection based on network warfare. What in particular is needed is the VISINT capabilities (especially from the air); the capability to "see through walls" in the urban battlefield; and advanced locating capabilities.
- Basic information systems about the enemy's infrastructure, which provide intelligence based on geography.
- The greater integration of collection, processing and analysis provides an information cross section based on geographic location as well as greater involvement of production and analysis in collection.

- A continued intelligence presence in an area gives a daily picture of the threats on the ground. Asymmetric warfare necessitates the ongoing presence of various sensors according to a specific plan as the key to early warnings and creating a picture of enemy intelligence and of targets.
- Broad, rapid conveyance systems make it possible to transmit all types of communications (audio, video, etc.).

Within the Combined Intelligence-Operational Range

- One response is waging integrated warfare, i.e., involving the operational side in intelligence information more thoroughly than before, and the active participation of intelligence in planning battles and constructing the systems that make that possible.
- Information is provided to the operational ranks, including the lowest rank possible, so that it may be implemented as effectively as possible. However, various limitations must also be taken into consideration.
- The work-circles of collection and attack are shortened. Because of the nature of the warfare and the elusiveness of the adversary, the time between the sensor's (or sensors') locating the targets and the information's reaching the attackers should be as short as possible. The final intention is one platform that can both collect and attack, and thus shorten the work-circles of collection and attack.

Conclusion

The confrontations of the current era are more complex and complicated than they were in the past, making the challenges for intelligence harder to meet. Intelligence is critical to operations, which have become almost surgical. To meet the challenges successfully, intelligence must be exact, provided in real time or almost in real time, continual and available to all the relevant ranks at the relevant time. That requires enormous financial and human resources, as well as cutting-edge technology in both collecting and processing information. The amount of intelligence collected and its quality are directly related to what is invested in them. Those are facts the decision makers have to recognize and understand, and no less important is their recognition of intelligence's limits in general and its limits in specific events in particular.

Relationship between the Decision Makers and the Head of Intelligence

Major General Meir Amit
Former Head of IDI and Director of the Mossad

The relationship between the head of an intelligence organization, an appointee, and the decision makers and especially the prime minister, who are elected officials, is intricate and complex. There is a lack of balance in the way they arrived at their positions.

The first question is how intelligence enters the decision-making process. The second is the worth of intelligence in the decision-making process. Intelligence has no intrinsic value, but acquires it when accompanied by interpretation. The mere acquisition of information and its transfer to the decision makers is insufficient; what is important is how it is used. There have been decision makers who do not understand that intelligence work is a vast mosaic, and wrongly perceive intelligence workers as prophets. As defense minister, Moshe Dayan preferred raw data, and would draw his own conclusions from snippets of information. In general, however, raw intelligence is not passed along before the picture is clear and the information has been confirmed by at least two other sources. That is because mistakes may be made if the whole picture cannot be seen. As noted, there are decision makers who prefer raw intelligence because they want to get a feeling for what is happening, but there is always a danger that incorrect decisions will be made based on misinterpretation of the information.

One of the difficulties in intelligence work is coping with the enemy. For example, often the enemy himself does not know what he would do if he had to make a decision. On the eve of the Six-Day War, when Egyptian President Gamal Nasser invaded the Sinai Peninsula, it was out of frustration with the outcome of the 1956 Sinai Campaign, which turned the peninsula into a demilitarized zone with a UN peace-keeping force, a situation he could not accept. In addition, the Soviet Union wanted to create another area of tension for the United States that would complement Vietnam. The Soviets, considering their influence in Egypt and Syria, regarded the Middle East as a suitable region. They exploited that influence by telling Syria that Israel was planning to attack, and advising them to pressure Egypt to come to Syria's aid by deploying Egyptian army forces in the Sinai Peninsula.

When Nasser entered Sinai, he gave the commander of the UN observer force the order to evacuate its stations and to either enter its camps or leave. The commander asked the UN Secretary General at the time, U Thant, what to do, and he was told to leave Sinai. All the events that followed would have been different if U Thant had decided to keep the forces in the camps. However, U Thant made his decision, which only increased Nasser's appetite, with the result that Nasser closed the Straits of Tiran, Israel's exit to the Red Sea and thence to Africa and Asia, to Israeli ships.

At first Nasser had not planned to go to war, but one thing led to another. There have even been claims that if Israel had done nothing, the Six-Day War would not have taken place. However, in retrospect it became clear – illuminated by documents seized after the war – that the Egyptians were in fact planning a defensive battle, hoping to halt the Israeli attack and then to counterattack, invade Israel's territory and cut off Eilat. They did not have the chance to carry out their plans because the Israeli attack succeeded in crushing them.

The story of the Six-Day War proves that rather than being static, intelligence is dynamic and complex, and sometimes leaves in doubt what can be expected from the enemy. That is especially true when the enemy does not himself know what his next step will be or cannot assess the importance of all the developments that may follow his decisions and moves.

Another issue concerning the relationship between the decision makers and intelligence is the question of responsibility: Who is responsible for an intelligence failure? In the United States, it is the decision makers. In the State of Israel it is always the military commanders: After the Yom Kippur War, it was Chief of Staff General David Elazar and the heads of Israeli military intelligence who were held accountable. Before that, it was the heads of military intelligence who paid the price for Operation Suzanna (the undoing of an Israeli intelligence network in Egypt in 1954).[1] The question repeated was, "Who gave the order?" However, the correct question would have been, "Who was responsible?" because that was who should have born the responsibility. Thus in Israel, responsibility always stops one level below the politicians.

How is the head of intelligence included in the decision-making process? To a great extent, it depends on the decision makers. Israel's first prime minister, David Ben-Gurion, knew how to receive assistance from the head of military intelligence. For example, following receipt of the information that the Egyptians were plotting to assassinate Jordan's King Hussein, I, as head of military intelligence, was sent to meet with the Jordanians to pass along the information, in the hope (and with good reason) that it would lead to the development of an intelligence and political channel between Israel and Jordan (which in fact did happen). The head of Jordanian intelligence was not available, so I met with the director of the king's office, to whom I gave the names of the potential assassins. That was a good example of how Ben-Gurion knew how to make immediate use of intelligence information for political needs.

---

1.   For further information, see the article by Shlomo Nakdimon, "Operation Suzanna," pp. 49–58.

Ben-Gurion was followed as prime minister by Levi Eshkol. He spoke to intelligence personnel as equals, and he listened with great attention to what we had to say. He projected an image of compromise and hesitation but it was sometimes an advantage: the faltering speech he made on the eve of the Six-Day War cast Israel as the underdog in the eyes of the world, and when the war broke out, after a tense waiting period of three weeks, the world was sympathetic.

Thanks to Eshkol's relaxed nature and ability to listen, as head of the Mossad I was smoothly integrated into the decision-making process. One night during the three weeks before the outbreak of the Six-Day War, while the IDF reserve forces were being called up, the CIA representative in Israel came to me with the following message: "If you fire the first shot, you'll be alone." Similar warnings had been received from De Gaulle and Harold Wilson, the British prime minister.

One morning, during our daily meeting with the prime minister – we were military intelligence director Major General Aharon Yariv, Foreign Minister Abba Eban, the director of the Prime Minister's Office Yaakov Herzog and myself as Mossad director – Yariv suggested sending me to the United States to examine its position. The next day I flew to Washington and met with CIA director Richard Helms, a good friend of Israel. He said the Americans were not making plans to resolve the crisis. I asked to meet someone in the upper echelons of the American administration, and he arranged a meeting for me with the American secretary of defense, Robert McNamara. After I explained the situation, he asked me two questions: How many casualties would Israel suffer and how long would it take? I told him it would take a week and there would be fewer casualties than in Israel's War of Independence. He said, "I read you loud and clear." Before we parted I asked him if it would be worth my while to remain in Washington for another day or two. He said, "No, go home, that's where you should be." No answer could have been clearer, and I understood that the United States would not object to an Israeli military action.

The Israeli ambassador to the United States, Avraham Herman, disagreed with my interpretation of McNamara's remarks. I suggested he come back with me to Israel to present his opinion to the government, and he agreed. At a small, classified government meeting, Herman and I presented our positions. The following evening, which was a Saturday, the entire government met and decided (with two left-wing abstentions) to go to war, and the Six-Day War began the following Monday morning.

There are several ways to present a picture of a situation to the decision makers or the government. One is to present a general intelligence picture and say, "That's what I know, make of it what you will," and the other is to present the picture and translate it into options. A third possibility is to present the picture and the options, and to recommend one of them. I remember a discussion I had about possibilities with the head of the CIA's research department. He said, "Present the picture, and let it go at that." I told him that was the wrong tack to take, and that in my opinion as head of an intelligence organization, the picture should be presented and the options given, and that sometimes it was also necessary to make a recommendation. I said I would choose the second possibility, that is, to present the picture and the options.

There has to be a close relationship between the decision makers and the head of an intelligence organization so that the intelligence worker can understand what the decision makers want and the decision makers in turn can understand the intelligence process. However, the head of an intelligence organization must preserve his independence and not surrender to the mindset of the decision makers.

When I began as Mossad director, the affair of the German scientists working in Egypt was exposed. It was feared they would help the Egyptians develop missile capabilities that would be turned against Israel. Isser Harel, my predecessor as head of the Mossad, considered it a serious problem. As far as I was concerned, the problem was mainly one of internal politics: Foreign Minister Golda Meir and the heads of

Mapai (the ruling party) versus Prime Minister Ben-Gurion. Meir and the heads of Mapai were convinced the Germans were helping in an Egyptian effort to destroy the State of Israel, but Ben-Gurion felt there was a different Germany, and that Israel had to think about relations with it in terms of what was good for its own future and strength.

An intelligence head's entanglement in internal political quarrels is unhealthy, and should be avoided insofar as is possible. That is one of the difficult dilemmas of the head of an intelligence organization: on the one hand, it is important for him to have close relations with the prime minister, because he has to know how the prime minister thinks so that the chemistry between them is good. On the other, his independence is important, as is his ability to present an objective picture, even if it is one the decision makers won't like. Thus the intelligence head has to know how to be close to the decision makers while preserving his independence, and to present them with findings even if those findings contradict their worldview. The greatest danger is for intelligence to become politicized, and this must be avoided at all costs.

The head of an intelligence organization is usually very much alone at the top. He has to take responsibility for many decisions he keeps to himself so that the decision makers do not suffer from too much stress. If he provides them with too many decisions to make, the bureaucracy involved will keep them from functioning. However, in the final analysis, responsibility rests with the prime minister. Deciding when to bring something to the attention of the prime minister is one of the central problems for an intelligence head.

An example of the issue of when an intelligence head should report to the prime minister was the affair of bringing the Iraqi MIG-21 to Israel in 1966. After the Iraqi pilot was recruited and debriefed in Europe, members of the Israeli air force approached me with a request to allow him to enter Israel so he could see the airfield where he would have to land. That posed a double dilemma for me: Whether or not to allow him into the country, and whether or not to inform the prime minister. At that point Levi Eshkol knew nothing about the operation because it was only in its initial stages, and there was no reason to concern him with it. Eventually I did tell him, because it was possible that something would go wrong, and it was better he knew about it sooner than later.

Two short notes in conclusion:

- From time to time in Israel, problems have been solved by nominating an intelligence advisor to the prime minister. In my opinion, that is not the correct solution. The correct solution would be to have a minister in the prime minister's office equal in rank to the deputy prime minister, whose role would be to coordinate with the heads of the intelligence services.

- An important issue for the activities and status of intelligence services and their relations with the decision makers is civilian oversight. There are various solutions. In Israel the solution was to appoint a Knesset subcommittee for secret services under the Foreign Relations and Defense Committee. It is the parliamentary body responsible for overseeing Israel's intelligence services. Although it has less authority than the oversight apparatuses of the United States Congress, it has proved itself an effective overseeing body.

The Revision Process in the Intelligence

Colonel (Ret.) Dr. Shmuel Even
Former Head of IDI's Revision Department

The revision department (RD, also known as the Devil's Advocate Department) of Israeli military intelligence is a small unit, atypical on the world military scene. Its main role is to think outside the box and to challenge the perceptions held by intelligence analysts at any given time. It deals not only with military matters but also with sensitive political issues, such as intelligence assessments of the peace process. Though it is directly subordinate to the head of military intelligence, it enjoys exceptional freedom of expression for a military unit. Furthermore, the head of the RD is one of the very few army officers whose documents reach the prime minister, the defense minister, chairman of the Foreign Affairs and Defense Committee, and others.

Why the Revision Department (RD) Was Established

On October 6, 1973, the State of Israel was surprised by an Egyptian-Syrian attack. With a tremendous effort and at the cost of many lives the IDF repelled the attack, but the country was rocked to its foundations. One of the conclusions of the Agranat National Commission, appointed after the war to investigate the debacle, was that military intelligence had failed to provide an early warning of the war. According to the committee's report, IDI had in fact received the necessary information, but had erred in interpreting it, as its perception of the enemy's intentions was clouded by a smokescreen set up by the Egyptians, who convinced IDI that it was preparing for an exercise. One of the main reasons behind the failure, the committee determined, was the lack of conceptual pluralism. According to the findings, the government of Israel had depended exclusively on the military intelligence assessments division of the general staff, and there was no other analytic body within the intelligence community to provide a counterweight to it. In addition, within military intelligence itself, a culture of openness to and patience for other opinions had not been developed.

The conclusions of the Agranat Commission led to organizational changes and the establishment of the RD, one of whose roles would be to examine the prevailing opinion and present alternatives. Other changes instituted to reinforce pluralism in intelligence assessment were reinforcing analysis bodies outside the IDF to counterbalance the political aspects of the IDI production and analysis division, and reinforcing the intelligence divisions of the various regional commands in the IDF to counterbalance the military assessment of the military intelligence division of the general staff. An advisor to the prime minister for intelligence was appointed, a role that had not existed for a long time.

The RD was established first within the IDI's production and analysis division, which created a conflict of interest. In 1983 it was made separate from the production and analysis division and became an independent department commanded directly by the head of IDI, with only two senior analysts. Thus, to a certain degree the modus operandi of the department is an extension of the personality and experience of its director, and its success is greatly dependent on the capabilities of the two intelligence officers and the support they receive from the IDI head.

The Department's Mission

The department's mission is to help IDI reduce the probability of a failure in evaluating issues with strategic importance for the State of Israel, such as providing early warning of war, large army maneuvers, strategic terrorist attacks, and the development and use of non-conventional weapons by Israel's enemies. However, it also deals with identifying opportunities for peace with the other countries in the Middle East, which are usually given the highest priority.

The Department's Functions and Methods

- To present different opinions for assessment to the intelligence bodies in the IDF and the head of the IDI analysis division to counterbalance group thinking.
- To note topics and directions for possible development that did not receive attention in military intelligence's assessments.
- To help improve the intelligence product by monitoring its quality and work processes within IDI.
- To provide a sounding board for other opinions expressed by lower-level analysts and support them in bringing their opinions to the attention of the heads of the system.
- To examine retrospectively the assessments of various production and analysis bodies to help them learn the necessary lessons and improve their analytical processes.
- To support IDI work when it may directly or indirectly influence the intelligence product.
- To advise the IDI's chief with issues he acknowledges are relevant.

The Department's Philosophy

In general, the department's methodology is critical analysis. That is, its analysts search for information and arguments that contradict the theses constructed by the intelligence community's various production and analysis departments. One anomaly is sufficient to refute a thesis, or at least to warrant a reexamination. However, the department often expresses its own analytical opinions, and in critical issues such as the early warning of a war, it investigates the matter thoroughly to develop its own thesis as a counterweight. It is especially important to initiate a critical discussion when the various intelligence bodies are in agreement.

On the other hand, its role is not to serve as another intelligence assessment department, which would destroy its uniqueness.

The RD is not in charge of the assessment processes of the apparatuses it monitors. Responsibility for internal control belongs to their commanders, such as the head of the production and analysis division, heads of the various arenas, the intelligence officers of the various commands, etc. In other words, it is not the role of the RD to replace independent internal examinations that are an integral component of the assessment process itself. The RD does not deal with evaluating the functioning of intelligence personnel, but rather examines the intelligence assessments they produce, although the connection between the two sometimes creates tension.

The Bodies Examined and the RD's Clients

The department examines the intelligence assessments of IDI, especially its production and analysis division, as well as occasional examinations of the Mossad, the Israel Security Agency and the Ministry of Foreign Affairs, at least for IDI needs. Often intelligence clients, such as the prime minister, the defense minister and the chief of staff, have inquired whether there were differences in the various intelligence assessments, and if so, why.

The RD's clients are the IDI director and various bodies, the prime minister, the defense minister, the foreign minister, the upper echelons of the IDF, the Knesset's Foreign Affairs and Defense Committee, other departments within the intelligence community and planning personnel both inside and outside the IDF. The department is one of the IDF's only units authorized to circulate its products to the most senior political and security offices, similar to the circulation of intelligence documents of the production and analysis division. For years, the RD's independent status gained the intelligence community's recognition.

The Department's Products

The department supplies a number of products. They are usually distributed as documents, and some are presented at various deliberations. The main ones are the following:

- Reports of the examination of intelligence deployment of the various factors: How accurate are the reports? To what extent are they based on information? Can the same assumptions and facts be used to reach completely difference conclusions? The reports sometimes include production and analysis assessments. As a general rule, the RD does not compete with other intelligence bodies. Its function is to show them and the intelligence clients that the same data can sometimes lead to different intelligence assessments, no less solid than those originally reached.

- Comparisons between the assessments of the various production and analysis bodies of the intelligence community: For example, a comparison is often made between IDI and Mossad assessments of the development of non-conventional weapons in the Middle East, and often serves to hasten an investigation of the factors behind the discrepancies, sometimes at the request of the political masters. For technical issues in which the RD does not have expertise, it seeks the help of external experts serving in the reserves.

- Annual examinations of the achievements and failures of the IDF's production and analysis branches: In presenting the annual intelligence assessment to the general staff, the head of the RD indicates intelligence successes and failures during the preceding year. The assessment is also distributed to other intelligence clients, including the prime minister and the defense minister.

- Playing the devil's advocate is an accepted way of challenging intelligence assessments. The director of the RD states a position opposed to that of the intelligence analysts. He presents all the logical data and information supporting the position. The analysts try to disprove his thesis. If they cannot, they must reexamine their own conclusions. For example, in May 1998 the RD issued a document titled "A unilateral Israeli withdrawal from Lebanon will significantly reduce the number rocket-fire attacks against Israel." Its objective was to challenge the opinion that withdrawing from south Lebanon without an agreement would increase the number of terrorist attacks carried out along Israel's northern border.

- Focus on the needs of intelligence clients: Intelligence needs are focused to make the decision makers aware of the specific intelligence matters the department feels are important. In that case, the relevant intelligence information – but not necessarily assessment – is circulated to the decision makers and those who make strategic decisions. For example, in April 1997 the RD distributed to the army and government a document entitled "Arafat still adheres to the political process but continues along the path of attacking Israel." The document, called "Spotlight," was written following a study done by the IDI's production and analysis division called "Whither Palestine?" The RD was of the opinion that a firmer stand could be taken regarding the Palestinians' use of violence and terrorism against Israel to achieve political goals, which is what happened during the Al-Aqsa intifada, which began in September 2000.

- Damage control assessment: On occasion there have been serious mishaps within the intelligence community that have influenced its end products. One was the case of a former Mossad agent who was detained in 1997 after it became evident that he had fabricated a false early warning and misled the Syrian desk of Israeli intelligence. As a result, the IDI director asked the department to examine the extent of the damage and its consequences for the intelligence picture.

- Recommendations: The department is asked to recommend improvements in producing intelligence and its end products.

To summarize: The IDI's revision department is an important tool for reducing lapses in assessment. We believe that the Israeli revision department might serve as a model to other intelligence services in the world, with the proper adjustments.

Problems with Collective Thinking

Major General (Res.) Shlomo Gazit
Former Head of IDI and the IDI's Production and Analysis Division

Every hierarchical organizational system runs the unavoidable risk of being subject to conceptual collectivism, the danger of an individual's being sucked into the mindset and evaluations of the group or person at the top of the pyramid. The situation is well known and familiar to everyone, and even the dangers are well known in almost every organizational system, both public and private. It is common even when a clear directive has been issued inviting full freedom of speech and giving unequivocal assurance that no one expressing an opinion different from the consensus or from the opinion of the person highest in the hierarchy will suffer in any way. It is also one of the greatest dangers lying in wait for an intelligence system, especially one dealing with evaluation and analysis.

I was part of IDI evaluation and analysis for almost fifteen years, from 1964 to 1979. I had firsthand knowledge of the wonderfully democratic tradition of open deliberations, in which a general and a second lieutenant sit at the same table and express opposing opinions, apparently without taking rank into consideration. However, the operative word is "apparently."

Having sat at the head of the table for many years, I watched as others looked and tried to guess, from a chance remark or perhaps even body language, what my position was, how I was planning to sum up the deliberations and which of the positions offered I would choose. Often one or another would change his mind after it seemed to him that my opinion was different from his. If that often happens during

316

discussions when all the participants are analysts, it is even more characteristic of discussions in the general staff, foreign minister's staff or the security staff.

I spent a great deal of time wondering how to overcome that perfectly human inclination. I felt it was one of the dangers threatening intelligence evaluations, and I knew it was one of the factors behind our mistaken collective evaluations on the eve of the Yom Kippur War.

The first and most logical step was to begin meetings by asking the participants to express their opinions with complete freedom, without bias and without fear of having an opinion different from or even contrary to those expressed by senior officers. During those years I can candidly say that no prejudicial action was ever taken against those who disagreed with their superiors.

I did my best not to utter a word until the end of the deliberations, not until I was asked to sum up. I hoped in that way no one would try to change his opinion to match what he thought my opinion or evaluation was.

Needless to say, what I did not know was the spirit of what had been said before the participants met in my office, and those earlier discussions are held every day in intelligence work, and often at two lower levels, the production and analysis division and in the relevant departments. I assumed – and hoped – that at those levels the same procedure of free expression had been followed.

To make sure, I circulated a personal letter to all the intelligence corps officers, instructing them to encourage independent thought and, should the path of unpopular thought be blocked for any reason, to approach me, the IDI director, personally, circumventing all the command channels on the way. Again, I promised that no prejudicial action would be taken. During my five-year stint as IDI head I was approached no more than four or five times. What was disturbing was that at no time did anyone claim to having had contrary opinions blocked by their superiors. They only wanted me, as IDI head, to notice them...

I also included Middle East experts from Tel Aviv University in important deliberations, despite the fact that there were analysts who resented the presence of such "civilians." All of those university analysts had previously worked for IDI and had three particularly desirable traits:

- They were not subordinate or answerable to me and would have no reason to want to agree with me.
- Regardless of their expertise, they were not party to any secrets and not familiar with classified intelligence material, and they used different sources.
- They were unaware of conceptions formulated during day-to-day evaluation and analysis work.

In conclusion, in certain instances we noted dissenting evaluations in our documents. In my assessment, that encouraged the expression of such opinions during deliberations. I am in no way convinced that I found a solution to the human problem, but the very fact that I was aware of the danger meant we did our best not to be trapped by it.

Appendices

Appendix 1

Historical Timetable

Amos Gilboa

This appendix gives the reader a timetable of various intelligence events that have taken place since the establishment of the State of Israel until spring 2011.

Several difficulties became apparent during its preparation. The main problem was that most of the important and even thrilling intelligence events are classified and will remain so for many years to come, if not indefinitely. Thus any timetable will be rife with information not included. There were various events that were publicized in one way or another, but the Israeli government never claimed responsibility for them and they therefore cannot be included.

Intelligence, especially Israel Defense Intelligence, has been a part of every war Israel has had to fight and all the IDF's various operations, and the Israel Security Agency has been involved in recent years in the IDF's counterterrorism activities as well. Therefore, a full chronological list of Israeli intelligence would include every battle ever fought by the IDF at every level in every war.

The question was which events to include? Everything dealing with organizational matters within the intelligence community (that could be divulged)? Changes in personnel? Small strategic events? What should be included and what should be excluded?

The system we decided on was to provide a table whose first column consists of purely intelligence events; it does not include changes in personnel (see appendix 3, "The Heads of the Israeli Intelligence

Community") or secondary organizational changes in the intelligence community. The second column gives the IDF's main wars and operations in which intelligence played an important and often decisive role; it includes national events that influenced intelligence, such as the assassination of Israeli Prime Minister Yitzhak Rabin. The third column contains important regional and global events that influenced intelligence evaluations and collection deployment.

Certain events may have been left out, but we hope the reader, especially intelligence personnel and those interested in intelligence, will find the list helpful.

Year	Intelligence Events	IDF and National Background Events	Regional and International Events – Influential Factors
1948–1959			
1948	The Arab department of the Palmach sends Israelis impersonating Arabs on sabotage and espionage missions in neighboring Arab countries. In the Beirut harbor they sink the *Igris*, a yacht formerly belonging to Hitler and purchased by the Egyptian army. Six Arab impersonators are killed and their grave sites are unknown. May 30: David Ben-Gurion begins the establishment of the Israeli intelligence community. (See appendix 2: Special Topics.) June: The intelligence department of the IDF's general staff is established and the Shabak is established.	The War of Independence	The armies of Egypt, Jordan, Syria, Lebanon and Iraq invade and attack the State of Israel as soon as it is established. From that moment on their military might is Israel's main intelligence challenge.

Year	Intelligence Events	IDF and National Background Events	Regional and International Events – Influential Factors
1949	April: The first coordinating committee is established for the intelligence services. November: Isser Be'eri, the first head of the IDF intelligence department, is removed from office.		
1950			
1951	February: The Mossad is established as an independent body for missions abroad.		
1952			
1953	December: The intelligence service of the IDF acquires the status of an independent branch at the general staff level.		
1954	From July on: Operation Suzanna – A network of Egyptian Jewish fighters operated by Israel Defense Intelligence		

YEAR	INTELLIGENCE EVENTS	IDF AND NATIONAL BACKGROUND EVENTS	REGIONAL AND INTERNATIONAL EVENTS – INFLUENTIAL FACTORS
	(IDI) is caught by the Egyptians after having carried out a series of attacks in Cairo and Alexandria. Two of them, Shmuel Ozer and Moshe Marzuk, are executed. Six others are sentenced to various prison terms and three are acquitted. In Israel the widely debated question is "Who gave the order?" Intelligence head Gibli resigns and is replaced by Harkabi.

December: A squad of fighters sent by intelligence Unit 504 is dispatched to deal with a listening device in Syria and caught. One, Uri Ilan, commits suicide in jail.

December 21: Lieutenant Colonel Max Bineth, from the Mossad, dies in Egyptian captivity. | | |

Year	Intelligence Events	IDF and National Background Events	Regional and International Events – Influential Factors
1955	January: A committee is appointed to investigate Operation Suzanna.	Throughout the year, attacks in retaliation for terrorist activities from Syria, Jordan, and Egypt.	
1956	February: A secret speech given by Khrushchev is smuggled to Israel by a Polish Jew named Viktor Grayevsky. The Mossad passes it on to the CIA, laying the foundation for the relations between the two and for the reputation of Israeli intelligence. As the year progresses, IDI institutes cooperation with French intelligence and later with American military intelligence. April: Zeev Avni is exposed as a spy in the Foreign Ministry. July 16: Mustafa Hafaz, a senior Egyptian military	The retaliation actions against Egypt continue. October 29– November 5: Operation Kadesh (the Sinai Campaign).	The Cold War goes global and molds world politics until the end of the 1980s. The Soviet Union enters the Middle East and Soviet weapons flow in. Nasserism takes hold in Egypt, the PLO is established, the Arabs attempt to divert the route of the Jordan River and the Joint Arab Command is established. All of the above influence the activities of the intelligence community and its missions until 1967.

Year	Intelligence Events	IDF and National Background Events	Regional and International Events – Influential Factors
	intelligence officer in the Gaza Strip, is terminated in an IDI operation.		
1957			
1958			
1959	April: A reserve call-up exercise is conducted without prior warning, causing panic throughout Israel and the Arab countries. Yehoshephat Harkabi, head of IDI, and Meir Zorea, head of Operations, are forced to resign.		
1960–1969			
1960	March: Lieutenant Colonel Israel Be'er, military historian, is arrested and accused of spying for the Soviet Union.\n\nMay: The Mossad (with the Shabak) abducts Adolf Eichmann in Argentina and brings him to Israel	Operation Rotem: The IDF sends the entire standing army south and later calls up the reserves.\n\nDuring the coming decade, the IDF prepares to face the Arab armies. Preparations include equipment, training, combat doctrine, deploying to face	The establishment of the UAR: In February 1958 Syriaand Egypt unite to form the United Arab Republic, and by the beginning of 1960 to all intents and purposes Egypt controls Syria. The Egyptians, afraid Israel will attack

YEAR	INTELLIGENCE EVENTS	IDF AND NATIONAL BACKGROUND EVENTS	REGIONAL AND INTERNATIONAL EVENTS – INFLUENTIAL FACTORS
	for trial. The Shabak becomes responsible for the security of VIPs.	the Soviet combat doctrine adopted by the Egyptian and Syrian armies.	Syria, send land forces into the Sinai Peninsula. From the beginning of the decade, the Syrian and Egyptian armies equip themselves with Soviet weapons and adopt Soviet battle doctrine.
1961	January: The ship *Egoz*, which smuggled Jews from Morocco to Israel in a Mossad operation, sinks on its way to Spain.		
1962	Toward the end of the year, in the assessment of the Mossad, headed by Isser Harel, the Egyptians are developing weapons of mass destruction with the help of German scientists. IDI rejects the assessment.	The affair of the German scientists causes a public outcry in Israel.	
1963	March: Mossad agent Yosef Ben-Gal is arrested in Switzerland and accused of operating		

Year	Intelligence Events	IDF and National Background Events	Regional and International Events – Influential Factors
	against the German scientists who helped Egypt. April: Ben-Gurion rejects Harel's evaluation and opinion, and Harel resigns. Meir Amit is appointed to replace him as Mossad director. In the fall, Amit meets King Hassan in Morocco and opens a new era in Israeli-Moroccan cooperation. July: A committee (the Yadin-Sherf Commission) is established to examine the areas of responsibility of the services of the intelligence community.		
1964		The war for water: Between June 1964 and July 1966, in accordance with an Arab League decision, the Syrians try to divert the course of the Jordan River to prevent	

YEAR	INTELLIGENCE EVENTS	IDF AND NATIONAL BACKGROUND EVENTS	REGIONAL AND INTERNATIONAL EVENTS – INFLUENTIAL FACTORS
		Israel from using its water. The IDF takes action against the Syrian attempts and a series of armed clashes ensues. Eventually the Syrians abandon the project.	
1965	January: Wolfgang Lotz, a Mossad agent operating in Egypt, is arrested and tried for attempting to sabotage the efforts of Egyptian scientists to manufacture missiles. May 18: Eli Cohen, a Mossad agent operating in Syria since 1961, is executed.		
1966	August 16: Operation Yahalom: An Iraqi MIG-21 lands his plane in Israel, the glorious conclusion of a Mossad operation. (See appendix 2, "Special Topics.")		

Year	Intelligence Events	IDF and National Background Events	Regional and International Events – Influential Factors
1967	Operation Yated: Using an agent, the Shabak fools the Egyptians about Israeli Air Force plans. Operation Katriza: At the end of the Six-Day War the intelligence corps and the intelligence division of the southern command conduct a thorough investigation of the Sinai Peninsula. Following an exchange of prisoners after the war, Mossad agent Shula Cohen is released from a Lebanese prison.	May 16: The Egyptian army enters the Sinai Peninsula. June 5–10: The Six-Day War. July: The War of Attrition begins along the Egyptian front. September 1967 to 1972: Campaign against terrorism in the Gaza Strip.	November 22: The UN Security Council adopts Resolution 242 for an Israeli withdrawal from the conquered territories to secure and recognized boundaries. To this day the resolution is the foundation for all political arrangements.
1968	February: The prisoners of Operation Suzanna return home as part of a prisoner exchange deal with Egypt. July: In the wake of the hijacking of an El Al plane to Algiers, the Shabak becomes responsible	May: Operation Karameh is undertaken against terrorists in Jordan. The War of Attrition begins along the Jordanian front, continuing until September 1970.	August 21: Russia invades Czechoslovakia.

YEAR	INTELLIGENCE EVENTS	IDF AND NATIONAL BACKGROUND EVENTS	REGIONAL AND INTERNATIONAL EVENTS – INFLUENTIAL FACTORS
	for security aboard planes. Following the Russian invasion, which began as a military exercise, IDI head Major General Yariv announces that every military exercise will be considered an indication of early warning.		
1969		During the year the IDF carries out a series of operations deep within Egyptian territory. The most prominent were: September 9: An armored incursion. December 25–26: A modern Soviet radar system is captured at Ras 'Arab.	March: Nasser officially announces the beginning of the War of Attrition against Israel.
		1970–1979	
1970	Collaboration between IDI and the Mossad on the one hand, and the American	January: The Israeli air force begins strikes deep within Egyptian territory. Nasser requests	March: The Soviet Union begins direct involvement in military affairs in Egypt and sends

Year	Intelligence Events	IDF and National Background Events	Regional and International Events – Influential Factors
	intelligence community on the other, becomes closer following Soviet intervention in Egypt.	aid from the Soviet Union. August: A cease-fire between Israel and Egypt ends the War of Attrition on the Egyptian front. It continues along the Syrian front until the beginning of 1973.	air squadrons and aerial defense forces to Egypt. September: "Black September" in Jordan, when the Jordanian army wages war on and overcomes the PLO. The Syrian army invades northern Jordan and retreats. The PLO moves to Lebanon, from which it wages a War of Attrition against Israel. September 28: Gamal Abdel Nasser dies and is replaced by Anwar Sadat as president of Egypt.
1971		Palestinian terrorists begin infiltrating from Lebanon into northern Israel.	
1972	December: The Shabak exposes a Jewish-Arab terrorist network operated by Syria.	May 9: Palestinian terrorists hijack a Sabena plane. It lands in Lod and an elite IDF force takes control of it. May 30: A Japanese Red Army squad, working for the	End of October: Sadat makes the strategic decision to attack Israel "with excellent Egyptian capabilities," and begins coordinating and making preparations for war.

Year	Intelligence Events	IDF and National Background Events	Regional and International Events – Influential Factors
		Popular Front for the Liberation of Palestine, massacres twenty-three people at the Lod Airport.	
		September 5: Eleven Israeli athletes are massacred at the Summer Olympics in Munich.	
		Throughout the year, the IDF attacks Palestinian terrorist bases in Lebanon.	
1973	January: The Shabak exposes Yuri Yelinov, a Soviet intelligence officer. He is arrested and released in a prisoner exchange deal. July: Six Mossad agents are arrested in Lillehammer, Norway, after mistakenly killing a Moroccan waiter, thinking he was head of the PLO's terrorist organization Black September. It marks the end of the series of targeted killings of Black September	April 9–10: Operation Aviv Neurim, in which special IDF forces raid the houses of terrorists and senior PLO figures in Beirut, killing three. October 6–24: The Yom Kippur War. From October 25 to January 18, 1974, a War of Attrition along the Egypt front. From November to May 31, 1974, a War of Attrition along the Syrian front.	In April, Syria becomes party to the secret of the upcoming war and begins preparation for it in coordination with Egypt. Various dates are chosen, until October 6 is finally decided upon.

Year	Intelligence Events	IDF and National Background Events	Regional and International Events – Influential Factors
	operatives after the murder of the Israeli athletes in Munich. Despite preparations and information about war, until the last minute IDI adheres to the evaluation that "the probability of war is very low." It was Israeli intelligence's worst failure.		
1974	April 1: In accordance with the conclusions of the Agranat Commission, the head of IDI and three intelligence officers are removed from office. The committee recommends several steps, especially evaluation pluralism. IDI reorganizes, expands the evaluation authority of the intelligence units of the various commands and establishes the Devil's Advocate Department.	January 18: Israel-Egypt separation of forces agreement signed at the 101st kilometer on the Cairo-Suez road. April 1: The Agranat Commission, appointed following the Yom Kippur War, issues its interim report. (See appendix 2 for a summary of the main committees and examinations.) May 31: Israel-Syria separation of forces agreement.	October: An Arab summit meeting is held in Rabat, Morocco, and recognizes the right of the PLO to the exclusive representation of the Palestinian people. The PLO begins to establish itself as a state within a state in Lebanon, a gradual process continuing throughout the decade, accompanied by thousands of shooting and other terrorist attacks along Israel's northern border.

Year	Intelligence Events	IDF and National Background Events	Regional and International Events – Influential Factors
	June: The production and analysis division is established in the Mossad, and the center for political research is gradually established in the Foreign Ministry.	From the middle of 1974 until the end of the decade: The IDF carries out hundreds of reprisals and preventive actions in the air, on land and at sea against the terrorist organizations in Lebanon.	
1975		September 1: An interim agreement with Egypt and a political "understanding" with the United States are reached. The end of the year: The "Good Fence" between Israel and Lebanon is opened, and Israel accepts refugees from the Lebanese civil war. Israel starts establishing a Christian militia, headed by Major Sa'ad Hadad, to control part of south Lebanon. The militia will eventually become the South Lebanon Army.	April: The Lebanese civil war breaks out and continues until its official end in 1989.

Year	Intelligence Events	IDF and National Background Events	Regional and International Events – Influential Factors
1976	From the middle of the year: The Mossad forms ties with the Christians in Lebanon, arms them and becomes important in determining Israeli policy toward Lebanon.	July 4: Operation Yonatan is carried out, in which the IDF liberates the passengers of a hijacked Air France flight that was on its way to Tel Aviv and diverted to Entebbe, Uganda.	July: Syria invades Lebanon on the side of the Christians against the Palestinians.
1977	July: Mossad Director Yitzhak Hoffi goes to Morocco to meet King Hassan and Egyptian Deputy Prime Minister Hassan Tuhami and lay the foundation for Sadat's visit to Jerusalem. IDI is compartmentalized from the contacts with Tuhami and does not assess Sadat as wanting peace.	September 18: Foreign Minister Moshe Dayan and Mossad Director Hoffi meet with Tuhami in Morocco. November 19: Sadat comes to Israel.	
1978		March 15–21: Operation Litani is held following the terrorist attack from the sea on a bus on the Coastal Road. The IDF takes over all south Lebanon as far north as the	

YEAR	INTELLIGENCE EVENTS	IDF AND NATIONAL BACKGROUND EVENTS	REGIONAL AND INTERNATIONAL EVENTS – INFLUENTIAL FACTORS
		Litani River, and then withdraws in accordance with Security Council Resolution 425. Control of south Lebanon remains in the hands of the Christian militia.	
1979	 	March 26: Israel and Egypt sign a peace agreement.	January: The Shah of Iran is deposed and Khomeini takes control of the regime, opening a new chapter in Iranian history and Iran's relations with Israel. April: The Arab world cuts off ties with Egypt. A military "eastern front" develops to face Israel to replace Egypt. December: The Soviet Union invades Afghanistan, and the Cold War heats up.
1980–1989			
1980		February: Israel and Egypt exchange ambassadors.	September: Iraq invades Iran, beginning a war that lasts for eight years.

YEAR	INTELLIGENCE EVENTS	IDF AND NATIONAL BACKGROUND EVENTS	REGIONAL AND INTERNATIONAL EVENTS – INFLUENTIAL FACTORS
		June 29: Escalation in the terrorism from Lebanon and the IDF's responses throughout the year.	
1981	Following Sadat's assassination, it is the IDI evaluation that President Mubarak will continue peaceful relations with Israel.	June 7: Israel destroys Iraq's nuclear reactor. July 24: The Americans broker a cease-fire with the PLO, reached in Lebanon. However, terrorist attacks continue. December 14: The Knesset passes a law annexing the Golan Heights.	October 6: Egyptian President Anwar Sadat is assassinated, and succeeded by Hosni Mubarak.
1982	November 11: Nine Shabak agents and sixty-six members of the security forces are killed when a military administration building collapses in Tyre, Lebanon.	June 5: The First Lebanon War begins. End of August: The PLO evacuates Beirut, its leadership moves to Tunis and its military forces disperse throughout the Arab countries. The focus of PLO activity moves to the Gaza Strip, Judea and Samaria.	September 16: The Sabra and Shatilla massacre, in which a Christian military force massacres residents of two refugee camps in western Beirut.

Year	Intelligence Events	IDF and National Background Events	Regional and International Events – Influential Factors
1983	January: The Shabak exposes Marcus Klingberg, a senior worker in the Israel Institute for Biological Research, as a Soviet spy. (See appendix 2: Special Topics for a summary of espionage affairs.) April: Following the recommendation of the Kahan Commission, Yehoshua Saguy relinquished his command as the director of IDI. November 4: Three Shabak agents and fifty-seven members of the security forces are killed in Tyre by a car bomb.	February 2: The Kahan Commission, established to investigate the Sabra and Shatilla massacre, releases its findings. September: The IDF withdraws from East Beirut and the Chouf Mountains to the Awali River north of Tyre.	
1984	April 12: The Shabak is involved in the Bus No. 300 affair, the killing of two terrorists who are taken alive after the attack. April: The Shabak exposes an underground	April 12: The Bus No. 300 affair begins. (See appendix 2.)	

YEAR	INTELLIGENCE EVENTS	IDF AND NATIONAL BACKGROUND EVENTS	REGIONAL AND INTERNATIONAL EVENTS – INFLUENTIAL FACTORS
	network of twenty-three Jews who engaged in terrorist activities against Arabs. November 1984 to January 1985: The Mossad undertakes Operation Moses and brings Ethiopian Jewry to Israel. They are brought to Sudan and from there flown to Israel.		
1985	November 21: Jonathan Pollard is arrested in the United States and charged with spying for Israel.	January: The government of Israel decides to withdraw from Lebanon and establish a security zone in the southern part of the country. The zone is held by the South Lebanon Army commanded by General Antoine Lahad, who succeeded Hadad, and by twelve Israeli outposts. October 1: The Israel Air Force attacks PLO headquarters in Tunis.	

Year	Intelligence Events	IDF and National Background Events	Regional and International Events – Influential Factors
1986	April: Shabak agents in London expose and prevent the attempted hijacking of an El Al plane.	October: Israeli Air Force navigator Ron Arad is shot down over Lebanon and captured.	
1987	December: The intelligence community is surprised by the outbreak of the first intifada. A commission is appointed to determine responsibility for collection and analysis of intelligence in the territories and of the PLO. An independent evaluation and analysis department is established within the Shabak.	December 8: The first intifada breaks out, continuing until the Oslo Accords in 1994, but beginning to wane by 1992.	December: The Hamas movement is founded in the Gaza Strip, Judea and Samaria.
1988	The Shabak and IDI organize to deal with the new situation in the territories.		July: The Iraq-Iran war ends. November 15: The Palestinian National Council holds a meeting in Tunis at which Yasser Arafat declares the establishment of an independent

YEAR	INTELLIGENCE EVENTS	IDF AND NATIONAL BACKGROUND EVENTS	REGIONAL AND INTERNATIONAL EVENTS – INFLUENTIAL FACTORS
			Palestinian state whose capital is Jerusalem, and recognizes the two-state principle. The PLO starts along a diplomatic road.
1989			October 22: The Taif Accord is signed by the various ethnic factions in Lebanon, formally ending the civil war and the legitimizing a Syrian presence in Lebanon.
			November 9: The Berlin Wall comes down. The Communist block begins to disintegrate. The Cold War is about to end.
1990–1999			
1990			August 2: Iraq invades Kuwait. Hezbollah, the remaining armed militia in Lebanon after the Taif Accord is signed, takes control of south Lebanon.

YEAR	INTELLIGENCE EVENTS	IDF AND NATIONAL BACKGROUND EVENTS	REGIONAL AND INTERNATIONAL EVENTS – INFLUENTIAL FACTORS
1991	Between the invasion of Kuwait and the First Gulf War, according to Israeli IDI evaluation Saddam Hussein will launch Scud missiles at Israel and has missiles with chemical warheads, but the probability that he will use them is very low. May 21: Operation Solomon brings 14,000 Ethiopian Jews to Israel, thanks to the special relations between the Mossad and the new Ethiopian regime.	January 18 to February 27: Iraq launches thirty-nine Scud missiles at Israel. Israel decides not to respond. October: Hezbollah begins attacking IDF soldiers, the Israeli posts in the security zone and the South Lebanon Army. The struggle against Hezbollah lasts throughout the decade.	January 17 to February 27: The First Gulf War is waged. The United States and the coalition forces conquer Kuwait and overcome Iraqi forces. October 30 to November 1: The Madrid Conference is held and puts into motion a process of negotiations and arrangements that will characterize the entire decade. December 16: The Communist regime falls and the Soviet Union collapses. The Cold War ends.
1992	Israeli intelligence accompanies the peace talks.	February 16: Hezbollah secretary general Abbas Musawi dies in Lebanon in a targeted killing carried out by the Israel Air Force. As the year proceeds, Israel conducts negotiations with	

YEAR	INTELLIGENCE EVENTS	IDF AND NATIONAL BACKGROUND EVENTS	REGIONAL AND INTERNATIONAL EVENTS – INFLUENTIAL FACTORS
		Syria, Jordan and the Palestinians in the territories.	
1993	Israeli intelligence is compartmentalized from the secret Oslo negotiations.	Summer: Terrorist escalation along the northern border causes the IDF to respond with Operation Accountability, July 25–31. September 13: The first public Oslo Accord between Israel and the PLO brings mutual recognition and an interim period of five years before the final status agreement.	February 26: The first terrorist attack on the World Trade Center in New York. Osama bin Laden and Al-Qaeda enter the world stage.
1994	Israeli intelligence faces the challenge of suicide-bombing terrorism (which breaks out after the Goldstein attack at the Cave of the Patriarchs in Hebron on February 25).	May 4: The Cairo Agreement gives the Palestinian Authority control over Jericho and the Gaza Strip. August 26: Peace agreement between Israel and Jordan. Throughout the year there are suicide bombing attacks on Israeli city buses (Afula, Hadera, Tel Aviv).	

Year	Intelligence Events	IDF and National Background Events	Regional and International Events – Influential Factors
1995	November 4: A disastrous failure of Shabak security procedures and a blow to the Shabak's image. The entire security system undergoes far-reaching changes.	Suicide bombing attacks continue, carried out primarily by Hamas. The worst is a double attack carried out in Beit Lid in January. November 4: Israeli Prime Minister Yitzhak Rabin is assassinated.	
1996	January 5: Yehiya Ayash, Hamas's "engineer," is killed. September: the intelligence community, especially IDI and the Shabak, begin a long-term process of organizing collection, evaluation and logistics for a possible future confrontation with the Palestinians.	February 25: A new wave of suicide bombing attacks begins, climaxing with the March 3 Dizengoff Center bombing. Spring: Escalation in the north. The IDF responds with Operation Invei Zaam, April 11–17. September 24–26: Fourteen IDF soldiers killed in Wailing Wall tunnel incident.	
1997	IDI reports that Iran is developing long-range surface-to-surface Shihab missiles and has begun the process		

YEAR	INTELLIGENCE EVENTS	IDF AND NATIONAL BACKGROUND EVENTS	REGIONAL AND INTERNATIONAL EVENTS – INFLUENTIAL FACTORS
	of acquiring nuclear capabilities. September 25: the Mossad fails to assassinate Khaled Mashaal, head of Hamas political bureau, in Amman, Jordan.		
1998	The intelligence community is compartmentalized from Ron Lauder's talks with the Syrians.	Israeli Prime Minister Binyamin Netanyahu holds talks with the Syrians through Ron Lauder, president of the World Jewish Congress.	
1999	The intelligence community is included in military and political issues concerning the Palestinian and Syrian-Lebanese moves.	July 6: Sworn in as prime minister, Ehud Barak says that within a year an agreement will be reached and the IDF will withdraw from Lebanon. September 4: The Sharm el-Sheikh agreement between Israel and the PLO is signed, implementing the interim agreement and launching negotiations for the final status arrangement.	February 7: Hussein, King of Jordan, dies, and is succeeded by his son Abdullah.

YEAR	INTELLIGENCE EVENTS	IDF AND NATIONAL BACKGROUND EVENTS	REGIONAL AND INTERNATIONAL EVENTS – INFLUENTIAL FACTORS
		December 8: American President Clinton announces the renewal of negotiations between Israel and Syria.	
2000–2010			
2000	IDI evaluation on the eve of withdrawal: Hezbollah will not attack by itself but will operate through the Palestinians, completely take over south Lebanon as far as the Israeli border and continue its buildup of long-range rockets. The intelligence community, led by IDI, provides full-time intelligence accompaniment for the negotiations for the final status arrangement with the Palestinians. Unlike previous instances, there is no IDI representation at Camp David.	January 3–9: The talks between Israel and Syria in Shepherdstown, West Virginia, fail. March 25: The Clinton-Assad talks in Geneva fail. Night of May 23: The IDF withdraws from the security zone in south Lebanon. July 12–25: The Barak-Arafat-Clinton summit meeting at Camp David is a failure. September 28: Ariel Sharon goes to the Temple Mount. September 29: The second intifada begins, lasting until August 2004.	June 10: Syrian President Hafez Assad dies and is succeeded by his son Bashar.

Year	Intelligence Events	IDF and National Background Events	Regional and International Events – Influential Factors
	IDI evaluation on the eve of the summit meeting: Arafat has been dragged to Camp David and his position will not be flexible. It is pointless to hold the meeting.		
2001	IDI and the Shabak enter into closer cooperation to engage in counterterrorism activities.		September 11: The World Trade Center in New York City is attacked and destroyed by terrorists. October 7: The United States attacks the Taliban in Afghanistan. The international war on terrorism begins.
2002	February 11: The Shabak law passes in the Knesset. (See appendix 2.)	January 2–3: The IDF takes over the ship *Karin A*, which was smuggling Iranian weapons, including long-range missiles, to the Palestinian Authority. Suicide bombing terrorism continues, reaching a peak with	

Year	Intelligence Events	IDF and National Background Events	Regional and International Events – Influential Factors
		the Passover Seder attack at the Park Hotel in Netanya on March 27, which left twenty-three dead and 140 wounded. March 29–May 10: In Operation Homat Magen the IDF takes over areas within the Palestinian Authority and destroys terrorist networks and the Palestinian Authority's military infrastructure.	
2003	Mistaken IDI assessment that Saddam Hussein has small amounts of non-conventional weapons capabilities, and that when he feels pressured the probability he will use them against Israel is low. Israeli intelligence community is surprised by Libyan announcement of intention to stop producing nuclear weapons.		March 20: The United States attacks Iraq (the Second Gulf War), conquers it within ten days and overthrows the regime of Saddam Hussein. From that time on there is an American military presence in Iraq. December 19: Libya announces it will no longer produce nuclear weapons (according to an agreement reached

YEAR	INTELLIGENCE EVENTS	IDF AND NATIONAL BACKGROUND EVENTS	REGIONAL AND INTERNATIONAL EVENTS – INFLUENTIAL FACTORS
			with the United States and Britain).
2004	IDI and the Mossad study the lessons of the Libyan surprise.	March 22: Hamas founder and leader Ahmed Yassin is killed in a targeted killing. March 28: The Steinitz (Chairman of the Knesset Foreign Affairs and Defense Committee) Commission issues its conclusions about intelligence during the Second Gulf War. (See appendix 2: Special Topics.) April 17: Abd Aziz Rantisi, who replaced Ahmed Yassin as Hamas head, is killed in a targeted killing.	September 2: The Security Council passes Resolution 1559 calling for the Syrian forces to withdraw from Lebanon and for Hezbollah to disarm. November 11: Yasser Arafat dies in France and Mahmoud Abbas replaces him as chairman of the PLO's Executive Committee.
2005	IDI (with Mossad support) presents the political echelons with a full picture of Hezbollah's firepower and an evaluation of its deployment and intentions, the result	August 15: Israel's unilateral disengagement from the Gaza Strip begins, continuing for eight days. A new situation comes into being in Gaza.	January 9: Mahmoud Abbas is elected president of the Palestinian Authority. February 14: Former Lebanese prime minister and Sunni faction head Rafiq

YEAR	INTELLIGENCE EVENTS	IDF AND NATIONAL BACKGROUND EVENTS	REGIONAL AND INTERNATIONAL EVENTS – INFLUENTIAL FACTORS
	of its intelligence collection and analysis since the Israeli withdrawal from Lebanon.		Hariri is assassinated in Beirut. March 14: The Sunni-Druze-Christian coalition known as the March 14 Group is established and calls for the Syrians to withdraw from Lebanon. March 25: The Syrian army begins its withdrawal from Lebanon after a presence which lasted for twenty-eight years. August 2: Ahmadinejad is elected president of Iran. Iran becomes a regional power and develops nuclear weapons capabilities despite international protests. Iran publicly threatens to destroy the State of Israel.
2006	The intelligence community does not foresee Hamas's victory in the Palestinian Legislative Council	June 25: Israeli soldier Gilad Shalit is abducted near the Gaza Strip border.	January 25: Hamas wins the Palestinian Authority's Legislative Council elections.

YEAR	INTELLIGENCE EVENTS	IDF AND NATIONAL BACKGROUND EVENTS	REGIONAL AND INTERNATIONAL EVENTS – INFLUENTIAL FACTORS
	elections, although it does predict a rise in its power. One of the lessons learned is the necessity to become more familiar with the workings of Palestinian society. IDI does not issue a concrete warning about abductions. The air strike is based entirely on a joint, long-term, Mossad-IDI intelligence effort. During the war, according to IDI evaluation, Syria will not attack Israel. With the end of the war IDI begins studying its lessons.	July 12: Eldad Regev and Ehud Goldwasser are abducted by Hezbollah near the Lebanese border. The night of July 12: The Israel Air Force attack on Hezbollah's long-range rockets in south Lebanon turns into the Second Lebanon War, which lasts until August 13. August 12: The Security Council passes Resolution 1701, calling for a cease-fire and other measures.	
2007	IDI and the Mossad make plans and deploy for eventualities in the northern arena, where the tension is great. They continue dealing with the Iranian threat. IDI publicly, and especially	April: Israel and Syria examine the possibility of preliminary contacts for negotiations, with Turkey as middleman. Israel struggles against the Qassam attacks from the Gaza Strip.	June 14: Hamas takes over the Gaza Strip in violent events that last but a few days. November 15: Lebanon does not have a president. According to a November report

Year	Intelligence Events	IDF and National Background Events	Regional and International Events – Influential Factors
	in clandestine contacts, indicates to the American intelligence community that its evaluation of the Iranian nuclear situation is incorrect, and presents proof. According to IDI evaluation, at the end of the year Hezbollah has 30,000 rockets and missiles (compared with the 20,000 it had on the eve of the Second Lebanon War).	Syria's secretly built nuclear reactor, located on the Iraqi border near Deir az-Zour, is completely destroyed. (According to the memoirs of former United States President Bush, the Israeli air force destroyed it and provided the United States with all the intelligence about the nuclear site.)	from the American intelligence community, in 2003 Iran waived the idea of developing military nuclear capabilities. Hezbollah continues its military buildup throughout the year and in the following years, stockpiling rockets and missiles from Iran and Syria smuggled into Lebanon, primarily through Syria.
2008	IDI is praised by the Winograd Commission for its strategic-operative actions, and criticized for lack of tactical intelligence and not providing the fighting forces with sufficient information. Intelligence lessons from the Second Lebanon War are implemented in Operation Cast	January: The Winograd Commission (which was appointed September 17, 2006, and issued a partial report on April 30, 2007) issues a full public report. May 21: Israeli and Syrian representatives meet in Turkey for indirect negotiations, and issue an official	February 13: Imad Mughnieh, Hezbollah's chief of staff, is assassinated in Damascus. May 21: The Doha Agreement is signed and made public, making it possible for Lebanon to elect a new president and giving Hezbollah and its supporters a veto in the newgovernment that will be formed.

YEAR	INTELLIGENCE EVENTS	IDF AND NATIONAL BACKGROUND EVENTS	REGIONAL AND INTERNATIONAL EVENTS – INFLUENTIAL FACTORS
	Lead. The fighting forces receive precise intelligence in real time.	statement to that effect. June 19: The Egyptian-brokered agreement for a lull in the fighting between Israel and Hamas begins. From August: Hamas steps up its shelling of western Negev communities, launching hundreds of rockets, the majority of them targeting the town of Sderot. December 27: Operation Cast Lead begins. The IDF attacks Hamas targets and takes control of some of the Gaza Strip. The Turkish-brokered talks with Syria are halted.	August 1: Muhammad Suleiman, head of Syria's nuclear program and "special projects," is killed in his house in Syria. November 5: Barack Obama is elected president of the United States.
2009	Following Operation Cast Lead an intelligence effort is invested to locate and identify weapons smuggled from Iran to Hamas in the Gaza Strip.	January 17: Israel announces a unilateral cease-fire. Operation Cast Lead ends and the IDF forces withdraw from the Gaza Strip.	January 20: Barack Obama is sworn in as president of the United States. March 26: A convoy of ammunition for Iran weapons intended for Hamas

YEAR	INTELLIGENCE EVENTS	IDF AND NATIONAL BACKGROUND EVENTS	REGIONAL AND INTERNATIONAL EVENTS – INFLUENTIAL FACTORS
	Intelligence finds continuous weapons smuggling to Hezbollah from Syria. During the summer it identifies Hezbollah operatives training in Syria to fire Scuds and surface-to-air missiles.

September 1: Organizational changes in IDI. A chief officer for intelligence collection is appointed, in terms of command subordinate to the land forces and professionally subordinate to the Intelligence Corps, and responsible for collecting combat intelligence. The IDI assessment for Iran is this: In 2008 Iran acquired the technology for full uranium enrichment, and during 2009 it amassed an amount sufficient for the | November 3: The Israeli navy, operating in the Mediterranean, intercepts the MV *Francop*, smuggling weapons from Iran to Hezbollah.

November 26: Prime Minister Binyamin Netanyahu announces a moratorium in construction in the Judea and Samaria settlements. | is destroyed in Sudan.

June 4: President Obama's speech in Cairo, calling for a new page to be turned in the United States' relations with the Muslim world.

June 12: Ahmadinejad is elected president of Iran for a second term. The following day riots break out throughout the country and are ruthlessly suppressed by the regime.

September 15: The Goldstone Report is issued, accusing Israel of war crimes during Operation Cast Lead. |

Year	Intelligence Events	IDF and National Background Events	Regional and International Events – Influential Factors
	production of one nuclear bomb (the material still at a low grade of enrichment). Iran works to improve its surface-to-surface missile capabilities and develops missiles that can reach Europe. Cracks appear in the Iranian regime, but the situation is well under control.		
2010	At the beginning of the year, IDI assessment is as follows: the probability of a war breaking out is low; the Palestinian issue treads water; the gulf widens between the Palestinian Authority in Judea and Samaria and the Hamas-controlled Gaza Strip; Hamas will spend the year emphasizing the rebuilding of the Gaza Strip and its own military buildup, especially regarding personal anti-aircraft	The Israel Intelligence Heritage and Commemoration Center (the source of this book) issues a detailed response to the Goldstone Report, refuting each of its claims. May 30–31: A provocative convoy of six ships sets sail from Turkey for the Gaza Strip and is intercepted by the Israeli navy. On board the largest ship, the *Mavi Marmara*, are forty mercenaries, most	January 19: Mahmoud al-Mabhouh, responsible for Hamas's arms smuggling, is assassinated in Dubai. February 7: Iran begins enriching uranium to 20 percent. Crisis in Israeli-Turkish relations following the affair of the *Mavi Marmara*. June 10: The UN Security Council imposes sanctions on Iran for the fourth time.

YEAR	INTELLIGENCE EVENTS	IDF AND NATIONAL BACKGROUND EVENTS	REGIONAL AND INTERNATIONAL EVENTS – INFLUENTIAL FACTORS
	weapons and long-range rockets; Hezbollah has a stockpile of 40,000 rockets. May 31: Israeli Prime Minister Binyamin Netanyahu publicly refers to intelligence reports of Syria's having provided Hezbollah with Scud missiles, currently in Syrian territory.	of them Turkish. Nine are killed in the violent confrontation aboard the ship; nine IDF soldiers are injured.	

Appendix 2

Special Topics

Amos Gilboa

with the assistance of Ephraim Lapid and Yochi Erlich

What follows is a short description of interesting topics that do not appear in the main articles of this book. They are the following: how the intelligence community was established; Night of the Ducks (1959); bringing an Iraqi MIG-21 to Israel in 1966; the ISA's Bus No. 300 Affair (1984); the most important of the various committees that investigated the intelligence establishment; the main espionage affairs that were exposed; and the ISA law.

How the Intelligence Community Began

The Israeli intelligence community was established along with the State of Israel and based on organizations already operating at the time: the Palmach's Arab division and the information services of the Haganah, the Etzel and the Lehi. The need to deal with the regular armies of the Arab countries (and not with local gangs of Palestinian Arabs) and the large number of intelligence bodies motivated Ben-Gurion to initiate the organization of an intelligence community on May 30, 1948.

To that end he was aided by Reuven Shiloah, his right-hand man in the process. The establishment of the services of Israeli intelligence lasted until February 1951. Since then there have been three main intelligence bodies: IDF intelligence, known as Israel Defense Intelligence (IDI); the Israel Security Agency (ISA), also known as the Shabak; and the Mossad.

The Night of the Ducks (1959)

On April 1, 1959, coded call-up messages were broadcast on the nightly edition of the news on *Kol Yisrael*, the only radio station then broadcasting in Israel. These codes were the signal for reserve army units to assemble. The announcements were made continually for several hours. In fact, it was only a mobilization exercise, but the radio announcements did not mention that fact, and there was no prior warning given. The broadcasts threw the country into a panic; people believed that the call-up was in response to a genuine emergency. The neighboring Arab states also believed that Israel was readying to attack, and they also went into a state of alert.

In the wake of the official committee of inquiry, Prime Minister David Ben-Gurion dismissed Major General Meir Zorea (chief of the operation branch) and Major General Yehoshephat Harkabi (the head of IDI) from their positions. The dismissal of the head of IDI was because he was responsible for the censorship of the media and the security of information communicated to the public. This episode became know as the night of the ducks, since one of the call-up codes repeated on the radio was the Hebrew word for "ducks."

Operation Yahalom: Bringing an Iraqi MIG-21 to Israel (1966)

On August 16, 1966, an Iraqi MIG-21 flown by Iraqi pilot Munir Radfa landed in Israel. It was the jewel in the crown of an unprecedented Mossad intelligence operation that had begun three years previously. An Iraqi Jew named Yosef who worked in Tehran told Mossad agents and the Israeli attaché that he could bring an Iraqi MIG-21 pilot to Israel with his plane. It sounded like a figment of his imagination, especially because at the time, the MIG-21, which the Egyptian and Syrian armies were supposed to receive shortly, was considered the most advanced Soviet fighter plane. However, examination showed that the pilot was a Christian and that Yosef had connections with his wife's family.

The matter was given a boost in April 1965 when Israel Air Force head Ezer Weizman asked Mossad director Meir Amit to make the effort to bring the IAF a MIG-21. At the time neither was aware of the ongoing contacts with Yosef. Amit put the Mossad into high gear to turn the vision into reality, and representatives of the IAF joined the effort. The Iraqi pilot was secretly brought to Israel for a "visit," meetings were held with him in Europe and arrangements were made to relocate both his family and Yosef's outside Iraq. On August 16 he landed his plane in Israel, escorted by two IAF fighter planes. The consequences of the operation went far beyond a simple intelligence achievement. The greatest contribution was to assist the IAF in dogfights in the Six-Day War against the enemy's MIG-21s. Information was also contributed to the United States Air Force, which until then did not have a working knowledge of MIG-21s, and it gave Israeli intelligence an international reputation for excellence.

The Bus No. 300 Affair (1984)

On April 12, 1984, four Palestinian terrorists took control of a no. 300 bus driving from Tel Aviv to Ashkelon with thirty-five passengers. The subsequent IDF takeover of the bus resulted in the deaths of two of the terrorists, and the other two were captured and taken to the ISA for questioning. At first it was reported that all four had been killed, but media photos showed that two had been captured alive. The issue was examined by an investigatory committee headed by Major General (Res.) Meir Zorea, and later by a commission headed by State Attorney Yonah Blatman.

In 1985 details of the incident were revealed by several senior ISA agents: the two terrorists were killed on orders given by ISA director Avraham Shalom after their capture; ISA agents who testified at the committee hearings perjured themselves, having been instructed to do so by the ISA head; and the ISA representative on the committee, Yossi Ginosar, coordinated perjured testimonies and reports about committee proceedings for the ISA head. Yitzhak Zamir, then attorney general, ordered a criminal investigation of all those who participated in the killings and cover up.

In June 1986 the president of the State of Israel pardoned those involved in the affair even before they had been brought to trial. In September 1986 the head of the ISA resigned.

The affair led to a severe crisis within the ISA because of the unethical norms rampant among its senior members, and to a deep lack of faith felt by the Israeli public and government institutions, especially the judicial system. That prompted the ISA to learn the moral and professional lessons of the affair and modify its behavior and standards in accord with the norms established by the bounds of law. The incident also led to the appointment of an internal inspector and later to the passing of the ISA law and the formulation of an ISA ideology. (See "The ISA Law" below.)

Investigatory Commissions

Since the founding of the intelligence community there has been a series of commissions appointed to investigate various failures and to improve overall intelligence functioning. Some of the main ones were the following:

- In 1954 Israeli prime minister Moshe Sharett appointed the Olshan (president of the Israeli Supreme Court)-Dori (former chief of staff) Committee to examine Operation Suzanna and determine who gave the order. No decisive conclusion was reached.
- On July 31, 1963, Israeli prime minister David Ben-Gurion appointed the Yadin (former chief of staff)-Sherf (former secretary of the government) Commission to examine the areas of intelligence community responsibility. Among its conclusions were that an intelligence advisor to the prime minister should

be appointed and the evaluation and analysis division within the Foreign Ministry should be strengthened.

- In 1973 the Agranat (president of the Israeli Supreme Court) Commission was appointed to examine the failures of the Yom Kippur War. With regard to intelligence, the committee made personal recommendations (such as removing IDI chief Zeira from his post) and organizational recommendations (especially creating pluralism in evaluating intelligence information, and reinforcing the intelligence units in the various regional commands). Most of the failures, the committee determined, were related to the "conception": the rigid conception of Israeli intelligence that it was unlikely Egypt would start a full-scale attack, despite the flow of information indicating the contrary.

- In 1982 the Kahan (president of the Israeli Supreme Court) Commission was appointed to examine the Sabra and Shatilla massacre. Its intelligence recommendation was to remove IDI head Yehoshua Saguy from his post.

- In 1987 the Landau (president of the Israeli Supreme Court) Commission was appointed to examine ISA interrogation methods following the "affair of Lieutenant Naffso." Its report demanded far-reaching changes in the ISA's interrogation of terrorist operatives.

- In 1995 the Shamgar (former president of the Israeli Supreme Court) Commission was appointed to examine the circumstances of the assassination of Yitzhak Rabin. ISA head Carmi Gillon and other senior ISA members were held responsible for the failure to protect the prime minister.

- In 2004 the Steinitz (chairman of the Foreign Relations and Security Committee) Commission, a subcommittee of the Foreign Relations and Security Committee, was appointed following the Second Gulf War and intelligence's failure to discover Libya's nuclear program. In March it recommended far-reaching organizational changes in the intelligence community, especially turning the IDI SIGINT unit, 8200, into a national agency. The recommendations were not implemented.

- In 2006 the Winograd (former judge) Commission was appointed following the Second Lebanon War. Its final report (issued January 2008) determined that intelligence at the strategic level was successful, but at the tactical level there were failures in providing the fighting forces with information.

- Various secret investigatory committees, especially during the second half of the 1980s, dealt with the delegation of authority and responsibility within the various branches of the intelligence community. Prominent was the agreement, known as the "Magna Carta," reached at the end of the 1990s between the IDI head, Amos Malka, and the ISA head, Ami Ayalon, regarding the division of responsibility for the Palestinian Authority arena.

Anti-Israel Espionage Affairs

Since its founding, one of the ISA's areas of activity has been preventing espionage directed against the security of the State of Israel. Most of the espionage effort came from the Soviet Union and its satellites until its final collapse in 1991, and some from various Arab countries. The lion's share of the spies were Jewish. The most famous cases exposed by the ISA were the following:

- Zeev Avni, a Soviet spy who infiltrated the Israeli Foreign Ministry. He was caught in 1956 and sentenced to fourteen years in prison.

- Levi Levi, a Polish intelligence agent who infiltrated the ISA. He was caught in 1957 and deported after seven years in jail.

- Kurt Sita, a world-famous professor, not Jewish, headed the nuclear physics department in the Technion, Israel's MIT. He worked for Czech intelligence and was exposed in 1960.

Sentenced to five years in prison, he was released before his sentence ended and left the country.

- Israel Beer, a lieutenant colonel in the IDF, well-known military historian and close to the upper echelons of Israel security. Worked for Soviet intelligence, arrested in 1969, sentenced to ten years and died in jail.
- Shmuel Sami Baruch, Israeli businessman, worked for Egyptian intelligence beginning in 1963, exposed and sentenced to eighteen years in jail.
- Udi Adiv, born on Kibbutz Gan Shmuel, belonged to a spy ring run by Syrian intelligence. Exposed in December 1972 and sentenced to seventeen years in prison. Released in 1984.
- Marcus Klingberg, senior member of Israel's biological institute and a Soviet spy, exposed in 1983. Sentenced to life imprisonment (usually twenty years in Israel), released in 1998 on medical grounds and allowed to leave the country for France in January 2003.
- Yosef Amit, a major in the intelligence corps, offered his services to the American embassy in Israel. Arrested in 1986, sentenced to twelve years in prison and released in 1993.
- Shimon Levinson, colonel who served on the armistice committees. Offered his services to Soviet intelligence when in Thailand working for the UN. Arrested in 1990, sentenced to twelve years in prison and released after serving eight years.

The ISA Law (2002)

The ISA is the only body within the intelligence community whose status, function and responsibilities are established by law. The law was issued in an official publication on February 21, 2002, the fruit of years of labor that began in the ISA as an internal activity in 1988. The law deals with determining four main issues:

- The institutional aspect: The status of the ISA, its director, how responsibility is determined and its subordination to the prime minister.
- The functional aspect: The ISA's purpose (protecting national security and Israel's democratic regime and institutions from terrorist threats, sabotage, subversion, espionage and the exposure of state secrets), its functions, general authority (including the authority to conduct interrogations) and specific authority (including frisk and interception from the communications networks and determining security clearance).
- The oversight and supervisory aspect: The status of the internal supervisor; the duty to report regularly to the Knesset, the government and the judicial advisor; the duty to secure external authorization for rules and regulations.
- Various orders resulting from the special nature of the ISA: Internal investigations, restrictions imposed on ISA workers during and after their employment, orders regarding security.

Appendix 3

The Heads of the Israeli

Intelligence Community

Amos Gilboa

Israel Defense Intelligence (IDI) Directors

Colonel Isser Be'eri
(1901–1958, born in Russia)
The IDF's first intelligence director, 1948; previously head of the Haganah's Shai. He was dismissed from his post following suspicion of complicity in the death of a double agent.

Major General Chaim (Vivian) Herzog
(1918–1997, born in Ireland)
Head of the intelligence service and intelligence division of IDF operations, 1948–1950; IDI director, 1959–1961; Israel's ambassador to the United Nations, 1975–1978; sixth president of Israel, 1983–1993.

Colonel Benjamin Gibli
(1919–2008, born in Israel)

From 1950 head of the intelligence division of IDF operations; IDI director, 1953–1955, dismissed following Operation Suzanna; Golani Brigade commander in the Sinai Campaign (1956). After his discharge from the IDF, he held executive positions in the private sector.

Major General (Professor) Yehoshephat Harkabi
(1921–1994, born in Israel)

IDI director, 1955–1959, promoted from deputy director; stepped down following the "Night of the Ducks," the public call-up of reserves on April 1, 1959. After his discharge from the IDF, he joined the academic world and published widely on the Israel-Arab conflict. He received the Israel Prize, the state's highest honor, in 1992.

Major General Meir Amit
(1921–2009, born in Israel)

IDI director, 1962–1963. Previously head of the operations branch and the southern and central commands. Headed the Mossad (for several months was head of both the Mossad and IDI), and later a member of the Knesset and minister of transportation, and held executive positions in the private sector. Founder, first chairman (1983–2005) and late president of the Israel Intelligence Heritage and Commemoration Center.

Major General Aharon Yariv
(1920–1994, born in Latvia)

IDI director, 1964–1972. Previously head of the command and staff school, IDF attaché to the United States, Golani Brigade commander, and deputy IDI director. After his discharge from the IDF, he was appointed counterterrorism advisor to the prime minister and served as minister of both transportation and information (1975). From 1977 till his death, he was head of the Strategic Studies Center at Tel Aviv University.

Major General Eli Zeira
(1928–, born in Israel)

IDI director, 1972–1974. Previously head of operations, head of collection, IDF attaché to the United States and deputy IDI director. Relieved of duties as IDI director after the Yom Kippur War in accordance with the recommendations of the Agranat Commission. After his discharge from the IDF, he entered the private sector.

Major General Shlomo Gazit
(1929–, born in Turkey)

IDI director, 1974–1979. Previously head of IDI's production and analysis division. After the Six-Day War he was chief coordinator of Israel's activities in the territories. After his discharge from the IDF, he held various executive positions, among them president of Ben-Gurion University and director general of the Jewish Agency.

Major General Yehoshua Saguy
(1933–, born in Israel)
IDI director, 1979–1983. Previously intelligence officer of southern command and of an armored division during the Yom Kippur War, and director of the IDI's production and analysis division. Relieved of duty following the conclusions of the Kahan Commission, which investigated the Sabra and Shatilla massacre. After his discharge from the IDF, he entered politics and was a member of the Knesset, mayor of Bat Yam and the Israeli ambassador to the Philippines.

Lieutenant General Ehud Barak
(1942–, born in Israel)
IDI director, 1983–1989. Previously commander of the General Staff Reconnaissance Unit (Sayeret Matkal), commander of a division, head of the planning branch of the IDF and head of central command. He was promoted to deputy chief of staff and appointed chief of staff. After his discharge from the IDF, he entered politics and served as minister of the interior, foreign minister and prime minister (1999–2000). Currently (2010) minister of defense.

Lieutenant General Amnon Lipkin Shahak
(1944–, born in Israel)
IDI director, 1986–1991. Previously brigade commander in the Paratrooper Corps, commander of a division and head of the central command. He was promoted to deputy chief of staff and appointed chief of staff. After his discharge from the IDF he became a member of the Knesset and served as minister of both tourism and transportation (1999–2001).

Major General Uri Saguy
(1943–, born in Israel)

IDI director, 1991–1995. Previously Golani Brigade commander, division commander and head of the ground forces headquarters. After his discharge from the IDF, he held various positions in national security, including responsibility for the talks with Syria.

Lieutenant General Moshe Yaalon
(1950–, born in Israel)

IDI director, 1995–1998. Previously commander of the Sayeret Matkal, brigade commander in the Paratrooper Corps, division commander and commander of the IDF forces in Judea and Samaria. Later head of the central command, deputy chief of staff and chief of staff. Since his discharge from the IDF, he has been a senior research fellow at the Shalem Center in Jerusalem. Currently (2010) minister for strategic affairs.

Major General Amos Malka
(1953–, born in Israel)

IDI director, 1998–2001. Previously commanded a brigade in the Armored Corps, commanded a division and was head of the ground forces headquarters. After his discharge from the IDF he turned to the private sector and held senior positions in various companies.

Major General Aharon Zeevi Farkash
(1948–, born in Romania)
*IDI director, 2001–2006. Previously commanded the IDI
SIGINT, was an aid to the head of the planning branch and
head of the Technology and Logistics Division. Since his
discharge from the IDF he has been a research fellow in the
National Institute for Security Studies.*

Major General Amos Yadlin
(1951–, born in Israel)
*IDI director, 2006–2010. Served as a fighter pilot in the
Israel Air Force and participated in the attack on the Iraqi
nuclear reactor in 1981. Was head of Israel Air Force
intelligence and staff, and IDF attaché to the United States.*

Major General Aviv Kohavi
(1964–, born in Israel)
*IDI director since November 2010. Previously served
as head of the operations division in the operations
directorate and commander of the Gaza division during
the Israeli unilateral disengagement.*

Mossad Directors

Reuven Shiloah
(1909–1959, born in Israel)

Founder and first Mossad director, 1949–1952. One of the founders of the intelligence community on instructions from David Ben-Gurion; Israeli minister to the United States and political advisor to the Israeli Foreign Ministry.

Isser Harel
(1912–2003, born in Russia)

Mossad director, 1952–1963, and concurrently responsible for the ISA. Head of the ISA, 1948–1952, and held senior positions in Shai before the founding of the state. Resigned after "the affair of the German scientists" and was a member of the Knesset and a businessman.

Major General Meir Amit
(1921–2009, born in Israel)

Mossad director from 1963 (when he was also IDI director) to 1968 (for his activities in the IDF see "Israel Defense Intelligence (IDI) Directors," above). After his post as Mossad head he was a member of the Knesset, minister of transportation, and held executive positions in the private sector. Founder of the Israel Intelligence Heritage and Commemoration Center and its president until his death.

Major General Tzvi Zamir
(1925–, born in Poland)
Mossad director, 1968–1974. Previously served in the IDF as head of the training division, headed the central command and was IDF attaché to Britain. After he was discharged from the army, he held executive positions in the private sector, including director of the oil refineries.

Major General Yitzhak Hoffi
(1927–, born in Israel)
Mossad director, 1974–1982. Previously served in the IDF as commander of a Paratrooper Corps brigade, headed the northern command and was acting chief of staff. After he completed his post in the Mossad he held executive positions in the private sector, including director of the electric company. Currently president of Agmon, a non-profit organization of former Mossad members.

Nahum Admoni
(1929–, born in Israel)
Mossad director, 1982–1989. Previously held a series of senior Mossad posts in Israel and abroad. After he completed his post in the Mossad he held executive positions in the private sector, including director of Mekorot, the national water company.

Shabtai Shavit
(1939–, born in Israel)

Mossad director, 1989–1996, the last director whose name was not made public. Previously held a series of senior positions in the Mossad in Israel and abroad. Since completing his post in the Mossad, he has held executive positions in the private sector, including director general of the Maccabi HMO.

Major General Danny Yatom
(1945–, born in Israel)

Mossad director, 1996–1998, the first director whose name was made public. Previously served in the IDF as a division commander, head of the central command and the prime minister's military secretary. Served as head of the prime minister's political-defense staff, was a member of the Knesset and served on the Foreign Affairs and Defense Committee.

Efraim Halevy
(1934–, born in England)

Mossad director, 1998–2002. Previously held a series of senior positions in the Mossad in Israel and abroad. Was Israeli ambassador to the European Union and head of the National Security Council. Currently head of the Shasha Center for Strategic Studies at the Hebrew University in Jerusalem and chairman of the Israel Intelligence Heritage and Commemoration Center.

Major General Meir Dagan
(1945–, born in the USSR)

Mossad director, 2002–2011. Previously served in the IDF as a brigade commander in the Armored Corps, commanded a division, was head of the operations division and commander of the liaison unit in Lebanon. After he was discharged from the IDF he was head of the counterterrorism staff.

Tamir Pardo
(1953–, born in Israel)

Mossad director 2011– present. Previously held a series of senior positions in the Mossad in Israel and abroad, including deputy of the Mossad director Dagan. During his military service he served in the Israel Defense Forces as a communication officer in the elite special forces unit Sayeret Matkal, and participated in Operation Entebbe.

Heads of ISA

Isser Harel
(1912–2003, born in Russia)
First ISA head, 1948–1952. Before the establishment of the state held senior positions in the Haganah's Shai. Was ISA head and responsible for the ISA until 1963. Resigned following the "affair of the German scientists." Was the prime minister's advisor for intelligence and later a member of the Knesset and businessman.

Izidor Dorot
(1916–1980, born in Poland)
ISA head, 1952–1953. Belonged to Shai before the establishment of the state and helped Shiloah (his deputy) to found the Mossad. Was deputy Mossad director until 1963. After completing his defense career he turned to the business sector.

Amos Manor
(1918–2007, born in Romania)
ISA head, 1953–1963. Previously was deputy ISA head. After completing his service in the ISA he held executive positions in the private sector.

Yosef Harmelin
(1922–1994, born in Austria)

ISA head, 1964–1974. After having held a series of positions in the ISA was called on to serve a second term, from 1986 to 1988, because of the Bus No. 300 affair. After completing his service he held senior positions in the foreign service.

Avraham Ahituv
(1930–, born in Germany)

ISA head, 1974–1981. Previously held key positions in the ISA, including head of the Arab division, and positions in Shai before the establishment of the state. After completing his service he held executive positions in the private sector.

Avraham Shalom
(1928–, born in Czechoslovakia)

ISA head, 1981–1986, resigned because of the Bus No. 300 affair. Previously headed the ISA's operational wing and held other important positions. After his resignation he turned to the private sector.

Yaakov Perry
(1944–, born in Israel)
ISA head, 1988–1995. Previously deputy head and in charge of Judea, Samaria and Jerusalem districts. After completing his service, he held a number of executive positions in the private sector. Currently a bank president.

Carmi Gillon
(1950–, born in Israel)
ISA head, 1995–1996. Previously held senior positions in the ISA, including head of the Jewish branch. Resigned following the assassination of Yitzhak Rabin. After completing his service he was Israeli ambassador to Denmark. Currently vice president of external relations for the Hebrew University.

Major General Ami Ayalon
(1945–, born in Israel)
ISA head, 1996–2000. Previously served in the IDF in a variety of positions in the navy, including navy commander. After completing his service he entered politics and became a member of the Knesset, minister without portfolio. Currently in the private sector.

Avraham Dichter
(1952–, born in Israel)

ISA head, 2000–2005. Previously headed the ISA's southern district, was head of the security division and second in command. After completing his service he was elected to the Knesset and served as minister of internal security. Currently a Knesset member.

Yuval Diskin
(1956–, born in Israel)

ISA head, 2005–2011. Previously was special advisor to the head of the Mossad. Held senior positions in the ISA, including responsibility for Judea and Samaria.

Yoram Cohen
(1960–, born in Israel)

ISA head, 2011–present. Previously was deputy of ISA head (2005–2008); head of the Jerusalem, Judea and Samaria area; and head of the Arab and Iranian anti-terror branch in the ISA headquarters.

About the Authors

Dr. Dmitry Adamsky is an assistant professor at the Lauder School of Government, Diplomacy and Strategy at the Interdisciplinary Center in Herzliya, Israel. He is also an affiliate of the National Security Studies Program, Harvard University.

Brigadier General (Res.) Dr. Daniel Asher is a military historian, university lecturer and researcher for the Israeli defense establishment. An intelligence officer with years of experience in research and field work, he specializes in the Arab-Israeli wars. He is the author of *The Egyptian Strategy for the Yom Kippur War*.

Dr. Shimon Avivi was formerly a senior intelligence officer and has extensively researched the Druze community. He has published two books and numerous articles about the Druze in Israel. His book *Copper Plate: Israeli Policy towards the Druze from 1948 to 1967* was awarded the Prime Minister's Prize for 2008.

Professor Uri Bar-Joseph teaches in the political science department at Haifa University. He has written more than thirty journal articles published on national security issues, intelligence and the Arab-Israeli conflict, and five books, the most recent of which is *The Angel: Ashraf Marwan, the Mossad, and the Yom Kippur War*.

Avner Barnea is a former senior member of the Israeli Security Agency (ISA). He is a competitive intelligence strategic consultant and lectures on competitive intelligence in the MBA program of Ono Academic College, Israel.

Colonel (Res.) Dr. Barak Ben-Zur is an expert analyst on strategic threats and risks. He specializes in strategic intelligence analysis, counterterrorism and Middle East studies.

Brigadier General Itai Brun is the head of IDI's production and analysis department since 2011. Formerly the director of the IDF's Dado Center for Interdisciplinary Military Studies (2006–2011), he was senior analysis assistant to the head of IDI's production and analysis division (2005–2006) and headed Israel Air Force Intelligence's analysis department (2001–2004).

Colonel (Ret.) Dr. Reuven Erlich held various positions in IDI's analysis department and field units of IDI. He is currently the director of the Meir Amit Intelligence and Terrorism Information Center (ITIC) at the Israel Intelligence Heritage and Commemoration Center (IICC).

Yochi Erlich has an MA in security studies from Tel Aviv University. She was formerly an intelligence officer in the IDI (1977–1999) and is currently an associate editor of the Israel Intelligence Heritage and Commemoration Center journal.

Colonel (Ret.) Dr. Shmuel Even was formerly head of IDI's revision department (the Devil's Advocate Department). He is a strategic and economic consultant to leading companies in Israel and a senior research fellow at the Institute for National Security Studies (INSS) at Tel Aviv University.

Dr. Boaz Ganor is the assistant dean of the Lauder School of Government and founder and executive director of the International Institute for Counterterrorism, both at the Interdisciplinary Center, Herzliya, Israel. He is also the founder and president of the International Academic Counterterrorism Community.

Major General (Res.) Shlomo Gazit was IDI director (1974–1979) after the Yom Kippur War. Previously head of IDI's production and analysis division. After the Six-Day War he was chief coordinator of

Israel's activities in the territories. After his discharge from the IDF, he held various executive positions, among them president of Ben-Gurion University and director general of the Jewish Agency.

Brigadier General Hanan Geffen was formerly commander of the IDI SIGINT unit (Unit 8200).

Brigadier General (Res.) Amos Gilboa was formerly head of the IDI's production and analysis department. He was advisor to the prime minister for Arab affairs, intelligence attaché to the United States, and lectures at the Interdisciplinary Center, Herzliya, Israel.

Eitan Glaser has an MA in political science from Haifa University. He served in ISA for thirty-two years.

Lieutenant Colonel (Res.) Shamai Golan was the IDF Air Force Intelligence operations officer for the attack on Iraq's nuclear reactor.

Shmuel Goren was formerly head of the HUMINT units of IDI and the Mossad.

Captain (Navy Res.) Shlomo Gueta was formerly head of the production and analysis division of Israel's naval intelligence. Formerly he fulfilled a variety of duties in naval intelligence, including research on maritime terror and shipping. He continues to serve as an officer in the reserves.

Efraim Halevy was born in London. He has been head of the Hebrew University's Shasha Center for Strategic Studies since 2003. Since 2004 he has chaired the Israel Intelligence Heritage and Commemoration Center. He was head of the National Security Council (2002–2003) and the Mossad (1998–2002), and wrote *Man in the Shadows*, 2006.

Brigadier General (Res.) Shalom Harari was an advisor on Palestinian affairs in the headquarters of both the Israeli Defense Ministry and the Civil Administration of Judea and Samaria for more than twenty years. Before that he served in the production and analysis and collection departments of IDI.

Colonel (Res.) Dr. Ephraim Kam was formerly the assistant director of the IDI production and analysis department. He is currently deputy head of the Institute for National Security Studies at Tel Aviv University and lectures on security at Tel Aviv University.

Brigadier General (Res.) Ephraim Lapid was formerly head of the collection department at IDI headquarters and IDF spokesman. He currently lectures at Bar-Ilan University.

Colonel (Ret.) Dr. Ephraim Lavie has been director of the Tami Steinmetz Center for Peace Research at Tel Aviv University since 2007. As an IDF officer he served as advisor for Arab affairs to the Israeli civil administration in the West Bank (1989–1998), and headed the Palestinian desk in the IDI production and analysis department (1998–2002).

Shlomo Nakdimon writes about contemporary Israeli history. He has received the Sokolov Prize for Journalism and the prize given by the Center for Strategic Studies of Tel-Aviv University. He wrote, among other works, *First Strike* about the bombing of the Iraqi nuclear reactor in 1981, and *A Hopeless Hope*, about the Mossad's support of the Kurdish revolt, 1963–1975.

Captain (Navy Res.) Arieh Oren served as a naval officer in the southern arena until he was wounded during the War of Attrition. He served in naval intelligence beginning in 1972. His last position was head of naval intelligence's production and analysis department. He continues to serve as an officer in the reserves.

Brigadier General Eli Pollak commanded a combat collection unit in IDI and was the intelligence officer for two divisions. He headed the Combat Intelligence School and the VISINT agency of IDI. Since 2009 he has headed the combat collection corps in the Ground Force Command.

Colonel Shay Shabtai is a senior IDI officer and researches strategic issues related to the Middle East and Israel's national security.

Colonel (Res.) Dr. Yigal Sheffy was formerly a senior intelligence officer in the IDI and is currently a senior lecturer in Tel Aviv University's diplomacy studies program. Among his books are *British Military Intelligence in the Palestine Campaign* and *Early Warning Countdown: The Rotem Affair and the Israeli Security Perception, 1957–1960*.

Colonel (Ret.) Shlomo Tirosh was formerly the commander of the IDI technological unit, and is the recipient of the Israel Security Prize.

Brigadier General (Res.) David Tzur was formerly the IDF's chief intelligence officer. He is currently the CEO of the Israel Intelligence Heritage and Commemoration Center. He commands a team of an intelligence directorate for strategic and operational exercises.

Major General (Ret.) Aviezer Yaari was formerly head of the IDI production and analysis department and commander of the military colleges.

Brigadier General (Ret.) Gadi Zohar served most of his tenure in IDI. He headed the Civil Administration in the West Bank and the terrorism research department.

10645461R10234

Printed in Great Britain
by Amazon